Kansai University
Institute of Oriental and Occidental Studies
Study Report Series

53

The Cultural Interaction of East Asia Seas in the Early Modern

Akira MATSUURA
Professor, Kansai University

Kansai University Press

Kansai University
Institute of Oriental and Occidental Studies

First Published in Japan in 2016
An imprint of Yubunsha Co., Ltd.

©2016 Akira MATSUURA
All rights reserved
ISBN 978-4-87354-642-1 C3022
Printed in Japan

Kansai University Press
3-3-35 Yamate-cho, Suita, Osaka, Japan

Foreword

"The Cultural Interaction of East Asia Seas in the Early Modern" by Professor Akira Matsuura is published from The Institute of Oriental and Occidental Studies. He has analyzed historical events, where vessels, voyages, marine transportations, exports and imports in East Asia mingle intricately with each other, with his discerning eyes and has advanced comprehensive findings from his broad intellectual horizon for many years. His research shows some characteristics, such as his cyclopedic and exhaustive ways of collecting data and materials, his excellent skill to construct the data and materials, and the brilliance of his new academic criterion utilizing the enormous amount of data and materials.

He already published nearly thirty sole author books, and has won renown, not to mention in Japan, in China, Taiwan, and South Korea. Moreover, his reputation has spread from East Asia to the U.S. and Europe. If a researcher is studying vessels and their operations at all, he surely knows the name "Akira Matsuura." Lots of data and materials excavated and introduced by him, and his research probing into them have extremely important meanings for researchers who aspire to study cultural and social science in East Asia. Researchers receiving benefit from his study are too numerous to enumerate.

Although many people often insist that "quality is more valuable than quantity" in the world of researchers, it goes without saying that "both quality and quantity are valuable" is the right attitude of researchers. The number of his research papers is more than 500, and his great achievements outclass others in quantity. Moreover, the fruits of his research are also remarkable in quality. It is the truth that we cannot create quality without making quantity in the field of cultural science. I cannot help being amazed to know that he was walking on the steep royal road for nearly a half century. Besides, he has been endeavoring in the past ten years to establish a new academic system called "cultural interaction studies" which will lead the Asia studies of Kansai University. The outline of the studies has started to be seen clearly in recent years. He presents the methodology of the studies in connection with vessel operations in this book. That can be called his unrivaled sphere of activity.

In addition, his work is outstanding not only in researches but also in educating students, and we must not overlook the fact that his young pupils are playing important roles in many universities and research institutes in East Asia. Sometimes he scolds young researchers or students strictly, but there is truly warm and instructive consideration in his reproofs. Many researchers follow him because the prominent intelligence coexists with the bright personality in his character. A researcher group which can be called Matsuura School has already spread into Mainland China, and he is producing great results in many places in East Asia in respect of nurturing younger men.

The result of his long years of research is concentrated in this publication. The research task of the Institute of Oriental and Occidental Studies is "comparative study of Eastern and Western cultures," whose core is the studies on Asian cultures. Unfailingly, this book will not only contribute to researchers who are interested in Asian cultures, but also advance greatly the studies on Asian cultures. I would like to express my deep respect to his sustained efforts and extraordinary talent, as well as the brightness of his personality.

        August, 2016
        Kansai University
        Director, The Institute of Oriental and Occidental Studies
        Nobuo Nakatani

Preface

Studies of global *maritime history* have frequently dealt with questions involving the Mediterranean and Atlantic, focusing on the history of Western Europe. However, there have been few studies dealing specifically with the waters surrounding East Asia. It would be fair to say that up until now historical studies looking at the seas lying within the area contained by the Chinese mainland, the Korean peninsula, the Japanese archipelago, the Ryukyu Islands, Taiwan, the Philippine and Indonesian archipelagos, the Malay peninsula, and mainland Indochina, namely the Bohai, Yellow, East China and South China Seas, have been slow to appear. This is perhaps because existing studies of Chinese history have mostly taken a *continental view of history*, as 'Maritime History' (*Kaiyō shi* 海洋史).

The activity of Chinese Junks was flourishing in Japan and Southeast Asia. It have great contributions to the cultural exchanges between China and other countries. In the Ming Dynasty, with the "Haiji 海禁" policy, coastal sailing activities were extremely limited. Until the Qing Dynasty, with the "Zhan Hailing 展海令" which was a policy to relieve "Haiji 海禁" policy was released, coastal sailing activities greatly improved. In Qing Dynasty, there were 4 representative Chinese junks called four sailing boats widely known by the people. They were sha-chuan 沙船 sand boats, niao-chuan 鳥船 birds boats, fu-chuan 福船 Fujian boats, guan-chuan 廣船 Guandong boats.

From the seventeenth century onward, four major types of Chinese seagoing ships, known as sand junks 沙船, bird junks 鳥船, Fuzhou junks 福船, and Guangzhou junks 廣船 respectively, were most active in marine transportation in East Asia.1 Of these ships, the flat-bottomed sand junks from Chongming 崇明 and Shanghai would leave the mouth of the Yangtze River, sail northwardly along the coasts of the Bohai Sea and reach Jinzhou 錦州, Niuzhuang 牛莊 and Gaizhou 蓋州. These ships were loaded with Shanghai cotton cloth, tea and other products from southern China. They brought back soya beans and other grains from north-eastern China.2 Bird junks, Fuzhou junks, and Guangzhou junks, on the other hand, had rounded bottoms. They were more suitable for sailing on the high seas.3 The activities of bird junks covered mainly the coastal regions of Fujian. They sailed into the Bohai 渤海 Sea to reach Jinzhou, Gaizhou, and Tianjin 天津.

The sea route that links the Yellow Sea, the Donghai (Tōkai 東海), the Korean Peninsula, the Japanese archipelagos, the Southwest Islands (the Ryūkyū Islands 琉球諸島), and Taiwan played an important role in the history of exchange among East Asian countries. When sailing on the sea, however, there was no guarantee for safety. And bad weather often led to sea disasters. In many cases, when a ship, its crew and passengers had been rescued in Japan, local authorities would conduct an investigation into the circumstance of the incident, and compile a report in Chinese *kanji* in order to convey the information to other countries in the Chinese cultural sphere.[1] We therefore have detailed *kanji* records of sea disasters. Becoming interested in sea disasters in East Asia, and the ways in which they were handled by the various governments in the region, I have recently examined these records.

19th century maritime trade with Vietnam near Hainan Island and Vietnam are still prosperous. Specific examples can be written by Charles Gutzlaff 1832. Hainan Island, the bulk of the output produced by the local leather, rice, and sugar. Especially its specialty sugar, were selling for transport to the coastal areas to the north of China. Hainan Island, China not only limited to the coastal areas, but also actively working with other overseas countries, such as Vietnam, Tokyo (Tungking), in the southern region of Vietnam (Cochin-china) and Siam (Siam), and Singapore trade. When one of its trading method is on the way to Siam docked in Champa (Tsiompa) and Cambodia (Cambojia) ports, marine timber procurement and other items used in shipbuilding, ship in the port temporarily. With this Junk ship, while the purchase while homing in Hainan and Guangdong, selling products to this form of trade. The Part I, IV article will focus on how the Chinese Junk ship in Vietnam maritime trade, especially that with the central Vietnam city of Hue (Hue) the trade center, specifically addressed at the time of trade patterns.

Part 2 article will focus Shino-Japanese Interaction on various issues, namely cultural exchange by the Chinese Junks, discussed the logistics, such as seafood and sugar and books.

To maintain its policy of national isolation during the Edo period, Japan restricted contact with the outside world to Dutch merchant ships and Chinese junks (called *Tō-sen* in Japanese) that arrived regularly at the Japanese port of Nagasaki. Sino-Japanese interaction consisted not only of trade in goods, but also of cultural and scholarly exchanges. In this paper I will be examining how this unofficial trade affected both Japan and China from a cultural perspective.

During the Edo period, the quantity of dried sea cucumber, dried abalone and shark fin (鱶鰭 *fuka-hire*), exported from Nagasaki to China grew considerably. Particularly during the Qing Dynasty, the growing popularity of seafood produced a taste for sea cucumber (海參 *haishen*), dried abalone (鰒魚 *fuyu*) and

---

1 For records about Chinese ships that suffered sea disasters, see the works published by the Kansai University Press in the bibliography.

shark fin (魚翅 *yuchi*) in China. As a result, export of these marine products increased steadily during the Genroku period (元禄時代, 1688-1703; Kangxi 康熙 27-42). Consumption was greatest in the Lower Yangzi delta region, but by the late Qing Dynasty consumption increased as dried sea cucumber, dried abalone and shark fin made their way into the interior, enlivening dining tables around China.

Tokugawa Yoshimune 徳川吉宗 also sought to learn about sugar production from merchants who arrived in Nagasaki. In other words, records show that Yoshimune used three methods to study sugar cane harvesting: observations of the cane harvest in Ryūkyū 琉球 and Satsuma 薩摩; study of Chinese texts; and conversations with Chinese merchants in Nagasaki. In this way, not only did overall sugar production increase, but the quality of sugar also improved.

It has long been known that the Japanese enjoyed Chinese books; their significance at the time is simply but vividly recorded in the *Wohao*[2] 倭好 (in Japanese *Wakō*). The *Wohao* reports that, of the Five Classics, the Classic of History (*Shujing* 書経 in Japanese *Shokyō*[3]) and the Classic of Rites (*Liji* 礼記 in Japanese *Raiki*) were well respected, whereas the Classic of Changes (*Yijing* 易経 in Japanese *Ekikyō*), the Classic of Poetry (*Shijing* 詩経 in Japanese *Shikyō*) and the Spring and Autumn Annals (*Chunqiu* 春秋 in Japanese *Shunjū*) were considered to be less important. As to the Four Books, we are told that the Analects (*Lunyu* 論語 in Japanese *Rongo*), Great Learning (*Dazue* 大学 in Japanese *Daigaku*) and Doctrine of the Mean (*Zhongyong* 中庸 in Japanese *Chūyō*) were well respected, whereas the Mencius (*Mengzi* 孟子 (in Japanese *Mōshi*) was less well regarded. It is thought that the Mencius was particularly unpopular due to the spread of its reputation as a revolutionary text which went against the Shogunate's policy, an idea that is clearly represented in the *Wohao*. Buddhist and Taoist scriptures were also popular, and medical texts, too, were inevitably purchased. In his *Xiuhaibian* 袖海編, Wang Peng 汪鵬, who traded in Nagasaki at the beginning of the Meiwa period 明和年間 between 1772 and 1780, wrote that the *dongren* (東人 Easterners), as he called the Japanese, would purchase any Chinese book imported to Japan however high the price.

During the first half of 19th century, the demand for steamers arose in East Asian countries after the English steamers came into China. The first steamer company set up by the Chinese government was China Merchants' Steam Navigation Company 招商局輪船公司 in Shanghai in 1872. However, the European

---

2 *Riben-fengtu-ji*, page unknown.
3 Where Chinese book titles have a well-known English translation, the book is referred to using that translation. Otherwise book titles are in the original language. The English translation of these titles is in [ ].

steamers had already been sailing in the waters along China's coast and they even sailed to the Hankou port at Yangtze River. These steamers played an important role not only in the international trade but also in the inner transportation of China.Mitsubishi was the first company to set up the regular route between Japan and China. In 1875, Mitsubishi started the regular route between Yokohama and Shanghai. In 1875, Mitsubishi Kaisha received thirteen steamers and the sponsorship of 250,000 Yen per year from the Japanese government. The company name was also changed to "Yūbin Kisen Mitsubishi Kaisha" (郵便汽船三菱会社). Then in 1885, because of the affiliation with "Kyōdo Unyu Kaisha"(共同運輸会社), "Nippon Yūsen Kaisha" was formally founded in Tokyo.

Contents

Foreword ·· Nobuo Nakatani ········ i
Preface ·· 1
List of Figures and Tables ·· 7

Introduction Human Movements and Goods Distribution through Chinese Junks on the East Asia and Southeast Asia during Qing Dynasty ············ 11

CHAPTER 1   Introduction ·· 13

Part 1: The Activities of Chinese Junks on the East Asian Sea in Early Modern Ages ············ 25

CHAPTER 2   Chinese Sea Merchants and Pirates ································ 27
CHAPTER 3   The Activities of Chinese Junks on East Asian Seas from the Seventeenth to the Nineteenth Centuries: Mainly Based on Sand Junks and Bird Junks ························ 57
CHAPTER 4   Junks ownen Yu Songnian 郁松年 and His Rare Book Collection ·· 71
CHAPTER 5   The Maritime Trade of Chinese Junks with Vietnam Hue (Huế) during 16-19 century ············ 79
CHAPTER 6   Maritime Rescue & Salvage in Early Modern East Asia and Its Modern Transfiguration ································ 89

Part 2: Sino-Japanese Interaction based on Chinese Junks in the Edo period ············ 107

CHAPTER 7   Sino-Japanese Interaction based on Chinese Junks in the Edo period ·· 109
CHAPTER 8   The Trade in Dried Marine Products from Nagasaki to China during the Edo Period ·· 125

CHAPTER 9	The Import of Chinese Sugar in the Nagasaki Junk Trade and Its Impact	159
CHAPTER 10	Imports and Exports of Books by Chinese Junks in the Edo Period	177

Epilogue Conflicts among the Shipping Companies over the Ocean Traffic in the Asian Seas 197

CHAPTER 11	Conflicts among the Shipping Companies over the Ocean Traffic in the Asian Seas	199

Appendix I: The Situation of Chinese Migrants Abroad
　　　　　　in the Newspaper of Singapore 211
Appendix II: The Situation of Chinese Migrants Abroad
　　　　　　in the Records of Chinese *Maritime Customs* 217
References 219
Afterword 227

List of Figures and Tables

List of Figures

1 Nagasaki arrived Chinese Junks and Dutch Ships
2 Junks at Youngjian estuary, 1981
3 'A Foreign Trader', Barrow, "Travels in China", 1804
4 Piracy Guo Badai, "Dai-shi-zha-huadao"
5 Chief ports on the route from the Yangtze River to the Bohai Sea
6 Sand Junks, Sha-chuan
7 Bird Junk, Niao-chuan
8 Xu-Hou-Hanshu Zhaji
9 Xu-Hou-Hanshu Zhaji, Vol. 1
10 Chinese Junk from Tokan Rankan to emaki(Picture Scroll of the Chinese and Dutch Residences) Printed by Ishizaki Yushi
11 Nagasaki Woodblock Print: Illustration of Chinese Junks Entering at Harbor
12 Scene inside the Chinese Residential Ares from Tokan Rankan to emai(Picture Scroll of the Chinese and Dutch Residences) Printed by Ishizaki Yushi
13 Illustration of Chinese in Shinsa showashu (Collection of Qing Raft Prayers)
14 Dried Sea Cucumber (Haishen)
15 Dried abalone
16 Dried shark fin
17 Dried sea cucumber
18 Trade value of return cargo of the seventh Nanjing ship, 1709 (by value in silver)
19 Trade value of return cargo of the seventh Nanjing ship, 1709 (by volume)
20 1762 seventh Ningbo ship, value of return cargo (by value in silver)
21 1762 seventh Ningbo ship, value of return cargo (by volume)
22 Volume of copper and dried marine products, return cargo of the third ship, 1764
23 Value in silver of return cargoes for Chinese Junks, 1803-1804 (in monme)
24 Average cargo volume of five Chinese Junks returning in 1833
25 Cargo on the ship Senzai-maru in 1862
26 Geographical origins of sea cucumber of Nagasaki in the early 19th century

27 Geographical origins of dried abalone
28 Map of CMSNCO's Asian branch 1920s
29 Map of CMSNCO's Line 1920s
30 The model of Aden
31 Map of CYK's Line

List of Tables

1 Table of Song dynasty sea merchants mentioned in Goryeosa
2 Number of ships entering seaports in Jinzhou, Niuzhuang and other places
3 Number of Sand Junks entering the port of Nanshi, Shanghai(1898-1902)
4 Activities of Junks harbored at Nanshi in 1899
5 Voyages by the Sand Junk
6 Transportation activities Sand Junks dispatched by Zhenkang in 1899 according to *Zhongwai Ribao*
7 Yu Songnian Edit, *"Yijian-tan Congshu"*
8 Cases of Qing sailboats drifting to Ryukyu, Korea and cargos
9 No. of Crew and arrival of 194 Chinese Junks in Nagasaki by Month; 1687
10 Return cargo of the seventh Nanjing ship, 1709
11 1762 Seventh Ningbo ship, value of return cargo
12 1761-1762 Chinese ships, return cargo; volume of copper and marine products(in kin)
13 Volume of copper and dried marine products, return cargo of the third ship, 1764(in kin)
14 Chinese Junks under the command of Qing merchant-officials returning to Zhapu
15 Value in silver of return cargoes for Chinese Junks, 1803-1804 (in kanme)
16 Principle cargo of Chinese ships returning 1833 (in kin)
17 Cargo on the ship Senzai-maru in 1862
18 Geographical origins of sea cucumber (Units: kin)
19 Geographical origins of dried abalone (Units: kin)
20 Status of consumption of various marine products in Chinese markes
21 Volume of sugar cargo on Chinese Junks serving Nagasaki, 1642-1653(in kin)
22 Cargo carried on Junks entering Nagasaki harbor, tenth month

23 Amount of sugar imported by Chinese Junks in 1831-1832 (Tempo 2-3)
24 Junks on which Li Daiheng arrived in Nagasaki
25 Comparison of the complete Xiaocaqng-shan-fang and the collection of selected works bought by Ichikawa Kansai
26 Muluti-volume texts shipped to China by Chinese Junks from 1794 to 1837, grouped by similar of identical books.
27 Sailing Steamers from Busan port in Jan. 1905
28 Sailing Steamers of ChosenYusen Kaisha in Aug. 1920

Introduction

Human Movements and Goods Distribution through Chinese Junks on the East Asia and Southeast Asia during Qing Dynasty

CHAPTER 1

Introduction

1 Initially

The "Haiji 海禁" policy, a ban on maritime activities imposed during China's Ming dynasty, was preserved in the turbulent era of the seventeenth century. It was used to against the force of Zheng Chenggong, an ex-Ming military leader located in Taiwan in Qing Dynasty. But after Taiwan's surrender, the "Haiji 海禁" policy was relieved in Kangxi 22 years (1683 year). After that, Chinese people began to take an active part in the foreign trade activities.

The activity of Chinese Junks was flourishing in Japan and Southeast Asia. It have great contributions to the cultural exchanges between China and other countries. In the Ming Dynasty, with the "Haiji 海禁" policy, coastal sailing activities were extremely limited. Until the Qing Dynasty, with the "Zhan Hailing 展海令" which was a policy to relieve "Haiji 海禁" policy was released, coastal sailing activities greatly improved. In Qing Dynasty, there were 4 representative Chinese junks called four sailing boats widely known by the people. They were sha-chuan 沙船 sand boats, niao-chuan 鳥船 birds boats, fu-chuan 福船 Fujian boats, guan-chuan 廣船 Guandong boats.[1]

This article focuses that Chinese Junks and its contributions to the movement of peoples and distribution of things on the waters of East Asia and Southeast Asia during the Qing Dynasty.

---

1 Zhou Shi-de 周世德, *Zhongguo Sha-chuan kaolüe* 中国沙船考略, *Kexue-shi ji-kan* 科学史集刊, vol. 5, 1963, pp. 34-54.
   Tian Ru-kang 田汝康, *Zhongguo Fan-chuan maoyi duwaiguanxi-shi lunji* 中国帆船贸易與对外关係史論集, Zhejiang People's Publishing House 浙江人民出版社, 1987, pp. 1-52.

2   The activities of the Chinese Junks during Qing Dynasty

Since the "Zhan Hailing 展海令" was released in early Qing Dynasty, the activities of four sailing boats called sha-chuan sand boats, niao-chuan birds boats, fu-chuan Fujian boats, guan-chuan Guandong boats were known by the people as the representative Chinese junks on the waters of East and Southeast Asia.[2]

Sailing in the Yangtze Delta to Chongming Island Northern shallow waters and the waters of the canal were sand boats. These boats had a strong thrust. It were used for carrying tea and cotton cloth along the coast of the Shandong Peninsula to the Northern Sea. And carrying soybeans, soybean oil and soybean meals that were produced in northeast, to the Yangtze River Delta region. Through this, these boats had important contributions to southern agricultural economy.[3]

Bird boats were major used in Fujian coast, specialized in ocean sailing routes extending to Japan and Southeast Asia, especially in the mid-18th century to the 19th century was an important connection between China and Japan.[4] Japanese historical records also left a lot of paintings about these bird boats . In the Edo period of Japan, Japanese called Chinese sailing as "Don boat", which all most were birds boat.[5]

Fujian boats and Guangdong boats were large ocean-going boats used in Fujian and Guangdong province, but the relevant historical records are not much left.

3   Human movements through Chinese Junks on the East Asian Seas during Qing

3.1   Japan

The following year of Taiwan surrendering (the year 1683), that is twenty-

---

[2] Zhou Shi-de, *Zhongguo Sha-chuan kaolüe*, *Kexue-shi ji-kan*, vol. 5, 1963, pp. 34.

[3] Matsuura Akira 松浦章、*Shindai Shanhai Sasen kouun-gyo shi no kennkyuu* 清代上海沙船航運業史の研究, Kansaidaigaku shuppannbu 関西大学出版部, 2004, pp.42-60.

[4] Matsuura Akira, *Shindai Kaigai boueki-shi no kenkyu* 清代海外貿易史の研究, Hoyu shoten 朋友書店, 2002, pp. 264-269.

[5] Matsuura Akira, *Shindai Kaigai boueki-shi no kenkyu*, 264-323頁。

three years of the Qing Dynasty Emperor Kangxi (康熙帝), in the September twenty-three years of Kangxi, Kangxi Emperor said: "In the seaside of Fujian and Guangdong, Ocean trade is beneficial to livelihood of these two provincial civil, the reduction of Government expenditure, and goods distribution. We should tax the merchants a little taxes, and pay the taxes as two provincial military expenditure so that the tael transportation cost can be reduced …"[6] In this way, Kangxi Emperor published a edict called "Zhan hailing" allowing people to engage in foreign trade.

Affected by the "Zhan hailing", lots of the Chinese Junks came to Nagasaki from Fujian and Guangdong. "Zhan hailing" released one year ago, 27 Don boats came into the territory of Nagasaki; "Zhan hailing" released that year, 24 Don boats came into Nagasaki. But in the following year of "Zhan hailing" released (the 24th year of Kangxi, that the second year of Johkyo (貞享), the year 1685), including the hadn't returned ships, amount to 85 Don boats stayed in Nagasaki.[7] This figure were three times and a half over the past.

The 4th year of Jyokyo (the 26th year of Kangxi, the year 1687), there were 137 Don boats came into Nagasaki (including the hadn't returned ships 22 Don boats). In the first year of Genroku (the 27th year of Kangxi, the year 1688), Chinese Junks quantity reached the highest peak, it were 194 boats (including the hadn't returned ships 77 Don boats).[8] Because there were too much Chinese Junks coming to Nagasaki, from the second year of Genroku (the year 1689), Japan published a statute to limit the quantity of Chinese Junks that would come to Nagasaki. With this statute, the quantity of Chinese Junks were imited to 70 boats every year by Japan.[9] But in the Genroku 11 year (Kangxi 37 year or the year1698), the statute was modified, the quantity of Chinese Junks were imited to 80 boats every year, volume of trade was imited to 13,000 silver every year.[10] In Enho 6 years (the 48th year of Kangxi, the year 1709), Japan's ban was modified again, the quantity of Chinese Junks were imited to 59 boats every year.[11] It is obvious that the main policy was to limit the number of trading boats and volume of trade.

In the Shotoku 5 year (the 54th year of Kangxi, the year 1715), the regula-

---

6 *Shengzu Renhuandi Sheng-xun* 聖祖仁皇帝聖訓, vol. 21, Xu-min 恤民. Shengzu Renhuangdi Shilu 聖祖仁皇帝實録, vol. 116.
7 *Nagasaki jituroku taisei seihenn*, vol. 11, Tosen nyuushinn narabini zatuji no Bu, Nagasaki bunnkenn sousho vol.1 no. 2, Nagasaki bunnken shuppannsha, 1973, pp.256-257.
8 Ibid, p.259.
9 *Dainipponn kinsei shiryou Totuuji kaisho nichiroku* vol.1, 1955, p.197.
10 *Ymawaki Teijirou, Nagasaki no Tojinn boueki*, 1964, p.316.
11 Ibid, p.326.

tion policy was more stricter by a law called "Kaihakugoshi shinrei" published. After that, this "Kaihakugoshi shinrei" was continued until the end of the shogunate with no fundamental changing.[12] This Nagasaki trade legislation was in order to control export volume of gold and silver and copper. Especially for Don boats, Chinese Junks quantity were limited to 30 boats, trade volume was limited to 9,000 silver. It also made a system that Japan government gave a card called "sinpai" to some approved Chinese Junks. Those Chinese Junks which had the card would been allowed to trade with Japanese, which hadn't the card would be forbidden to land in Nagasaki.[13] Therefore, from Shotoku to Kyoho period (Chinese Kangxi to Yongzheng 雍正era), Chinese merchants had a heavy competition around the "sinpai".[14] After Shotoku era, in order to control the export volume of copper and other reasons, the numbers of Chinese Junks coming into the Nagasaki were limited as follows:

  The second year of Kyoho (The 56th year of Kangxi,the year 1717) 40 boats

  The 5th year of Kyoho (The 59th year of Kangxi, the year 1720) 30 boats

  The 18th year of Kyoho (The 11th year of Yongzheng, the year 1733) 29 boats

  The 5th year of Gen bun (The 5th year of Qianlong, the year 1740) 20 boats

  The second year of Kanpou (The 7th year of Qianlong, the year 1742) 10 boats

  The second year of Kan-en (The 14th year of Qianlong, the year 1749) 15 boats

  The second year of Meiwa (The 30th year of Qianlong, the year 1765) 13 boats

  The third year of Kansei (The 56th year of Qianlong 56, the year 1791) 10 boats[15]

Although the numbers of Chinese Junks coming into the Nagasaki were limited by Japan, but due to climatic reasons, every year the quantity of Chinese Junks coming into Nagasaki actually were not fixed. We can make a form as

---

12 Matsuura Akira, *Edojidai Tosen niyoru Nicchuu bunnka kouryu*, Shibunnkaku, 2007, pp.99-110.
13 Tokugawa kinrei ko, vol. 6, Kaihaku goshi jyourei.
14 Ohba Osamu, *Tokugawa Yoshimue to Daishin kaiten, Hosei shi kenkyu*, vol. 21, 1972.
15 Yamawaki, ibid, pp.318-320.

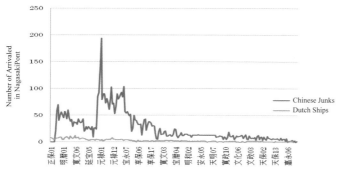

Figure 1　1644–1862 Nagasaki arrived of Chinese Junks and DutchShips

following to look the basic quantity.

Every Chinese Junk can take about 100 people engaged in the trade between China and Japan. So, after the mid-18th century, each year nearly 1,000 Chinese people engaged in trade stayed at Nagasaki.

The last year of Sino-Japanese trade was the year 1861 (The first year of Bunkyu 文久, the 11th year of Xianfeng 咸豊). In this year, Chinese merchants employed 2 English ships arrived at Nagasaki.[16]

3.2　Taiwan

There are some historical records about the relations between Taiwan and the mainland shipping, such as a general called Hao Yulin 郝玉麟 written in his letter in Yong Zheng 13th year (the year 1735).

> "Luerhmen (鹿耳門) is located in the key location of the entrance of Taiwan. A patrol has been set up in Luerhmen".

"*Tai-wan fu-zh*, (a history book of Taiwan prefecture)" Volume 2, also have a description about the Luerhmen Port as following:

> "The large merchant ship from Xiamen to Taiwan and the small merchant ship from Taiwan to Danshui, are all going out and coming in Taiwan through this Luerhmen port".

From this record, we can see that Luerhmen Port was the bond linking the

---

16　Matuura, *Edojidai Tosen niyoru Nicchuu bunnka kouryuu*, pp. 346-354.

Taiwan and mainland in the beginning of the Qing Dynasty. After that, some ports also were opened between Taiwan and mainland, such as the 49th year of Qianlong (1784), Lukang port was opened in Zhanghua County; the 53th year of Qianlong (1788) Danshui 淡水 (near Taipei) was opened, in the 6th year of Daoguang (1826), Haifeng port of Changhua County and Wushi port of Yilan County was opened.

In addition, smuggling activities were frequently happened. The most typical representative was called "Smuggling to Taiwan"[17], that meant immigrants smuggling into Taiwan from mainland. One of the fact is recorded in the document which was written by Su Mingliang 蘇明良, a general of Guangdong province, in the September10th of the 8th years of Yongzheng (the year 1730).

> "A refugee ship taking 129 people drifted on Guangdong…They said they were going to smuggle to Taiwan from Fujian province. In the august 12th, they left Xiamen. But due to heavy waves, the ship damaged and drifted on Guangdong."[18]

It can be seen men and women of 129 persons along the coast were going to smuggle to Taiwan, but due to storm the ship damaged and drifted on Guangdong.

In the 26th year of Qianlong (the year 1761), Xiamen government also had a investigation about smuggling problem. From this investigation we can know "over 48 families (277 people) had been smuggled to Taiwan"[19] in that year in Xiamen. In the 25th year of Qianlong (1787), Qing government also had a report about smuggling problem as following.

> "From the October of the 23th year of Qianlong until December of the 23th year of Qianlong, the cases that sneaked into Taiwan had happened twenty five cases, 999 persons had smuggled to Taiwan, Among them 34 persons had drowned."[20]

---

17 Zhuan Ji-fa 莊吉發、*Qing Shi-zong jinzhi toudu Taiwan de yuanyin* 清世宗禁止偷渡臺灣的原因、*Shi-huo yuekan, fukan* 食貨月刊 復刊、vol.18, no. 8, 1983.
18 National Palace Museum国立故宮博物院編、*Secret Place Memorials of the Yungcheng period Ch'ing Documents,* 宮中檔雍正朝奏摺、No. 16, 国立故宮博物院、1979、p.903.
19 Guoli Zhongyangyanjyuyuan Lishiyuyan yanjiusuo ed. 國立中央研究院歷史語言研究所編, *Ming-Qing shiliao* 明清史料, *Wu-bian* 戊編, vol. 2, p.29b.
20 National Palace Museum ed., *Secret Place Memorials of the Ch'ien-lung period Ch'ing Documents,* 宮中檔乾隆朝奏摺, vol.66, 1987, p.592.

The above are some historical evidences about smuggling problem between mainland and Taiwan. The smuggler often used the small port to smuggle into Taiwan[21].

3.3 Southeast Asia

According to a memorials from Fujian customs affairs management to the throne in the November 15 of 8th year of Yongzheng (1730), it had a record about the relations between China and Southeast Asia.

> "In the 11th of this month, a Siamese boat drifted on Xinghua county of Fujian province. According to castaways confession, Siamese merchants' ancestors in this boat were from Fujian, lots of sailors' ancestors in this boat were from Zhejiang, only 6 sailors were Siamese. The boat were going to Ningpo to do business with Chinese, but the boat suffered the storm in the half way, so they drifted on Xinghua county.[22]
> "In the August 11th, a Siamese boat also drifted on Xiamen because of the strom. After 15 days, a Annam boat also drifted on Xiamen because of the strom. According to the confession of castaways in two boats, they all were Chinese living in overseas, the boats also were China Junks."[23]

From these records, it can be seen that overseas Chinese were leading the trade between China and Siam. Chinese merchants act a pivotal role in the China-Southeast Asia trade. There also have some records about Chinese merchants in Southeast Asia as following.

A report from a admiral called Xu Liangbin in the 15 March of the 9th year of Yongzheng (the year 1731): "In the 12th February of this year, a boat bounded for Philippines carrying illegal immigrants 127 persons, had been found out on the Fujian maritime space."[24]... "Through further inquiry, a fact have been found out that lots of coastal Chinese had lived in Annam and Philippines and other Southeast Asia nations. Overseas Chinese accepted official position from those Southeast Asia nations. The coastal Chinese pretended to be sailors to go

---

21 National Palace Museum ed., *Secret Place Memorials of the Ch'ien-lung period Ch'ing Documents,* 宮中檔乾隆朝奏摺, vol.66, 1987, p.592.
22 National Palace Museum ed., *Secret Place Memorials of the Yung-cheng period Ch'ing Documents,* No. 17, 1979, p.193.
23 National Palace Museum ed., *Secret Place Memorials of the Yung-cheng period Ch'ing Documents*, No. 17, 1979, p.194.
24 National Palace *Museum ed., Secret Place Memorials of the Yung-cheng period Ch'ing Documents*, No. 17, 1979, p.789.

through the customs…. From now on it's best to check the merchant ship carefully."[25]

Another report was from the Fujian governor called Hao Yulin in the April 25 of the 11th year of Yongzheng (the year 1733): "In last December, a boat bounded for Philippines carrying illegal immigrants 157 persons, had been found out on the Fujian maritime space. According to their confession, about 10 to 20 thousand Chinese people from Zhangzhou county and Quanzhou county had lived in Philippines. The Overseas Chinese were engaged in doing business with mainlanders by taking ocean ship to home country. Most of the residents of Philippines port were Chinese".[26] …Smuggler paid 5 or 6 silver per person to organizers, and pretended to be sailors to go through the customs, so it was hard to be found out them"[27].

4 Goods circulation through Chinese Junks between East Asia and Southeast Asia

Chinese Junks regularly arrived in Nagasaki of Japan every year. These Chinese Junks contributed to the cultural exchanges between China and Japan. The following will introduce the goods which brought by Chinese Junks and Ryukyu Chinese Junks to Japan.

The goods carried by Chinese Junks from China mainly were high-grade silk, sugar and traditional Chinese medicinal materials. For example, in anei six years (1823), a Chinese Junk which carried 275000 pounds of sugar arrived at Nagasaki.[28] The largest quantity of trade goods between China and Japan was sugar. According to a local chronicles called *Zhapu Bei Zhi* which published in Daoguang 23 year (1843), mainly sugar which was carried to Japan were from Fujian and Guangdong Province.[29]

25　National Palace Museum ed., *Secret Place Memorials of the Yung-cheng period Ch'ing Documents*, No. 18, 1979, pp.360-361.

26　National Palace Museum ed., *Secret Place Memorials of the Yung-cheng period Ch'ing Documents*, No. 21, 1979, p.353.

27　National Palace Museum ed., *Secret Place Memorials of the Yung-cheng period Ch'ing Documents*, No. 21, 1979, p.354.

28　Matsuura Akira, *Kinsei higash ajia kaiiki no Hansen to Bunka koushou, Kansaidaigaku shuppannbu*, 2013, p.168.

29　*Zhapu bei-zhi* 乍浦備志、vol.14, *Zhongguo difangzhijichengXiang-zhen-zhi zhuan-ji* 中国地方志集成 郷鎮志専輯、vol.20, Shanghai shudian 上海書店、1992, pp.229-230.

Ryukyu imported the goods from Fujian province through the tribute trade.[30] The variety of goods can be seen from a cargo list noted in Daoguang five year (1825) as following.

> The custom duties of goods were about 2099 silvers, had been exempted. The first largest goods that were carried by Ryukyu boats were ginsengs. The total quantity of traditional Chinese medicinal materials were about 120 thousand jin. The second largest goods was the tea. Other goods was sugar, porcelain, brazilwood and so on.[31]

Because Ryukyu was Chinese dependency, lots of the custom duties were exempted. Ginsengs maybe were used as traditional Chinese medicine. Because Ryukyu could produce sugar, the number of imported sugar was much smaller than Japan.

Compared the goods imported by Japan with Ryukyu, the most obvious difference was that Japan didn't import tea from China. That was because Japan had introduced tea bushes from China and could processed their own tea. Ryukyu hadn't own tea bushes, cultivation also was difficult, so Ryukyu had to import tea from China. For example, in the September of Qianlong 32 year (1767) Ryukyu imported 21740 jin tea from China. In the November of Qianlong 38 year (1773) Ryukyu imported 20020 jin tea from China. In the January of Qianlong 40 year (1775) Ryukyu imported 10320 jin tea from China. In the December of Qianlong 40 year Ryukyu imported 65370 jin tea from China[32]. If convert to current counting unti, Ryukyu imported about 6 ton to 38 ton tea from China every year.

The most expensive inputed foods from Fujian province to Ryukyu was high-grade fabric. But by the time of late Qing dynasty, most high-grade fabric in China were imported from Europe, the high-grade fabric exported from China to Ryukyu also maybe were from Europe, Fujian province became a entrepot trade place in the late Qing dynasty.

In the same time of late Qing dynasty, China also exported goods to Singapore. From a report of British Parliament testimony in March 29 of 1830, it was described that "I got a cargo list about a Chinese Junk from Xiamen to Singapore. The ship arrived at Singapore in January 25 of 1824. The weight of goods

---

30 *Matsuura Akira, Kinsei Higashi-Ajia kaiiki no Hansen to Bunka-koushou*, pp.147-150.
31 Zhongguo diyi lishi dangan guan ed., *Qingdai ZhongLiu guanxi dangan xuanbian*, pp.632-633.
32 Zhongguo diyi lishi dangan guan ed., *Qingdai ZhongLiu guanxi dangan xuanbian*, p. 111, 155, 157, 166, 173.

were about 200-250 tons...The main variety of goods were porcelain, paper umbrellas, sweets and tea "[33]. Comparing the variety of exported goods between Japan and Singapore from a comparative perspective, it can be seen that the main goods exported to Singapore were articles for daily use. That was because lots of the overseas Chinese lived in Singapore. They needed to buy goods from their homeland. There also had a historic records about Singapore overseas Chinese which recorded in the October of 1880 as following.

> Singapore was under the jurisdiction of the United Kingdom, there were 6621 miles from Shanghai to Singapore.... More and more Chinese arrived in Singapore after the late of Qing dynasty. At the beginning, the largest numbers of overseas Chinese in Singapore were from Fujian Province, the second numbers were from Guangdong Province. But after Daoguang 18 year, the largest numbers of overseas Chinese in Singapore were from Guangdong Province, overseas Chinese from Fujian Province were the second. And every year more than ten thousand people arrive in Singapore from Guangdong Province. their leader called Hu Yuji 胡玉基."[34]

5 Conclusion

Chinese junks regular arrived at Nagasaki, and stayed for 4 months. In this 4 months, about 100 persons would stayed at Nagasaki. The main goods of Chinese junks were sugar and traditional Chinese medicinal materials. Comparing the variety of imported goods between Japan and Ryukyu, the same goods were traditional Chinese medicinal materials, others were different. In order to maintain balance, on the way to Japan, Chinese junks ballasted the sugar, and ballasted the copper and marine products when returned to China.

Ryukyu boats carried the copper, sulfur and sea foods to China. Chinese Junks also carried the same goods from Japan to China. The different place was that Ryukyu boats carried a large amount of tea and papers from China to Ryukyu. But Japan had their own native tea and papers, so Japan didn't carry tea and papers from China. The exception was that Japan liked importing Chinese books from China.

---

33 *First Report from the Select Committee on Affairs the East India Company*, China Trade, vol. 8, 1830, p.322.
34 Zhongguo diyi lishi dangan guan ed., *A Collection of Archives on the Relations between China and Southeast Asian countries in Qing Dynasty* 清代中国與東南亞各国関係檔案史料匯編、vol.1, Guoji wenhua chuban 国際文化出版, 1998, p.217.

Chinese Junks also carried a large amount of articles for daily use to Southeast Asia. There were many overseas Chinese need those goods. When returned to China, Chinese Junks would carry a large amount of grain from Southeast Asia. The industrial structure of every islands in Southeast Asia was different, so the goods from China to Southeast Asia by Chinese Junks also were not exactly the same.

the main goods that imported from China to Ryukyu were

Chinese junks had arrived at Nagasaki and was going to trade Sino-Japanese trade with periodic regularity, into the territory generally had stay after about 4 months. Chinese Junk's of crews were about 100 or so and to stay at Nagasaki. These carried large quantities of sugar that was produced in the southeast part of Fujian and the Shantou area, Chinese herbal medicine 漢方薬剤 to Nagasaki. In the same period of Ryukyu is Chinese Tributary country, the annual tribute Ryukyu dynasty dispatch boat carrying Chinese goods return. Japan and the Ryukyu buy Chinese goods are common Chinese herbal medicine, but other than that the purchase of goods different. Chinese Junks at sea must have ballast, starting from China when ballast is sugar, compared to copper and dried seafood China when returning from Japan.[35]

Ryukyu vessels for tributary to China carried Ryukyu of goods to China, in addition to copper, sulfur, also dried seafood. This is sailing with Qing China returning from Japan equipped cargo were similar. However, the Ryukyu tributary states carry large quantities of paper, tea leafs, which is very different from the situation in Japan. Japan conducted the domestic tea cultivation and processing, so no need to import Chinese tea. And Japan's domestic production, processing and paper, and therefore needs no special paper to China's purchase. Instead, historical data show that the situation has books published in Japan by the Qing Dynasty sailboat shipped back to China.

Chinese junks carried Chinese goods to Southeast Asian countries, most Chinese people living locally to provide daily necessities, while returning from Southeast Asian countries to carry a large number of Chinese junk food is rice cereal category.

Also located above the island country in East Asia and Southeast Asia waters, but because of differences in their respective countries, such as the industrial structure, although both belong to the same period of the trade, but the demand for goods varies.

---

35 Matuura Akira, *Kinsei Higashi-Ajia kaiiki no Bunnka-kousho, Shibunnkaku*, 2010, pp. 327-333.

Part 1:

The Activities of Chinese Junks on the East Asian Sea in Early Modern Ages

CHAPTER 2

Chinese Sea Merchants and Pirates

1 Introduction: The course of research in Chinese maritime history

Studies of global *maritime history* have frequently dealt with questions involving the Mediterranean and Atlantic, focusing on the history of Western Europe. However, there have been few studies dealing specifically with the waters surrounding East Asia. It would be fair to say that up until now historical studies looking at the seas lying within the area contained by the Chinese mainland, the Korean peninsula, the Japanese archipelago, the Ryukyu Islands, Taiwan, the Philippine and Indonesian archipelagos, the Malay peninsula, and mainland Indochina, namely the Bohai, Yellow, East China and South China Seas, have been slow to appear. This is perhaps because existing studies of Chinese history have mostly taken a *continental view of history*, as Kawakatsu Heita points out in 'Launching Maritime History' (*Kaiyō shikan no funade*): 'postwar Japanese have not had a view of history that takes account of the sea.'

It has been said that Chinese history emerged from the Yellow River basin. Although the importance of the culture of the Yangtze River basin has recently been acknowledged, the cultural activity of the maritime regions, with their broad coastline, has been neglected and for a long time has received little attention. As archaeological surveys of the coastal regions have progressed, the history of the maritime life of Chinese people living in coastal areas has gradually come to be re-thought. Especially as China's policy of opening up to the outside world has progressed since the 1980s, the history of its coastal regions has been re-evaluated. With historical studies of the special economic zones (SEZs) being particularly prolific, research focused on the port cities of the coastal regions has received a lot of attention, and historical studies focused on the famous trading ports of Tianjin, Shanghai, Ningbo, Wenzhou, Fuzhou, Xiamen and Guangzhou have begun to be published.

Research on port cities and their economic relations with the hinterland surrounding them is developing from the previous court-centered history into research on regional history. I would like to reflect this research into regional history in looking at what we can find out if we look at the previously land-focused Chinese history from a marine perspective, and especially looking at the Chinese sea merchants (*haishang*), who have played a central role in its maritime life.

'Chinese sea merchants' refers to the Chinese merchants who traded by sea, and among the important results of Japanese research into Chinese sea merchants, mention must be made of Kuwahara Jitsuzō's[1] *The Exploits of Pu Shougeng* (*Ho Jukō no jiseki*). Kuwahara first reported on his research on Pu Shougeng[2] at the 1915 meeting of the Tokyo Historical Society, and published the results of his studies in five editions of *Shigaku zasshi* between October 1915 and October 1916. These were published in book form, with the addition of subsequent research, as *The Exploits of Pu Shougeng, State Agent Trade Supervisor from the West* (*Sō-matsu no teikyo shihaku seiikijin Ho Jukō no jiseki*) in 1923. This book does not appear from the title to be directly related to Chinese sea merchants, but it is one of the best and most indispensable Japanese studies on East Asian history, as it contains various research on the diverse activities of Chinese sea merchants. Other studies worthy of note include Kuwahara's *Essays on the History of East-West Communication* (*Tōzai kōtsūshi ronsō*), Fujita Toyohachi's[3] *Studies on the History of East-West Interaction: South Seas* (*Tōzai kōshōshi no kenkyū: nankai hen*), and Ishida Mikinosuke's[4]

---

1   **Kuwahara Jitsuzō** (1870-1931): Japanese scholar of East Asian history. Professor at the College of Letters of Kyoto Imperial University, he made a great contribution in the areas of the history of east-west communication, cultural history and the history of law, and established the basis of education in East Asian history. His work is collected in *The Complete Works of Kuwahara Jitsuzō* (*Kuwahara Jitsuzō zenshū*) published by Iwanami Shoten in five volumes plus appendix.

2   **Pu Shougeng** (dates unknown): a Muslim south seas trader of Arabian or Persian origin in China's Southern Song and early Yuan dynasties. He became a trade official in Quanzhou, Fujian province in the mid-thirteenth century.

3   **Fujita Toyohachi** (1869-1929): Japanese scholar of East Asia. After graduating from the Tokyo Imperial University College of Letters, he worked in education in Qing China, where he contributed to the development of Chinese academia, before becoming a professor at Waseda and Tokyo Imperial Universities. In 1928 he became director of the History Department at the newly established Taipei Imperial University, but died soon afterwards. His research is collected in *Studies on the History of East-West Interaction* (*Tōzai kōshōshi no kenkyū*, in two volumes: *Nankai hen* and *Seiiki hen*).

4   **Ishida Mikinosuke** (1891-1974): Japanese scholar of East Asia. After graduating from the Tokyo Imperial University College of Letters, he devoted his energies for

Chinese Sea Merchants and Pirates

Figure 2   Junks at Youngjian（甬江・寧波）estuary, 1981

Chinese Historical Documents on the South Seas (*Nankai ni kansuru Shina shiryō*), and these earlier studies built up a repository of research focused on Chinese historical documents in the area of interaction between east and west. However, although these studies have been taken up in the history of the various nations and in regional history, they have not been developed from the viewpoint of maritime history. In this book, I would like to pursue these historical documents with a focus on maritime history.

2   Problems concerning Chinese sea merchants

2.1   The business of Chinese sea merchants

There are few concrete examples to clarify the economic activity of Chinese sea merchants, but I would like to relate the following example, which is known in some detail.

It is a story of foreign trade, found in volume 12 of *Yue Jian* by Wang Zaijin

---

many years to managing Tōyō Bunko (Komagome, Bunkyō-ku, Tokyo), which collected important books on East Asian studies. He seems to have published over 400 volumes of research, but apart from his generally know *Spring in Changan* (*Chōan no haru*, Kōdansha Gakujutsu Bunko), part of his research is collected in *A Library of East Asian Cultural History* (*Tōa bunkashi sōkō*, Tōyō Bunko) and the four-volume *Collected Works of Ishida Mikinosuke* (*Ishida Mikinosuke chosakushū*, Rokkō Shuppan).

from the latter half of the sixteenth century. In the Wanli era (1567-1619), a certain Lin Qing from Fuqing in Fujian province built a large ship with a ship owner, Wang Hou, and employed Zheng Song and Wang Yi as *baduo* (helmsmen), Zheng Qi, Lin Cheng and others as *shuishou* (lower ranking sailors), along with Jin Shishan and Huang Chenglin as silversmiths, Li Ming, who was familiar with navigation, as a guide, and Chen Hua, who spoke *woyu* (Japanese), as an interpreter. The ship set sail for Japan, loaded with *shaluo*,[5] pongee, silk, *bupi*,[6] white sugar, porcelain, fruit, scented fans and combs, sewing needles, and paper. They planned to trade these in Japan for Japanese silver, which the silversmiths would smelt onboard for them to bring back. This account gives a concrete example of what shipping operations in overseas trade were like at that time. This kind of practice followed from the immense profits that could be made from overseas trade.

It was not necessarily the case that those onboard ships were all of the same nationality. The crew of a shogunate ship that arrived in the Korean peninsula in 1604 included Japanese and Portuguese, as well as Chinese. Wen Jin, from Haicheng county in Zhangzhou, Fujian province, who was 35 at the time, had set off the previous February on a trading journey from Fujian to Giao Chi in Vietnam, but was attacked by a Japanese ship just before landing. Over one hundred were killed, with only twenty-eight survivors. Wen Jin and the other survivors went with the Japanese ship to Jianpuzhai, the present day Cambodia, where they bought leather goods, wax, pepper, *sumu*,[7] ivory, rhinoceros horn, *daimei*,[8] gold and silver before heading for Japan. The Portuguese onboard were involved in trade between Macau and Jianpuzhai, and had joined the ship to trade with Japan along with the Japanese crew. The Japanese had set out with Chinese living in Nagasaki and Satsuma, with the intention of trading with Cambodia.

The ship with these people onboard had encountered a storm on the way to Japan and been blown off course to the Korean peninsula. This ship was one of the so-called *shuinsen*,[9] that had been granted licenses in the form of a red seal

---

5   *shaluo* (silk gauze): silk woven into a thin fabric, which was highly prized because of the complexity of its manufacture.

6   *bupi*: generally a woven cotton cloth, in which China had the most advanced technology in the world at this time. From the eighteenth century onwards, cotton cloth exported to Europe was highly prized as 'Nankeen cotton.'

7   *sumu*: sappan wood, an evergreen tree grown in the tropics, the bark of which is used for red dye.

8   *daimei*: a turtle, which grows up to one meter in length. Its shell is boiled and used for tortoiseshell work.

9   *shuinsen*: ships which made trading voyages to south-east Asia, licensed with a

(*shuin*) to voyage overseas by Tokugawa Ieyasu. One of the Japanese on board had been provided with five hundred taels of silver in trading capital from Ieyasu, in addition to the license.

What kind of profit could be made from overseas trade at this time? For example, one hundred catties of Chinese-made Huzhou silk[10], which Chinese merchants took Luzon in the Philippines in the mid-seventeenth century could make one hundred taels of silver, but if it was exported abroad it could apparently fetch as much as three hundred taels. If one could overlook the danger and succeed in the venture, huge profits were guaranteed. Both in the East and in the West, in commerce that sought to exploit interregional price differences, the greater the danger the greater the riches it offered.

The shipping business that targeted instant riches of this sort saw the appearance in the Qing dynasty of ships specializing in ocean-going transport. Taking the example of Jiang Longshun's ship from Yuanhe county in Suzhou, Jiangnan (later Jiangsu) province, which was carried off course to the Ryukyu islands in January of 1786 (year 51 of the Qianlong era), it was hired with a crew of twenty in (intercalary) March of year 49 of the Qianlong era by a Mr. Huang of Zhenjiang to transport ginger to Tianjin. It was then hired in Tianjin by a Mr. He from the port of Niuzhuang in the northeast to transport rice from Niuzhuang to Tianjin. Then it was hired by a Mr. Shi of Shandong province to take spices from Tianjin to Huang county. Unable to find an employer in Huang county, it headed for its port in the northeast, where it was chartered by a Mr. Huo to take rice to Huang county again. It headed back to its northeast port again and was chartered by Mr. Huo to take rice to Lijin county in Shandong province. When that was finished, it went again to its northeast port, where it was chartered to transport rice to Tianjin. In Tianjin, it was chartered by You Huali, a merchant from Fujian, to go to Ningbo, and it was loaded with jujubes in Haifeng county in Shandong before setting sail, but it got into difficulty at sea

---

permit to travel overseas, in the form of a *shuin* (red seal), from the Momoyama period to the early Tokugawa period. Those who traded using the licensed ships included the *daimyō* of western domains, such as Shimazu and Hosokawa, and merchants from Kyoto, Osaka, Sakai and Nagasaki. Exports included silver, copper and lacquer ware, while imports included raw silk, silk cloth, deerskins, sappan wood and sugar. Between 1604 and 1635, as many as 350 such licensed ships were sent to what are now Vietnam, Thailand, Cambodia, the Philippines and Taiwan.

10 **Huzhou silk** (*husi*): raw silk from Huzhou, a famous centre for the production of raw silk, in Zhejiang province, south of Lake Tai. Rice and mulberry cultivation and sericulture progressed from the late Song dynasty onwards, and from late Ming and early Qing the manufacture and weaving of silk developed. 'Huzhou silk' in particular established itself as a brand name.

on the way to Ningbo and was blown off course to the Kingdom of the Ryukyus. In this actual example, the ship was chartered seven times in the space of two years, earning transportation fees in the process.

As for the transportation fees for ships engaged in this shipping and transportation business, Xu Wansheng's ship from Ninghaizhou in Dengzhou, Shangdong province was chartered with a crew of twenty in July 1862 (the first year of the Tongzhi era) by timber merchant from Niuzhuang to transport 1,350 pieces of timber from Ninghaizhou, near the city of Yantai, to Niuzhuang, for which the charter fee was four hundred taels of silver. The same ship was chartered by a traveling merchant in Niuzhuang to transport twenty *lou* (bamboo crates) of oil and 630 piculs of soybeans to the Jiangnan area, for which the transportation fee was 535 taels of silver. The first of these journeys was from Ninghaizhou, the present day Muping county, to Niuzhuang, the second from Niuzhuang to, presumably, Shanghai, which is four times the distance by sea, but the charter fee was around 1.3 times. It is impossible to generalize, since it depends on the volume of cargo, but fees must have been decided by the distance traveled and the volume carried.

In the case of coastal sand-junks in the reign of the Qing emperor Daoguang, if they were requisitioned by the government to carry loads of 70% designated rice and 30% other cargo for unloading in Tianjin, they were paid a fee of five *qian* per picul of rice. The fee for transporting a cargo of 3,000 piculs to Tianjin, with 2,100 piculs of rice, was therefore 1,050 taels, and for a cargo of 1,500 piculs, with 1,050 piculs of rice, it was 525 taels. Since money would also have been earned from trading the cargo, the transportation earnings from one sand-junk would seem to have been from seven or eight hundred taels up to over one thousand taels, and since it would likely have made over a thousand taels on the return journey as well, high earnings would seem to have been obtainable as long as the journey was accomplished safely. On the other hand, as far as the costs of building a ship are concerned, large seagoing ships of this sort, carrying 3,000 piculs, cost as much as 10,000 taels of silver. Medium-size ships cost several thousand taels, but, given the earnings that could be made from a single journey, the cost could be recovered within a few years if several safe journeys could be accomplished. The merchants who operated these Chinese ships had a wide range of activities in a variety of forms, making large profits in the process.

2.2 Cargo carried by Chinese ships

The cargo carried by these seagoing ships varied enormously between times and regions. Carried from the south seas to China were pepper and sappan

Figure 3   'A Foreign Trader', Barrow, *"Travels in China"*, 1804

wood, cloves[11] and other spices, while exports from China to other countries generally included woven silk, china and porcelain. China and porcelain in particular are found even today in the wrecks of sunken ships that are discovered from time to time. A well known wreck, a long-distance ocean-going sailing ship thought to be from the end of the Southern Song dynasty, which was discovered off Quanzhou in Fujian in 1974, was carrying a variety of objects, including spices, medicine, bronze coins, china and porcelain, bronze- and woodenware, textiles, and leather products. A wreck found off the coast of Mokpo, in southwest Korea, the 'Xin'an ship,' thought to be an ocean-going sailing ship from the Yuan dynasty, was found to have been carrying more than twenty thousand pieces of china and porcelain, including celadon and white porcelain, eight million bronze coins weighing as much as twenty-eight tons, and red sandalwood.

Up until the Song dynasty, low volume, high value products, which had a large interregional price difference, were common, but from the beginning of the Qing dynasty cargoes of coastal ships in particular are often large volumes of commodities. These would include rice, soybeans, and sugar. Fujian, which had constant shortages of rice, shipped it in from Jiangsu, Zhejiang and Taiwan. Soybeans, which were used as food and soil fertilizer in the Jiangnan region, were transported by ship from the coastal areas of Huabei and the Northeast to Shanghai and on to Zhejiang and Fujian.

---

11   **cloves**: the dried buds of *syzygium aromaticum*. Used as a spice or medicine. Cloves originate from the Moluccas, and are a scented shrub of the *Myrtaceae* family that grows in the tropics.

Part 1: The Activities of Chinese Junks on the East Asian Sea in Early Modern Ages

The cargoes of a Chinese ship that sailed from Zhapu in Zhejiang to Nagasaki in Japan in January 1824 and another that sailed in the same month from Xiamen in Fujian to Singapore were very different. Whereas the Chinese trading ship that went to Nagasaki carried mostly silk textiles, sugar and a wide variety of medicine, the ship that went to Singapore carried mostly everyday items that seem to have been for Chinese living there, and which were of various kinds. There were 660,000 pieces of china and porcelain of thirty-two kinds, ten thousand tiles, twelve thousand paper umbrellas, and various items that one might find in a department store today: sweets, dried mushrooms, salted fish, shoes made from silk, cotton or straw, tobacco, combs, writing brushes, pickled vegetables, cotton cloth, yarn, and tea. It seems perfectly natural that two Chinese trading ships that left China at the same time for different destinations should have carried different cargoes, but there is little historical evidence to make this clear.

2.3 The construction of Chinese ships

Recent archaeological surveys have revealed the construction of Chinese junks, which could operate over a wide area as long as there was wind.

Sunken ships have been found and studied in archaeological surveys since the 1970s. The site of a Qin or Han dynasty shipyard, which was the subject of a dig in Guangzhou in late 1974, suggests that sailing ships of up to twenty meters in length and weighing twenty-five to thirty tons were built there. Previously, in August 1974, the hull of the wooden seafaring ship mentioned above, known as the 'Quanzhou Bay Song dynasty ship,' was discovered in the ground at the port of Houzhu, in the southeast of Quanzhou, Fujian province. The structure of this ship already had something like a keel, timber that functioned like a backbone, running along the bottom of the ship from the prow to the stern, called the *longgu*. If the ship got into difficulty at sea, this seems to have acted to limit flooding even if part of the hull was damaged, giving the vessel an excellent structure. Studies of the excavations suggest that this was a ship from around the end of the Southern Song in the second half of the fourteenth century, measuring around thirty-four meters in length and weighing around four hundred tons. Studies of the 'Xin'an ship' found off the coast of southwest Korea between 1976 and 1984 show that it was a seafaring three-masted sailing ship from the Yuan dynasty, thirty-four meters in length and weighing around two hundred tons.

The discovery of sunken Chinese ships has thus made up for the lack of written historical material on ships, and provides much more concrete information than excavated material.

Chinese junks were an environmentally friendly form of transport, requiring no oil like today's cars. Of course, from the perspective of an age that stresses speed, they are slow. However, if we think of the history of Chinese seafaring ships, particularly junks, as the 2,000 years of the Western calendar, then we should remember that, dividing it at Fulton's invention of the steamship at the start of the nineteenth century, the period when junks were in use, covers the not inconsiderable period of 1,800 years. This also suggests that the history of Chinese junks is of great significance.

2.4 Chinese piracy

The slowest area of maritime historical studies to develop has been the history of piracy, which is seen as anti-history. In the field of Japanese history, these began with Naganuma Kenkai's *Japanese Piracy* (*Nihon no kaizoku*) and *Studies in Japanese Maritime History* (*Nihon kaijishi kenkyū*) and have seen major developments recently in Amino Yoshihiko's *Ruffians and Pirates* (*Akutō to kaizoku*) and elsewhere, but in relation to specifically Chinese history, piracy has been largely ignored, with the exception of the *wokou* (Japanese pirate) problem in the Ming dynasty (see page 38) and the problems of piracy by Cai Qian (see page 80) and others.

Research into Chinese piracy has been almost ignored up until now. From the perspective of orthodox history, it has been seen as anti-history, but there were some pirates who surrendered to the government and were given positions something like that of the navy by the government, in order to put down pirates, as was seen in the late Song and Yuan dynasties and again in the late Ming dynasty. The question cannot therefore be understood just in neat terms of positive and negative.

As the development of Chinese society gradually spread from the hinterland of the Yellow River delta to the coastal regions, Chinese piracy began to appear over a wide area, but the region where it left most of a record was the coast of southern China. The reason it occurred frequently in southern China is probably because pirates, always used to the sea, made their bases in the islands, where it was easier to evade capture by the authorities after their depredations, and in the complicated geography of the coastal areas.

In this chapter, I would also like to discuss these records of piracy and look at the role of piracy in maritime history through the ages.

3 Sea merchants and pirates in the Tang, Song and Yuan dynasties

3.1 The origins of Chinese overseas trade

The term '*haishang*' (sea merchant) seems to have come into general use from the Tang dynasty onwards, but mentions of maritime trade can be found in official histories before that.

China's trade with countries to the west was at first carried out overland. One person who thought of sending an envoy to the country of Da Qin'Da Qin in the west, thought to be the Roman Empire was the Later Han Protector General of the Western Regions (*xiyu dufu*[12]) Ban Chao. Ban Chao tried to send his subordinate, Gan Ying, to Da Qin in 97 AD. Gan Ying passed through the Western Regions to reach the country of Tiao Zhi'Tiao Zhi (thought to be Syria), where he reached the 'great sea.' Planning to cross the great sea, he was told by a sailor from the country of An Xi 'An Zi (thought to be Parthia) that the voyage would take three months even with a favorable wind, and that, considering the prevailing winds, he should prepare at least two years' and up to three years' provisions for the sea crossing. He therefore gave up on sailing to Da Qin. However, around seventy years later, an envoy was sent by sea from Da Qin. In 166 AD an envoy of An Dun, king of Da Qin, thought to be the Roman emperor Marcus Aurelius Antoninus, arrived from Nhat Nam in central Vietnam, initiating relations with China with an offering of ivory, rhinoceros horn and tortoiseshell. Consequently, it seems people traveled from Da Qin to Funan, and people from Nhat Nam, Giao Chi and elsewhere traveled to Da Qin.

In 226, under Sun Quan of Wu in the Three Kingdoms era, Qin Lun, a merchant from Da Qin, arrived in Giao Chi, and met Sun Quan with the support of Wu Mo, prefect of Giao Chi. Sun Quan asked Qin Lun about the manners and customs of Da Qin and was given a substantial report. It is recorded in the *Zhong tian zhu guo* chapter in volume 54 of the *Liang Shu* that Wu Mo, prefect of Giao Chi, later tried to take Qin Lun to China proper, but Qin Lun decided to return to his country when Wu Mo died on the way.

Thus it seems that communication with countries overseas became active

---

12 *Xiyu dufu*: A *dufu* (Protector General) was appointed for the first fifty-nine years of the Former Han dynasty to suppress the Western Regions, managing the colonies and protecting communications and trade. After the Protector General was killed at the end of the Former Han, in the Xin era of Wang Mang, no appointment was made. Subsequently in 74 AD in the Later Han the post was revived but soon abolished, and in 91 AD Ban Chao was appointed. It was abolished in 107 AD.

from around the Later Han, and sea merchants began to arrive in China. Later, as overseas relations became more active, mentions of Chinese sea merchants become more frequent in official histories as well.

3.2 Birth of the maritime trade supervisor

Officials responsible for work relating to overseas trade in the Tang dynasty were known as *shiboshi*[13] (maritime trade supervisors). The first appearance of the title *shiboshi* is around the time of Emperor Xuanzong. In 714 You Wei, appointed *shiboshi* of Annan, and Commander Zhou Qingli reported to the court that Persian priests could make intricate works of art. The next record is found in 763, when the eunuch and *shiboshi* Lü Taiyi expelled the governor (*jiedushi*) of Guangnan, Zhang Xiu, and instigated a revolt in Guangzhou. It is recorded in the *Jiu Tangshu* that, when the rebel forces of Huang Chao, from Shandong, joined the rebellion of Wang Xianzhi[14] and threatened Guangzhou, the centre of overseas trade, in 879, there were great fears that the profit from maritime trade and gems including the south sea pearls brought in every year, would be stolen by the rebels and that the exchequer would be bankrupted. The *Tangguo shibu*, which records the history of the Kaiyuan era (713-741) to the Changqing era (821-824), records that overseas trade was carried on actively from the eighth century, mainly in Guangzhou, and that for this purpose the post of *shiboshi* was established to take charge of trade affairs.

The *Xin Tangshu* says that it was a rule in the past that, if a sea merchant sank, his property would be disposed of by the government, and if the merchant's wife did not report to the authorities within three months, the whole of it would be appropriated. As this makes clear, the activities of sea merchants were not entirely free, but were subject to certain forms of government restric-

---

13   **shiboshi** (or *shibosi*): The first appointment of an official to supervise overseas trade in China was that of the *shiboshi* in Guangzhou in the second year of Kaiyuan (714) in the Tang dynasty. Under the Tang, only the title *shiboshi* is known, but in the Song dynasty we find '*shibosi*' established as a title. The Song *shibosi* dealt with all affairs relating to the business of trade, including inspecting the cargo of trading ships entering port and imposing import taxes. The Yuan dynasty largely carried on the Song system of *shibosi*. However, in the Ming dynasty, as a policy of isolation was pursued, the *shibosi* became mainly a post for dealing with tribute ships. In the Qing dynasty, there was no *shibosi* as under previous dynasties, but the same work of dealing with the arrival and departure of trading ships was handled by customs (*haiguan*).

14   **Rebellion of Wang Xianzhi**: Wang Xianzhi (?-872), a salt trader at the end of the Tang dynasty, led a revolt of three thousand landless peasants around 875 to 878 from the mid and lower reaches of the Yellow River to the mid-Yangtze.

tion.

Cases of Chinese sea merchants who ventured overseas in the Tang dynasty are also frequently mentioned in Japanese sources. From around the time when Japan stopped sending envoys to China in 894, a large number of sea merchants started coming to Japan from the Chinese mainland. It is easy to find cases of people visiting China on these Chinese merchants' ships in the records of Japanese monks.

Names of Chinese sea merchants are also found in Ennin's *Record of a Pilgrimage to China in Search of the Law*, made famous by Reischauer's[15] Ennin's[16] *Travels in T'ang China*. The entry for 8 January of the sixth year of Shōwa (839) in Volume 1 of Ennin's diary records that in 819 the Chinese merchant Zhang Jueji set sail with a cargo of various items for trade, but encountered adverse winds and was adrift for three months before blowing ashore in the province of Dewa. The entry for 5 July in the fifth year of Huichang (Shōwa 12, or 845) states that the Japanese priest Egaku made a pilgrimage to Wutaishan in the second year of Huichang (842) and that when he returned to Japan he went on the ship of Li Linde, presumably a Chinese sea merchant.

These examples also show that the overseas activity of Chinese sea merchants increased from around the first half of the eighth century.

These Chinese sea merchants faced not only shipwreck from the forces of nature, but also frequent man-made disasters, in the form of piracy. Jianzhen[17] (Ganjin), who founded Tōshōdaiji in the western part of Nara after reaching Japan on his sixth attempt, was plagued by the fear of piracy, as well as natural disasters at sea. The entry in the *Tōdaiwajō tōseiden* for his first attempt to reach Japan, in the second year of Tianbao (743), states that his voyage to Japan was prevented because pirates were very active and the coasts of Taizhou, Wenzhou

---

15 **Reischauer**: Edwin O. Reischauer (1910-90), born in Tokyo to Presbyterian missionaries who had come to Japan, after graduating from high school, he obtained his degree from Harvard, after which he became a professor at Harvard, and the US ambassador to Japan.

16 **Ennin** (794-864): a priest of the Tendai school in the early Heian period. He went to Tang China in 838, and spent ten years in China, including Tiantaishan in Zhejiang province. His diary from the period is *Record of a Pilgrimage to China in Search of the Law*. After his return to Japan, he became chief priest of the Tendai school and was given the posthumous name of Enkaku Daishi.

17 **Jianzhen** (689-763): born in Yangzhou in present-day Zhejiang, he became a monk at the age of fourteen and subsequently trained and became a priest in Changan. He taught in Yangzhou, but resolved to go to Japan in response to the request for monks, and reached Japan in 753 after five unsuccessful voyages. He later established Tōshōdaiji and is known as the founder of the Ritsu school in Japan.

and Mingzhou (known as Ningbo since the Ming dynasty) had suffered at their hands. Since the *Zizhi tongjian* reports that pirates including Wu Lingguang attacked Taizhou and Mingzhou in February of 744, the third year of Tianbao under the Emperor Xuanzong, the pirate who prevented Jianzhen from reaching Japan at this time was presumably the same Wu Lingguang. The leader of Hainan, Feng Ruofang, who rescued Jianzhen when he was blown off course there, was in fact a pirate who had grown rich by attacking a Persian ship that was on its way to China along the coast of Hainan.

The Tang capital of Changan is described as the start of the Silk Road, but that is clearly a perception that focuses on overland communication. However, if we take a different perspective and look at communication between China and other countries by sea, it is clear that an increasing number of countries were visiting China by sea as the Tang court internationalized. The starting point for this communication by sea was Guangzhou, which was visited by merchants not only from southeast Asia, but from far-off Arabia as well. The *Tales of China and India*, written in Arabic in the second half of the ninth century, makes clear that Guangzhou gathered goods brought by Arabs and Chinese.

3.3 Expansion of overseas trade

Song China established a *shibosi* in Guangzhou in 971, soon after the founding of the dynasty, to oversee ships from overseas and the movement of Chinese merchant ships, and subsequently established them in Hangzhou and Mingzhou as well. Consequently, Arabian merchants and others began visiting for trade from overseas countries such as Da Shi (Arabia), Zhan Cheng (Champa) and Sanfoqi (Srivijaya), carrying foreign products such as spices, ivory, rhinoceros horn, and sappan wood, and seeking Chinese-made silk textiles and porcelain. In response to this, in 989, sea merchants heading overseas from China for the purposes of trade were required to have papers issued by the authorities at the Liangzhe *shibosi*. Sea merchants not in possession of official papers were punished and had the goods they were carrying seized by the authorities. The official papers that sea merchants were required to have when venturing abroad named their cargo, the destination of their voyage, and a guarantor, and were only issued once they had confirmed that they were not carrying arms, articles for the manufacture of arms, or contraband.

One example of Song dynasty sea merchants is found in the *Record of a Pilgrimage to Mt Tiantai and Mt Wutai* by Jōjin[18], who went to China during the

---

18 **Jōjin** (1011-81): A priest of the Tendai school in the late Heian period. He became a monk at the age of seven, and went to Song China in 1072 at the age of 62, where he

Song dynasty and visited Mt Tiantai in Zhejiang and Mt Wutai in Shanxi. According to Volume 1 of his *Record*, he crossed to China from Matsuura in Hizen on one of three Chinese ships in March of the fourth year of Enkyū (fifth year of Xining, under the Northern Song, 1071). The captain of the first of these three Chinese ships was Zeng Ju, called Zeng Sanlang, from Nanxiongzhou, the captain of the second ship was Wu Zhu, called Wu Shilang, from Fuzhou, and the captain of the third was Zheng Qing, called Zheng Sanlang, from Quanzhou. The captains' homes were in present day Nanxiong in Guangdong, and Fuzhou and Quanzhou in Fujian, so they were presumably sea merchants from Guangdong and Fujian. There were many such Chinese sea merchants who visited Japan.

The entry in the *Chōya gunsai*[19] for 20 August in the second year of Chōji (fourth year of Songning under the Northern Song, 1105) records that a trading ship arrived in Shigashima at Hakata, in Kyushu. The *gangshou*, or owner, of this ship was Li Chong, from Quanzhou in Fujian. He was in possession of a *gongping*, in other words a certificate of passage, issued by the Director of the Liangzhe Shibosi in Mingzhou (Ningbo). The certificate reads: 'This ship is the property of Li Chong, who has recruited its crew of sailors to go to Japan to trade, and has already paid taxes at the *shibosi* in Mingzhou and received a permit to sail.' It also lists the names of Li Chong and his crew of sixty-nine, and mentions the cargo, including forty rolls of inlaid work, ten rolls of raw silk, and twenty rolls of figured silk.

Japanese records are not the only historical documents revealing the activities of sea merchants in the Song dynasty. The names of many Chinese traders are also found in the *Koryo sa*, which is the record of the Koryo dynasty that came to power in the Korean peninsula. In the *Koryo sa*, the names of Chinese are frequently recorded as '*Song shang*' or '*Song dugang*.'[20] In either case, geog-

---

visited Mt Tiantai in Zhejiang and Mt Wutai in Shanxi, and was highly revered by both the government and people in the Song capital, Bianliang (the present day Kaifeng, in Henan). *Record of a Pilgrimage to Mt Tiantai and Mt Wutai*, which is a diary of his voyage to and sojourn in China, was entrusted to a traveler returning to Japan, who brought it back. Jōji himself died of illness in China, without returning to Japan.

19 *Chōya gunsai*: Compiled by the mathematician Miyoshi Tameyasu, with an introduction from 1116, but with later additions. An important historical document containing Heian period official writings.

20 *dugang*: Particularly interesting entries give the titles *dugang* and *gangshou*. The authority on the history Song dynasty commerce, Shiba Yoshinobu has written of *dugang* that 'the representatives of trading ships coming from China are frequently described in the *Koryo sa* as "*dugang* Such-and-such,"' interpreting *dugang* to be the representatives of ships, and that *gangshou* 'must have been the leaders of the crew,' or the captain. Saeki Tomi interprets it as follows in his *Gazoku kango yakkai* (*Under-*

Table 1 Table of Song dynasty sea merchants mentioned in the *Goryeosa* (高麗史) (only those with Chinese place names stated)

Year	Koryo reign year	Date	Song	Place of origin	'*Shang*' or '*dugang*'	Name	Number of crew
1017	Hyongjong 8	5 July	Song	Quanzhou		Lin Renfu	40
1018	Hyongjong 9	11 April*	Song	Jiangnan		Wang Xizi	100
1019	Hyongjong 10	14 July	Song	Quanzhou		Chen Wengui	100
1019	Hyongjong 10	17 July	Song	Fuzhou		Yu ?	100+
1020	Hyongjong 11	27 Feb	Song	Quanzhou		Huai Zhui	
1022	Hyongjong 13	17 Aug	Song	Fuzhou		Chen Xiang-zhong	
1022	Hyongjong 13	28 Aug	Song	Guangnan		Chen Wensui	
1026	Hyongjong 17	9 Aug	Song	Guangnan		Li Wentong	3
1027	Hyongjong 18	20 Aug	Song	Jiangnan		Li Wentong	
1028	Hyongjong 19	5 Sep	Song	Quanzhou		Li Shanye	30+
1029	Hyongjong 20	13 Aug	Song	Guangnan		Jiang Wenbao	80
1030	Hyongjong 21	18 July	Song	Quanzhou		Lu Zun	
1031	Tokjong 1	19 June	Song	Taizhou	*Shangke*	Chen Weizhi	64
1033	Tokjong 2	1 Aug	Song	Quanzhou	*Shangdougang*	Lin Ai	55
1038	Chongjong 4	24 Aug	Song	Mingzhou	*Shang*	Chen Liang	147
				Taizhou		Chen Weiji	
1045	Chongjong 11	11 May	Song	Quanzhou	*Shang*	Lin Xi	
1049	Munjong 3	9 Aug	Song	Taizhou	*Shang*	Xu Zan	17
1049	Munjong 3	21 Aug	Song	Quanzhou	*Shang*	Wang Yicong	62
1059	Munjong 13	6 Aug	Song	Quanzhou	*Shang*	Xiao Zongming	
1059	Munjong 13	5 Aug	Song	Quanzhou	*Shang*		

* intercalary month

raphy suggests that they had come to Koryo by ship, and they were surely Song dynasty sea merchants.

Looking at mentions of Chinese sea merchants in the *Koryo sa*, we find that many are listed just as Chinese merchants, without giving their place of origin. The table below lists only those where the place of origin is stated. Based on the few cases where the place of origin is stated, as the table shows, most of the sea merchants were from Quanzhou in Fujian, and Mingzhou (Ningbo) or Taizhou in Zhejiang, in other words from the present day provinces of Zhejiang and Fujian. It is also known that some Chinese sea merchants made regular trips

standing Classical and Colloquial Chinese): '*Gangzhu:* owner. Cargo is referred to as *gang*. This refers to cargo tied up with rope.'

between China and Koryo over several years. These various Song dynasty sea merchants sailed repeatedly to Koryo with goods for trade and took Koryo-made products back to China. The trade items taken from Song China to Koryo included new learning and culture, such as the Chinese *Taiping yulan*[21] and other publications.

3.4 Sea merchants, pirates and trade supervisors under the Southern Song

When the Northern Song fell in 1126, as the Jin army advanced south, the Imperial family fled to Jiangnan and re-established the Southern Song dynasty with their provisional capital of Lin'an in Hangzhou. The Southern Song era saw development spread to the south of China, as the area under Song control was to the south of the Yangtze and as its capital was in Hangzhou, in the coastal part of Zhejiang. The maritime activities of sea merchants in the provinces of Fujian and Guangdong, on the coast south of Zhejiang, therefore increased.

In July of the fourth year of the Jianyan era (1130), the Southern Song government prohibited sea merchants from Fujian, Guangdong, Huai and Zhe from going to trade in Shandong and acting as guides for the Jin army. Sea merchants from the coast were actively engaged in maritime trade even in a time when the Jian and Southern Song were facing each other across the Huai River, as we know from the fact that powerful families in the Jiang, Zhe and Fujian regions were ordered to bolster their defenses by conscripting armies.

Quanzhou Yang Ke in *dingzhi* volume 6 of the *Yijianzhi*[22] contains the following anecdote. In over ten years as a sea merchant, Yang Ke built a fortune of two million taels. Whenever he got into difficulty at sea, he would pray to the gods to save him and would vow to build temples in various places, but when land came into view he would forget his promises and not give them another thought. When he was becalmed at sea in the tenth year of the Shaoxing era (1140), a god appeared to him in a dream and admonished him for his previous insincerity. Yang Ke told the god in his dream 'I am just on my way to Lin'an

---

21 **Taiping yulan:** (*Imperial Readings of the Taiping Era*) 1,000 volumes in 55 sections in all. An encyclopedia of the Song court, completed around 982/983, thought to have been published in woodblock print in the reign of Emperor Renzong (1022-62). It was subsequently in demand throughout East Asia. A feature of the book is its almost 1,700 types of quotations, which quote books that have not survived into the present.
22 **Yijianzhi**: 180 volumes, 25 additional volumes and one further addition. Completed by Hong Mai (1132-1202) around 1198. It was compiled by Hong Mai as a collection of various unusual popular stories during his term of office as a regional official, and is an important historical source for matters not found in official compilations.

now' and it is recorded that he subsequently fulfilled his promises to the gods. This story suggests that there were sea merchants who had made huge profits from the maritime trade centered on Fujian and Zhejiang.

An inscription from the eighth year of Shaoxing (1138) in Putian in Fujian records that Zhu Fang, a *gangshou* from Quanzhou, offered incense to the Xiangying Temple to pray for a safe sea voyage to Srivijaya. This is clear evidence that merchants went as far as present day Indonesia for trade.

We know that the thirty years or so of the Shaoxing era (1131-62) saw the rise not only of sea merchants, but also of many pirates. According to the *Songshi* (*History of the Song*), the pirate Zhu Cong raided Guangzhou and then Quanzhou in the fifth year of Shaoxing (1135). In (intercalary) February, the pirate Chen Gan raided Leizhou. In March, the Southern Song court ordered the capture of Zhu Cong. In August, Zhu Cong surrendered to the authorities and was appointed a naval commander.

Han Yanzhi, eldest son of General Han Shizhong, who served with distinction in the founding of the Southern Song, was administrator of the Zhejiang region around 1174, and it is said that the seas became peaceful while he was regional administrator, as he captured alive the leader of pirates who had been engaged in pillaging there. There are frequent mentions of the appearance and subjugation of pirates later under the Southern Song. This presumably is partly due to the Southern Song court having its capital near the coast at Hangzhou and to its aggressive promotion of overseas trade.

Among those active in Quanzhou in Fujian at the end of the Southern Song and the start of the Yuan dynasty was Pu Shougeng, mentioned earlier. Pu Shougeng's ancestors had come to Guangzhou from somewhere towards Arabia, and had apparently moved from Guangzhou to Quanzhou in his father's generation. Pu Shougeng was appointed to the Southern Song court for his service, along with his brother, in suppressing pirates in the southern seas at the end of the Southern Song era, and was appointed Trade Supervisor (*tiju shibo*) in Quanzhou. As the office of trade supervisor dealt with the comings and goings of foreign ships, and consequently brought the privilege of receiving various gifts for his involvement in negotiations with foreign merchants, and as he also engaged in overseas trade himself, he would have accumulated considerable wealth. When the Southern Song court fell a short time later, he changed his allegiance to the Yuan court that succeeded it. As the Yuan court also treated Pu Shougeng well as regional administrator for Fujian, he also took steps to expand trade with invitations to the countries around the southern seas. Between the late Southern Song and the early Yuan dynasties, Pu Shougeng was active in the role of trade supervisor, overseeing foreign ships and foreign trade, for around thirty years.

3.5 The sea and the people of the plains

In 1277, before Khubilai Khan subjugated the Southern Song south of the Yangtze in 1279, the Yuan court established a *shibosi*, equivalent to a modern customs office, in Quanzhou. They subsequently established *shibosi* in Qingyuan (Ningbo), Shanghai and Ganpu (on the coast of eastern Zhejiang), and also had them in Wenzhou (Zhejiang), Guangdong (Guangzhou) and Hangzhou. The purpose of thus establishing *shibosi* was to promote trade with foreign countries and consequently increase tax receipts. The *shibosi* issued all ships leaving or entering the harbor with official documents detailing their destination and cargo, which were largely based on the Song dynasty system. The law code of the Yuan court, the *Yuan dian zhang*, required that sea merchants pay duty at the *shibosi* when returning to China from foreign countries or Hainan, and provided that, if there were any concealed goods that had not been declared, these should be seized by the authorities and a heavy penalty applied.

Quanzhou in Fujian, where the Yuan government established its first *shibosi*, was an important port for overseas trade at the time. This is known from mentions in Marco Polo's[23] *Description of the World*.

For every one ship that arrives in Alexandria and other ports to sell pepper to the lands of Christendom, a hundred ships arrive in Zaytun. Judging from the volume of trade, Zaytun is undoubtedly one of the two greatest seaports in the world.

(*The Travels of Marco Polo volume 2*, translated by Atago Matsuo, Heibonsha, p.114)

As this quotation shows, Quanzhou, which Marco Polo calls Zaytun, was the largest port in the world in the thirteenth century, along with Alexandria in Egypt. Naturally, not only merchant ships from India and other countries to the west, but also many Chinese ships passed through it.

The Mongols who founded the Yuan dynasty were people of the plains, but they were more aggressive in advancing overseas than the successive dynasties of Han Chinese. Not only did they voyage to Java and Japan, but they also transported grain paid as tax from the Jiangnan region to their capital of Dadu

---

23 **Marco Polo** (1254-1324): A Venetian merchant. He traveled with his father and uncle through central Asia to Yuan China, where he was favored by the Yuan Emperor Khubilai and served the Yuan court for around fifteen years. He left from Quanzhou by sea in 1290 and arrived back in Italy in 1295. The *Description of the World (The Travels of Marco Polo)* is thought to be a record of Marco Polo's account of his great journey. He is also well known for introducing Japan as 'Zipang.'

(Beijing) by sea rather than rowing it up the Grand Canal.

3.6 South Sea trade in the Yuan dynasty

The *Zhenla feng tu ji*[24] by Zhou Daguan shows that many people traveled to south-east Asia in the Yuan period. It states that many Chinese went to Zhenla (Cambodia) because it was easy to trade there, as clothes were simple, rice was easy to come by, women were many, it was easy to build a house and there was an abundance of daily goods.

The *Dao yi zhi lüe*[25] by Wang Dayan is an important Yuan geographical work on the countries of the southern seas, and the entries for most countries mention their products and the (presumably Chinese) goods for which they traded them. It is not difficult to imagine that the blue-patterned and white porcelain that was popular everywhere at that time refers to Jingdezhen porcelain, which was produced in great quantities in the Yuan dynasty.

Another work that is of interest as an important historical source on the southern seas in the Yuan dynasty is the Yuan *Dade nanhai zhi*, remains of which are preserved in the Beijing Library and parts of which are quoted in the *Yongle dadian*.[26] It is said to have been originally written by Chen Dazhen in 1304, and books six to ten are known today. It is a regional gazette of present day Guangdong Province, and what is left of it includes entries on trade with countries of the southern seas. On 'cargo' (*bohuo*) 'sent to barbarian lands' it states at the beginning that 'goods are sent to *Shiziguo* (Sri Lanka)' and that Guangzhou is a focal point for foreign ships where many treasures are to be found, listing among the treasures imported from abroad: ivory, rhinoceros horn,

---

24　**Zhenla feng tu ji**: The Mongol Zhou Daguan accompanied an embassy from the Yuan court to Cambodia in 1296 and returned to China in 1297. This is an account of what he saw and heard during his stay in Cambodia. It was written in 1297.

25　***Dao yi zhi lüe***: Completed in 1351, this relates the experiences of Wang Dayan, from Jiangxi, who spent several years visiting the countries of the southern seas. Its importance lies in the fact that it is said to have been composed from Wang Dayan's actual experiences in personally visiting these countries. It is invaluable for understanding Chinese people's knowledge of the countries of the southern seas in the Yuan dynasty. It mentions one or two hundred areas, and Ishida Michinosuke points out that the *Dao yi zhi lüe* already uses the terms 'East' and 'West' in the sense in which they were used from the Ming dynasty onwards.

26　**Yongle dadian**: Compiled on the orders of Emperor Yongle. It was ordered phonetically, based on the *Hong wu zheng yun*, from existing works in all fields. It included works of which the originals had already been lost and most of it was destroyed in the Second Opium War.

houding,[27] pearls, coral, and tortoise shell; and mentioning among the 'barbarian lands' overseas: Giao Chi, Zhancheng (Champa), Zhenla, Xianguo (Siam), Danmalingguo (Tambralinga on the Malay peninsula), Sanfoqi (Srivijaya), and Shepo (Java). These were presumably places from which ships came and to which ships went from Guangzhou.

4 Sea merchants and pirates in the Ming dynasty

4.1 Maritime trade in the Ming dynasty

The Ming court imposed a maritime ban (*haijin*),[28] forbidding maritime trade to civilians, but permitted the visits of foreign tribute ships. It was only in the latter half of the Ming period that overseas trade by civilians became common.

It was in the sixteenth century, from the Jiajing era (1522-66) onwards, that the word *haijin* (maritime ban) came into use. The maritime ban, conventionally described by the phrase 'The Hongwu Emperor, Zhu Yuanzhang,[29] will not permit a single ship's timber to set sail,' was not established at a stroke. In 1371, when he discovered that Li Xing and Li Chun, who were in command of the Xinghua guards in Fujian, were secretly employing others to engage in overseas trade, the Emperor Hongwu ordered the *dadu dufu*[30] to ban all coastal troops from engaging in overseas trade. In 1381, he also banned the populace along the coast from trading with foreign countries. Then in 1394, Emperor Hongwu cut off travel with overseas countries on the grounds of frequent counterfeiting, and

---

27 *houding*: Thought to be the skull of a water bird the size of a peacock or a bird similar to a crane, used to make ornaments.
28 **Maritime ban**: This was a policy of restricting or prohibiting voyages or activities at sea by ships in China, but these were often imposed to maintain order or prevent smuggling for political reasons, or to prevent disputes with foreign countries. The chief instances of this policy were the *haijin* policy imposed for almost the whole of the Ming dynasty, and the *qianjieling* ban announced by the Qing government to deal with Koxinga in Taiwan.
29 **Zhu Yuanzhang** (1328-98): The Emperor Hongwu, first emperor of the Ming dynasty. He made his capital in Nanjing, laying the foundation for 250 years of Ming rule.
30 **dadu dufu**: The highest military body established in the Ming dynasty, with the power to control the army.

allowed tribute only from the Ryukyus, Zhenla (Cambodia) and Xianluo (Siam). He also strictly prohibited not only the coastal people's frequent journeys abroad to trade spices, but also their invitation of foreigners for immoral purposes.

Thus, the *Da Minglü* compiled in 1397 provided for laws forbidding secret trips abroad and illegal journeys overseas; in particular, the construction of illegally large ships, with two or more masts, journeys abroad to trade with cargos of goods prohibited from export, and conspiring with pirates were strictly forbidden.

While it prohibited the Chinese populace from traveling overseas, for the sake of envoys coming from abroad, it established a method to confirm the authenticity of envoys in 1383, by providing authentication documents for three countries that brought tribute to China: Xianluo, Zhancheng (Champa), and Zhenla. These countries were identified as countries that came to bring tribute out of devotion to the Chinese emperor. They were each enfiefed by the Emperor Hongwu as the kings of Xianluo, Zhancheng and Zhenla, and treated as the official envoys of their countries, and the imperial gifts bestowed in return for their tribute provided these countries with their only opportunity to obtain Chinese products.

However, Emperor Hongwu's limited relations with overseas countries were greatly changed by the later Emperor Yongle. Emperor Yongle dispatched the eunuch Zheng He[31] to countries overseas and welcomed tribute from many more countries. Japan was one of these countries, and in 1404, Ashikaga Yoshimitsu was enfiefed as the king of Japan, Yuan Dao Yi, and tribute trade with the Ming court began with his dispatch of tribute ships.

Countries were not free to send tribute ships whenever they chose; there were times for sending tribute (*gongqi*) set by the Ming court. Different times were set for each country: once per year, once every two years, once in ten years, and so on. One tribute per year was possible, as in the case of Koryo/Korea. The Kingdom of the Ryūkyūs sent tribute once every two years. Japan was only allowed to send tribute once every ten years. There was also a tribute route, stipulating the place at which China could be entered when bringing tribute. For south-east Asian countries, this was Guangzhou, for the Ryūkyūs it was originally Quanzhou in Fujian, but this was later changed to Fuzhou, which it remained until the Qing period. For Japan it was Ningbo in Zhejiang. Coun-

---

31 **Zheng He**: A Muslim from Yunnan, who is said to have become a eunuch of the Emperor Yongle after King Yan when the Ming army subdued Yunnan around 1382. He made seven voyages to the southern seas after the Emperor Yongle succeeded to the throne in 1405.

tries that brought tribute overland also had a designated point of entry. In the case of Korea, after the capital was moved to Beijing, entry to China was near the mouth of the Yalu River, and the designated route ran through Liaoyang in present day Liaoning Province, along the coast of the Bohai Sea and to Beijing via Shanhaiguan. In charge of their first entry to China from overseas were the Ming *shibosi*, who judged the validity of the authentication documents provided in advance by China and brought by the tribute bearers of each country.

Items presented as tribute to the Ming emperors were *gongwu* (tribute), and these were designated for each country. From Japan, they included horses, armor, short swords and sulphur, while from the Ryūkyūs they included horses and sulphur and south-east Asian spices such as costus root, cloves and pepper. Siam's included ivory, rhinoceros horn and peacock feathers, and specialties of each country were designated as tribute. The gifts given by the Ming emperors in return for the offering of tribute were mainly high quality silk textiles, as well as products from among those offered by other countries, which were not available in the receiving country. Books were also important imperial gifts. In the Yongle era, apart from silk textiles, Japan received gold and silver, antiques, and pictures and books.

4.2 Pirates and *wokou* in the Ming dynasty

References to the *wokou* (Japanese pirates) who attacked coastal regions of Ming China can be found almost throughout the Ming period. Looking particularly at records of attacks by *wokou*, their main targets were from the Korean peninsula to the northern coastal regions of the Chinese mainland in the early Ming period, but in the second half of the period, from the Jiajing era onwards, there are reports of them attacking Jiangsu, Zhejiang and southwards to Fujian and Guangdong. Records frequently show that *wokou* and pirates were associated with each other.

One of the reasons for the appearance of Japanese pirates in the Jiajing era, as given in the entry for 6 April in the thirty-fifth year of Jiajing (1556) in the *Shizong shilu*, is that Wang Zhi (see page 50), Mao Haifeng and others led bands of pirates on raids because they were unable to make great profits due to the severity of the maritime ban. It theorizes that another reason was that famine in Japan had caused the price of rice to rise and people were suffering from starvation, while pillaging was rife, but the rulers of Japan were unaware of this. As this analysis points out, this clearly coincided with a rise in demand for maritime and overseas trade among the Chinese population in the coastal regions.

The appearance of Japanese pirates came during the rule of Ashikaga

Yoshiteru,[32] the thirteenth shogun of the Muromachi *bakufu*, and reflects the fact that the authority of the Muromachi *bakufu* had collapsed, with the warring daimyos dividing up the country. It is difficult to distinguish between *wokou* and pirates in this period. The historical terminology *beilu nanwo* (Mongols in the north and Japanese pirates in the south) that has been used in the past results from *nanwo* and *wokou* having been studied in terms of Japanese history or the history of Sino-Japanese relations. However, since Ming era pirates are indivisible from *wokou*, as explained above, research on *wokou* needs to be refocused in terms of the history of maritime East Asia and the history of the East and South China Seas.

4.3 The reality of Chinese pirates in the Ming dynasty

Where did most periods in the Ming period originate? Did the people especially in the coastal regions seek a living at sea and overseas because they were unable to bear the burden of heavy taxation? Or were they ex-officials forced out of the Ming political system at the time, and other dissatisfied elements? Which coastal regions were most involved, for example merchants from Fujian? I shall illustrate what they were actually like mainly from records in the most fundamental historical source for the Ming dynasty, the *Ming shi lu* (*Veritable Records of the Ming Dynasty*).

According to an entry for 19 August in the twenty-fourth year of Hongwu (1391) in the *Taizu shi lu* within the *Ming shi lu*, the pirate Zhang Ama carried out a raid with a band of Japanese barbarians, but government forces repelled them. It is recorded that Zhang Ama was a scoundrel from Huangyan County in the district of Taizhou in Zhejiang, who was a frequent visitor to Japan and led other gangs to ravage the coast, bringing great misery to people on the coast. This Zhang Ama must be the first pirate known in the Ming period. As is recorded in the *Records*, he was a dissolute man from Huangyan County in the district of Taizhou in Zhejiang. The men Zhang Ama used as his accomplices were clearly gangs of Japanese pirates. This is because he is said to have had constant contact with Japan. This shows that there were close connections between what the Ming called *wokou* and Chinese pirates.

In 1407, Chen Zuyi, a pirate from Jiugang (Palembang) was taken by the

---

32 **Ashikaga Yoshiteru** (ruled 1546-65): Thirteenth shogun of the Muromachi *bakufu*. Eldest son of the twelfth shogun, Yoshiharu. He succeeded his father as shogun when the authority of the Ashikaga shogunate had slipped following the Ōnin War, and was shogun in name only, as his father Yoshiharu had ceded power to the *Kanrei* Hosokawa Takakuni, and Yoshiteru's rule was a time when the power of the Hosokawa *Kanrei* was growing, as was that of the Miyoshi and Matsunaga families.

eunuch Zheng He, who had been sent to the West. Chen Zuyi, who had been captured alive, was sent to the capital and sentenced to death. He was a Chinese pirate who had laid waste to the southern seas.

In 1449, Chen Wanning, a pirate from Fujian, attacked Chaoyang County, on the coast north-east of Guangdong. Chen Wanning had lured people from the coast of southern Fujian and Chaozhou to go to sea with him and engage in piracy.

4.4 The expansion of trade in the South China Sea

When, in the first year of the Longqing era (1567-72) the Governor of Fujian, Tu Zemin sought to trade with the countries of south-east Asia – except for Japan, which was seen as the ringleader of the *wokou* – the maritime ban was relaxed and overseas trade flourished. The number of Chinese ships venturing to south-east Asia, especially in the second half of the sixteenth and early part of the seventeenth centuries, grew from fifty in around 1567 to eighty-eight in 1589, one hundred in 1592, and 137 in 1597. This subsequently grew to forty per year from Fujian alone by 1612. Forty-three ships are recorded for 1628. So dozens of Chinese merchant ships were traveling to south-east Asia every year.

The destinations for Chinese merchants from the coast, principally Fujian, were port cities in Luzon in the Philippines, the Moluccas, the Indonesian archipelago, and the Malay peninsula, where they traveled to trade. In these island ports they encountered trading ships from Europe, which was entering its so-called Great Age of Sail. One of the best known ports at the time, Bantam (Xiagang) in the east of Java, was known for the visits of Dutch and British ships seeking to import raw and woven silk and other Chinese products brought there by visiting Chinese vessels. In 1623 a sea merchant from Fujian went trading, as he did every year, in the Kingdom of Dani (Sultanate of Pattani) on the east coast of the Malay peninsula, in what is now Thailand, and in Java in Indonesia. The merchant, Pan Xiu, met a Dutchman in Pattani and recommended him to trade in the Penghu Islands west of Taiwan. The Dutchman therefore tried to trade with Chinese in Penghu, but was rejected by the Ming authorities.

5 Sea merchants and pirates since the Qing dynasty

5.1 Maritime trade in the Qing dynasty

Overseas trade in the Qing dynasty was characterized by greater entrenchment, compared to the Ming period, of the countries with which coastal merchants traded. Chinese merchants ventured abroad with large volumes of Chinese goods designed to satisfy the demands of the countries with which they traded.

The cargo of a Chinese merchant vessel that reached Singapore from Xiamen in 1824 included around 660,000 pieces of porcelain of thirty-two kinds, 10,000 floor tiles, 200 coping stones, 15,000 paper umbrellas, confectionery, dried foods, silk products, tobacco, pickled vegetables, cotton, and tea, while the cargo of another Chinese merchant vessel that visited Nagasaki at the same time consisted almost entirely of drapery, sugar and medicine. In the case of Singapore, these were mostly goods for the *huaqiao*[33] (overseas Chinese) living there, building materials and ordinary tableware, foodstuffs, and fancy goods, without which the lives of the local Chinese would clearly have been difficult, while in the case of Japan they were so-called *hakuraihin* (imported goods) and luxury goods.

Trade which had been irregular in the Ming period became regular and frequent in the Qing. This was also why Japanese who had been shipwrecked in various parts of south-east Asia were able to make their way back to Japan. As Chinese merchant ships frequently visited the islands in the South China Sea and elsewhere, shipwrecked Japanese went with them when they returned to China proper and were taken from their port of arrival to ports from which ships departed to Japan. A broad network had been built up by Chinese merchants, which allowed them to return from here on ships going to Japan.

This network developed not only for overseas trade, but also as a coastal trading network. Along the coast of the Chinese mainland, sailing ships from Tianjin and Shandong in the north, sand junks from the vicinity of Shanghai, *ningchuan* from Ningbo, and *niaochuan*[34] from Fujian traversed the Bohai,

---

33 *huaqiao*: A word that came into use at the end of the nineteenth century, meaning Chinese, or people of Chinese descent, who had moved or were staying abroad. '*Qiao*' suggests temporary settlement, and recently the term '*huaqiao* and *huaren*' has become more widely used, including '*huaren*' (foreign nationals of Chinese origin).

34 *niaochuan (bird boats)*: Ocean-going sailing ships developed mostly in the coastal areas of Fujian from the end of the Ming dynasty onwards. In the Qing period increas-

Yellow Sea, East Sea (East China Sea), Taiwan Straits, South Sea (South China Sea) and other seas, engaged mostly in the transport of goods.

There were also ports that linked this coastal activity with overseas trade. A good example is Zhapu in Zhejiang, which specialized in trade with Japan. Chinese sugar imported into Japan was produced in southern Fujian or at Chaozhou in south-east Guangdong, and in the first half of the Edo period it was shipped directly from these locations to Nagasaki. From the mid-Edo period onwards, Zhapu became a base for trade with Japan, and sugar was brought by coastal trading boats to Zhapu, from where it was exported on specialist ships for the Japan trade.

5.2 Chinese sailing ships in the Qing dynasty

Thus, in the Qing dynasty, there was a flourishing of maritime activity that had not been seen in Chinese history before the Qing. In particular, coastal transport and overseas transport were seen to be integrated, with a network developing throughout almost all the coastal regions of the Chinese mainland. Sea transport in these regions was carried out by Chinese sailing ships. Coastal and ocean-going ships sailed these waters and their names reflected the contemporary construction of the ships: the *weichuan* found mostly in Tianjin, the *shachuan* (sand junks) that were based in Shanghai south of the Yangtze and that plied the northern coastal waters, the *ningchuan* that traveled to northern waters from Ningbo in Zhejiang, and the ocean-going *niaochuan* that were mostly from Fujian and were found in all sea areas. Some of these also visited Nagasaki, and they were often seen in commemorative photographs taken by visitors to Nagasaki and in the *Nagasaki hanga* that were used as postcards.

As maritime activity flourished using these sailing ships, among those who were unable to participate in their commercial activities were some who pursued illegal activities at sea, and pirates made an appearance. The areas where pirates made their bases were the coastal islands from the Zhoushan archipelago to Wenzhou in Zhejiang, and islands along the coast from Fujian to Guangdong, while the range of their activities extended over the whole coast of mainland China. The names of many pirates throughout the Qing period are known, but the most famous was Cai Qian, from Dong'an County in Fujian, who appeared in the Jiaqing era. He grew to be a rebel who caused considerable trouble to the

---

ingly large ships were used, and the *niaochuan* that went to Japan in the second half of the nineteenth century in the Edo period for the Nagasaki trade carried a large amount of cargo and a crew of over one hundred. They seem to had been so called because, as they floated on the sea, they resembled resting birds.

Qing government, tried to occupy Taiwan, and almost made a maritime empire for himself.

5.3 Piracy in the Qing dynasty

Who looked enviously on these ships that crisscrossed the oceans, as described above? Of course there must have been people who targeted the merchant ships laden with treasure. At the start of the Qing dynasty, any political forces who opposed the Qing, such as Koxinga, were called pirates. However, apart from these forces, there were also pirates, known as *haidao* or *yangdao*.

In the first year of the Yongzheng era (1723), Guangdong and Fujian had the most pirates, followed by Zhejiang. Within Guangdong, Chaozhou on the north-east coast and Huizhou on the central coast were problem areas for piracy. Places on the coast of Jiangnan and Zhejiang where pirate boats congregated were the islands scattered where Jinshan and the ocean side of Huaniao meet Xiabashan and Yangqushan, which belong to Zhejiang, where present day Hangzhou Bay meets the East China Sea, which were places where it was difficult for the eyes of the government to see, located as they are on the provincial border of Jiangsu and Zhejiang.

Gao Qidao's report to the Emperor Yongzheng dated 21 April in the sixth year of Yongzheng (1728) reads: 'The Nan'ao area is most important and is the entry and exit point for pirates from Guangdong and Fujian. It will allow us to search the area thoroughly and block off the entrance for pirate ships, and to search out the pirates' hideaways.' The Nan'ao Islands were a good place to escape from the authorities, as they are made up of a complex series of islands.

Towards the end of the Qianlong era frequent mention is made of *yangdao*, as pirates who terrorized the seas.

> Recent pirates are mostly gathered on islands at sea, and investigations into the criminals Wang Kunshan and Wang Masheng, who were arrested in Zhejiang and Guangdong, have shown that they are originally from Fujian. It is currently difficult to investigate all of the islands in the short term. However, the Zhangzhou and Quanzhou regions in Fujian are places where pirates frequently appear, and laws must be established to prohibit them.
>
> (*Qianlong shang yu dang*, volume 15, p. 29)

This shows that around the fifty-fourth year of Qianlong (1789) pirates known as *yangdao* made frequent appearances in the seas from Zhejiang to

Part 1: The Activities of Chinese Junks on the East Asian Sea in Early Modern Ages

FIgure 4　Piracy Guo Badai（郭婆带）
　　　　　"Dia-shi-zhai-hua-dao（點石齋畫報）" Vol.3

Guangzhou.

An edict dated 7 April in the fifty-sixth year of Qianlong (1791) shows that bandits appeared in the seas off Jinzhou in Shengjing, who turned out to be from Fujian. Damage from raids at sea off Jinzhou and Gaizhou was very costly, and since the pirates were originally from Fujian, it was deduced that they had local guides throughout Jinzhou and Gaizhou. So pirates were also found on the coast of the Bohai, in the north east. The remote cause was said to be the coastal activity of Fujian merchants.

According to an edict dated 2 March in the fifty-sixth year of Qianlong, bandits appeared at sea throughout Zhejiang and Fujian, not only attacking merchant vessels, but even attacking a naval patrol boat on patrol in the area. These pirates were all people from coastal regions, who were short-tempered by nature, and as the regional administrators had been unable to change them or show leadership, they had turned bad and become people who were only too willing to break the law. An important function of the navy was originally to suppress piracy, and it had been successful in this, but there were those in the navy who illegally sold weapons to pirates.

As mentioned already, the members of pirate gangs had local characteristics from their places of origin. An edict for 18 March in the fifty-sixth year of Qianlong mentions four *huodao*, including Gao Zao, captured by a Zhejiang patrol boat, and the *daoshou* (pirate leader) Lin Qi and twenty-eight *huodao*, including Chen Qiu, from Fujian, as well as more than twenty *yangdao*. As the mention in this edict shows, there were pirates known as *daoshou* and *huodao*. This shows that pirate gangs had an order of precedence, with pirate leaders known as *shoudao* and their subordinates known as *huodao*, with the addition of '*huo*,' meaning 'comrade.'

6 Conclusion

In *Relations Between Taiwan and Southern China, Current Institutions and Future Strategy*, compiled in the sixth year of Taishō (1917) by the Police Headquarters in the Welfare Department of the Governor General's Office of Taiwan, Part 1 Chapter 3, 'The Control of Piracy and Relations with Southern China' states that pirates operating in the coastal regions of southern China were frequently seen in the seas around Taiwan, especially in the Taiwan Straits, attacking ships, and engaging in brutal activities that terrorized the inhabitants. The season when pirates appeared was summer, to benefit from the seasonal winds, and every year between June and September they attacked ships sailing the coast of Taiwan or traveling between Taiwan and the mainland. In terms of the pirates' origin, it was reported that the most brutal were 'those based in the region of Xiaoxi, Meizhou, Da Niaogui, Xiao Niaogui, and Nanridao' along the coast of Fujian. It is clear that the activities of pirates were also a problem in Taiwan under Japanese rule.

The same book also mentions forty-one cases of pirate attacks in the Taiwan Straits and elsewhere between the thirty-first year of Meiji (1905)nd the fifth year of Meiji (1916). The earliest case is from 6 June Meiji 31, when a Taiwanese ship, the *Shunwanyi*, was attacked by pirates. The ship was suddenly ordered to stop in mid voyage and, in addition to the killing of one crew member and serious injuries to two others, 190 *koku* of brown rice and various articles were stolen. When the Taiwanese *Xinrifa* was attacked by pirates on 24 June Taishō 4 (1914), '127 bags of rice, thirty *hakamas*, five coils of rope, one lock, three sails, two yen and forty sen in cash, with an estimated value of over 650 yen' were plundered from onboard. The pirate ship that attacked the *Xinrifa* was a three-masted sailing junk with a capacity of around three hundred *koku*, painted red above and white below. On 3 September Taishō 5 (1916), the Taiwanese ship the *Jinlianmei* was attacked by three pirate ships at sea off the Chinese mainland; the pirates stole its cargo of timber worth 1,167 yen 98 sen at the time, as well as the crew's clothing worth 402 yen, and also the ship and its fittings worth 2,716 yen and 50 sen.

I have discussed the questions of Chinese sea merchants and pirates, and what is clear throughout is that, although it has received little treatment in studies of Chinese history to date, the people of China have left many traces of their involvement with coastal waters and the high seas.

The history of the coastal regions of mainland China, from Liaoning in the north to Hebei, Tianjin, Shandong, Jiangsu, Shanghai, Zhejiang, Fujian, Guangdong, the Guangxi Zhuang Autonomous Region, and Hainan cannot be told without mentioning their relationship with the sea. The present, and future economic development, are intimately connected with the sea. The inland provinces adjacent to these also affect, and are affected by, the sea to some extent. Sea merchants have been responsible for one part of economic activity in the coastal regions, and the wealth they have brought from overseas has contributed to the economic development of China. From overseas, Chinese sea merchants brought back spices, silver, rice, dried goods and marine products. In return, to countries overseas they took raw and woven silk, ceramics, Chinese medicine, tea and all kinds of necessities, for which many countries yearned. Harming the operations of these Chinese sea merchants, and sometimes living off them, were the pirates, some of whom gave a serious jolt to the government of the time. In this sense, too, China's involvement with the sea is an indispensable angle from which to look at the country's history.

CHAPTER 3

The Activities of Chinese Junks on East Asian Seas from the Seventeenth to the Nineteenth Centuries: Mainly Based on Sand Junks and Bird Junks

1 Introduction

From the seventeenth century onward, four major types of Chinese seagoing ships, known as sand junks, bird junks, Fuzhou junks, and Guangzhou junks respectively, were most active in marine transportation in East Asia.[1] Of these ships, the flat-bottomed sand junks from Chongming and Shanghai would leave the mouth of the Yangtze River, sail northwardly along the coasts of the Bohai Sea and reach Jinzhou, Niuzhuang and Gaizhou. These ships were loaded with Shanghai cotton cloth, tea and other products from southern China. They brought back soya beans and other grains from north-eastern China.[2] Bird junks, Fuzhou junks, and Guangzhou junks, on the other hand, had rounded bottoms. They were more suitable for sailing on the high seas.[3] The activities of bird

---

1 Zhou Shide, 'Zhongguo shachuan kaolüe', *Kexue shi jikan*, 5 (Beijing, 1963), 34-54. Tian Rukang, 'Shiqi shiji zhi shijiu shiji zhongye Zhongguo fanchuan zai dongnan Yazhou hangyun he shangye shang de diwei', *Lishi yanjiu*, 8 (Beijing, 1956), 1-21. This article was later published in his *Shiqi - shijiu shiji zhongye Zhongguo fanchuan zai dongnan Yazhou* (Shanghai, 1957), 1-45. See also his 'Zailun shiqi shiji zhi shijiu shiji zhongye Zhongguo fanchuan ye de fazhan', *Lishi yanjiu*, 12 (Beijing, 1957), 1-11 and 'Shiwu shiji zhi shiba shiji Zhongguo haiwai maoyi fazhan chihuan de yuanyin', *Xin jianshe*, 8-9 (Beijing, 1964), 45-62. These two articles have been incorporated into his *Zhongguo fanchuan maoyi yu duiwai guanxi lunji* (Hangzhou, 1987), 1-99.
2 Matsuura Akira, *Shindai Shanghai shasen kōungyō shi no kenkyū* (Osaka, 2004), 207-335.
3 For illustrations and discussions of Chinese junks with flat bottoms and rounded bottoms, see Oba Osamu, 'Hirado Matsuura shiryō hakubutsukan zō 'Tōsen no zu'' ni tsuite – Edo jidai ni raikō shita Chūgoku shōsen no shiryō', *Kansia Daigaku Tōzai Gakujutsu Kenkyūjo Kiyō*, 5 (Osaka, 1972), 13-49; 'Scroll paintings of Chinese junks which sailed to Nagasaki in the 18th century and their equipment', *Mariner's Mirror*, 60:4 (1974), 351-62. See also his *Edo jidai ni okeru Chūgoku bunka juyō no kenkyū*

junks covered mainly the coastal regions of Fujian. They sailed into the Bohai Sea to reach Jinzhou, Gaizhou, and Tianjin.

A record in Japanese the *Official Gazette* (*Kampō*) published in June 1890 reported that in Zhifu (present-day Yantai, Shandong province) more than 300 sand junks came from the mouth of the Yangtze River, 30 to 40 ships from Ningbo, ten from Guangdong, and five to six from Fujian. There were also some 3,000 ships from the nearby coastal areas in the north-east, and more than 100 from Tianjin.[4] Obviously, sand junks from the mouth of the Yangtze River played a pre-eminent role in long-distance voyages. As for the bird junks, they sailed not only along the Chinese coasts but also to foreign countries. From the mid-eighteenth to the late nineteenth centuries, when Japan adopted the policy of 'national isolation', more than ten bird junks visited the port of Nagasaki annually.[5] These oceangoing ships linked the Chinese continent with Taiwan, which was isolated by the sea. They also sailed to South East Asia, enabling the Chinese to migrate from China to both of these areas. So far, research on Chinese sailing vessels by European and American scholars has focused mostly on junks named after their places of construction, or their homeports.[6]

This article, however, will focus on ships by their types, such as sand ships and bird ships, and on their activities in East Asia from the seventeenth to the nineteenth centuries.

2 The Scope of Chinese Junk Activity

In 1684 after its suppression of Zheng Chenggong in Taiwan, the Qing court lifted the ban it had once imposed on maritime activities. Junks from Chinese coasts actively began to conduct maritime transportation in deep-sea areas. Research in recent years indicates that the activities of these junks covered a vast area of thousands of kilometres, stretching from the Bohai Sea to the Yellow Sea, the East China Sea and all the way to the South China Sea. Coastal shipping by Chinese junks flourished from the mid-seventeenth century and lasted to the latter part of the nineteenth century when steamships appeared regularly along the Chinese coasts. In 1886, a report compiled by the Japanese

---

(Kyoto, 1984), 489-536.

4 *Kampō*, 2083, 11 June 1890, 116.

5 Matsuura Akira, *Shindai kaigai bōeki shi no kenkyū* (Kyoto, 2002), 63-75.

6 See, for example, I.A. Donnely, *Chinese junks and other native craft* (Shanghai, 1924), 1-142.

The Activities of Chinese Junks on East Asian Seas from the 17th to the 19th Centuries

Figure 5   Chief ports on the route from the Yangtze River to the Bohai Sea.

Consulate described the trading activities of these Chinese junks.[7] According to this report, although steamship transportation had started to develop in China, junks remained important in shipping. These junks used three major sea routes and their activities were mainly in the Bohai Bay, the areas near the mouth of the Yangtze River and the adjacent coasts in Zhejiang province, and the coastal areas around Xiamen, Fujian province. This report also pointed out that owing to its central location, Ningbo was a centre for transportation by junks. Local ships as well as those from other ports harboured in Ningbo. Sailing between Ningbo and Fujian, they brought such Fujian products as granulated sugar, paper, olives, tangerines and timber to Ningbo. From Ningbo, they sailed to neighbouring ports as well as to Zhenjiang, near the mouth of the Yangtze River, which served as the point at which to link with the Grand Canal. Annually, more than 200 such ships brought rice and pigs from Zhenjiang to Ningbo; and from Ningbo they carried paper, granulated sugar, and mats to Fujian. Every year, about 110 ships left Ningbo for places along the coasts of the East China Sea, the Yellow Sea, and the Bohai Sea. They reached Zhifu on the Shandong peninsula, Niuzhuang and Jinzhou in Liaoning province, and Tianjin in the middle reaches of the Haihe River. Ships heading toward Tianjin were loaded mainly with grains, which would eventually be transported to Beijing. Other cargos on

---

7   The following discussions of the activities of Chinese junks are based on records from the 'Shinshiki hansen bōeki gaikyō', in *Tsūshō hōkoku* (Dai ni kai, 1886), 108-9.

these ships included medicines, alum, paper, bamboo poles, and timber.When sailing back to Ningbo, these ships carried back such local products from northeastern and northern China as soya beans, bean cakes, vermicelli, dates, peanuts and peanut oil. Ships from Ningbo not only conducted long-distance transportation, they also sailed to such ports as Taizhou and Wenzhou in central and southern Zhejiang province. When these ships came back to Ningbo, they were usually loaded with charcoal, alum, pigs, tangerines, materials for making mats, and raincoats. Ships leaving Ningbo for home brought back seeds, medical herbs, cotton, cakes of cottonseeds and oil. According to the same report, the coastal areas of Fujian were also important in marine transportation. Once every year from December to January of the following year, these ships, loaded with granulated sugar, tea and timber would sail to areas north of Taiwan. And they brought back to Taiwan, soya beans, vermicelli, dates, animal fats, liquor and sheepskins.

Ships from southern China sailing toward South East Asia, particularly those headed toward Singapore, carried bamboo poles, charcoal, palm fibres, fire wood, tangerines, paper, planks, lumber, potatoes, and water jars, as well as household supplies commonly used by local Chinese. When these ships sailed home, they brought back bark, lumber, beans, clams, cotton, dates, granite, lychees, dried longan, medicated oil, planks, salted fish, granulated sugar, sweet potatoes, seaweed, walnuts, and rice, which had a ready market in south China. In its discussion of the importance of the activities of these Qing-dynasty junks, a report indicated that Chinese seamen demonstrated superior navigational skills, that the important seaports these junks often visited included Tianjin and Yingkou along the Bohai Bay, Shanghai, and Ningbo, which were centrally located on the Chinese coast, and that the circulation of commodities was facilitated by junks active along the coasts of Ningbo.

3 Sand Junks and Bird Junks on East Asian Seas

Sand junks as previously stated were flat-bottomed sea-going vessels built and frequently used in areas near the mouth of the Yangtze River. They were of light draught, and thus suitable for sailing in shallow waters.[8]

In the First Historical Archives of China, Beijing, there is a document of

---

8   Akira, *Shindai kaigai bōeki shi no kenkyū* (Kyoto, 2002), 264-9.

Table 2 Number of ships entering seaports in Jinzhou, Niuzhuang and other places.
From *Jinzhou, Niuzhuang dengshu zhengshou shuiyin qingdan*, Jiaqing period.

Seaports	Type of junk	No. of junks entering the ports (this year)	No. of junks entering the ports (two years previously)
Jinzhou: Tianqiaochang, Xiaomatigou	*sha, niao, wei*	1,365 (41.5%)	1,090 (31.5%)
Niuzhuang: Mogouying, Genglongtun	*sha, niao, wei*	728 (22.2%)	1,053 (30.5%)
Gaizhou: Lianyundao, Hongqigou, Dagushan, Qingduizi	*sha, niao wei, dong*	147 (4.5%)	163 (4.7%)
Xiuyan: Jianshanzi, Yingnahe, Baojia matou, Xiaoshahe	*sha, dong*	570 (17.3%)	620 (17.9%)
Fuzhou: Niangnianggong, Wuhuzui, Piziwo, Qingshantai	*sha, niao wei, dong*	114 (3.4%)	136 (3.9%)
Jinzhou: Jinchang, Shicao, Hongyan, Heshangdao	*sha, niao, wei*	362 (11%)	395 (11.5%)
Total		**3,286 (100%)**	**3,457 (100%)**

the Jiaqing period entitled 'A list of taxes collected from ships harboured in Jinzhou, Niuzhuang and other places', (*Jinzhou, Niuzhuang dengshu zhengshou shuiyin qingdan*) which provides us with first-hand information on ships active on the seas in northeastern China.[9] **Table 2** summarizes the relevant information from this document.

Although the exact year in which these ships called on a port is unknown, the list nevertheless provides us with the total number of ships that had entered the seaports in the coastal areas in Liaoning province. From this list, we learn the names of more than twenty ports, from Tianqiaochang and Xiaomatigou in Jinzhou to those in Niuzhuang, Gaizhou, Xiuzhou, Yanzhou and Jinzhou. We also learn that four different types of junks, known as *sha, niao, wei*, and *dong* respectively, entered the ports. *Sha* was the abbreviation for sand junks from areas south of the lower reaches of the Yangtze River, *niao* for bird junks from Fujian and southern China, *wei* for junks from Tianjin, and *dong* for junks from Shandong province. Of these ships, the sand junks reached all the seaports listed in the table above. The total number of ships amounted to more than 3,000 with the majority of these ships being sand junks from areas near the mouth of the

---

9 *Qingdai zhupi zouzhe caizhenglei guanshui*, document no. 0371-012 (Jiaqing period).

Part 1: The Activities of Chinese Junks on the East Asian Sea in Early Modern Ages

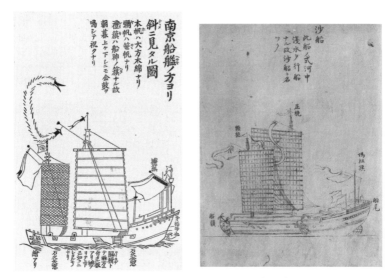

Figure 6　Sand Junk, Sha-chuan（沙船）

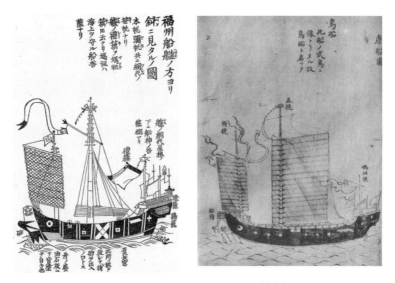

Figure 7　Bird Junk, Niao-chuan（鳥船）

Yangtze River. More specifically, many sand junks and bird junks from Fujian called on seaports in Jinzhou and Niuzhuang.

After the Jiaqing period, there were no detailed records of the activities by sand junks. However, in the late nineteenth century, records concerning such activities in Shanghai appeared in two local newspapers: the *Shiwu Ribao* (*Current Affairs Daily*, first published in May 1898) and the *Zhong Wai Ribao* (*Daily News of China and Foreign Countries*, which was the continuation of the *Shiwu Ribao*). A 'local news' section in the two newspapers contains reports about the Nanshi (south market). Nanshi referred to the area along the bank of the Huangpu River south of the seat for the old Shanghai County, which corresponds to present-day Dongjiadu in Huangpu District (known also as Puxi) where the Nanpu Bridge has been build over the Huangpu River. In Shanghai, such names for places as Nanshi and Beishi (north market) came into use after 1861, when France, having helped Qing troops to suppress the Small Swords Society, whose members had once occupied the seat for the Shanghai County during the Taiping Rebellion, extended its concession in Shanghai to Shiliupu on the bank of the Huangpu River. From then on, the area from Shiliupu to the French concession was referred to as Beishi, and the area south of Shiliupu and Xiaodongmen, as Nanshi.[10]

Shiwu Ribao was first published in Shanghai on 5May 1898. In issue no. 2,

Table 3 Number of Sand Junks entering the port of Nanshi, Shanghai (1898-1902) From *Shiwu Ribao*, May 1898 to April 1902.

Year/month	1898	1899	1900	1901	1902
January	—	29	10	48	33
February	—	45	30	39	30
March	—	46	40	25	0
April	—	49	54	90	23
May	24	59	39	89	0
June	18	54	61	114	0
July	62	85	107	75	0
August	2	7	12	20	—
September	0	37	0	18	—
October	0	24	10	8	—
November	2	34	48	30	—
December	28	39	65	100	—
Total	**(136)**	**508**	**476**	**664**	**86**

---

10 Zheng Zuan, *Shanghai diming xiaozhi,* (Shanghai, 1988), 18.

Part 1: The Activities of Chinese Junks on the East Asian Sea in Early Modern Ages

Table 4　Activities of Junks harbored at Nanshi in 1899: From *Shiwu Ribao*, 1899.

Name of the firm	No. of voyages to Nanshi	No. of junks owned by the firm	Port of departure
Xietai	33	29	Qingkou, Jiacang, Laiyang, Jiaozhou, Niuzhuang
Tongkang	31	14	Niuzhuang, Pizihe, Qishan
Shenji	25	7	Niuzhuang
Hetai	21	15	Qingkou
Jinde	16	15	Qingkou, Shahe, Shidao, Wendeng, Niuzhuang
Guangji	14	11	Qingkou, Jiacang
Yongji	14	11	Jiacang
Fulai	13	10	Jiacang
Yuchang	11	8	Qingkou, Jiacang
Taisheng	11	11	Lidao, Shidao, Yanghe, Wendeng
Lianji	10	6	Niuzhuang, Pizihe
Zhenkang	10	3	Niuzhuang
Guangsheng	9	2	Shidao, Niuzhuang
Yishun	9	6	Jiacang, Boer
Total	**227**	**148**	

dated 6 May 1898, an item appeared in the 'Local News' section stating 'The day before yesterday five sand junks arrived at Nanshi: three from Niuzhuang, one from Shidao, and one from Laiyang'. Here, 'the day before yesterday' refers to 4 May. Shidao and Laiyang were places located in eastern and southern Shandong peninsula respectively. **Table 3** shows the activities of sand junks in Nanshi.[11]

According to this table, as many as 508 sand junks entered the port of Nanshi in Shanghai in 1899. Information in the 'local news' section also indicated that in 1899 junks dispatched by various trading firms sailed to Nanshi at least nine times. **Table 4** is a summary of the number of junks owned by different firms and their ports of departure.

The information in **Table 4** clearly indicates that sand junks were instrumental in forming very close connections between Nanshi in Shanghai and various seaports along the coasts in northeastern China and the Shandong Peninsula.

The trading firm, Xietai, which sometimes appeared in the *Zhongwai Ribao*

11　The information has been collected from copies of the *Shiwu Ribao* preserved at the library of the Research Institute of Modern History, Chinese Academy of Social Sciences, and microfilms at the Shanghai Library.

Table 5 Voyages by the Sand Junk, *Qianzengyu* according to *Shiwu Ribao* and *Zhongwai Ribao*

Month & date of publication	Source of information	Duration of the voyage	Remarks
18 Jun. 1898	No. 45 of the *Shiwu Ribao*		Returning from Niuzhuang
16 Feb. 1899	No. 177 of the *Zhongwai Ribao*		Returning from Niuzhuang
4 Jun. 1899	No. 285 of the *Zhongwai Ribao*	109 days	Returning from Niuzhuang
1 Aug. 1899	No. 343 of the *Zhongwai Ribao*	59 days	Returning from Niuzhuang
28 Sep. 1899	No. 401 of the *Zhongwai Ribao*	59 days	Returning from Niuzhuang
5 Dec. 1899	No. 469 of the *Zhongwai Ribao*	69 days	Returning from Niuzhuang
15 Apr. 1900	No. 593 of the *Zhongwai Ribao*	132 days	Returning from Niuzhuang
1 Jun. 1900	No. 640 of the *Zhongwai Ribao*	48 days	Returning from Niuzhuang
18 Jul. 1900	No. 687 of the *Zhongwai Ribao*		Returning from Niuzhuang
23 Jul. 1900	No. 692 of the *Zhongwai Ribao*	53 days	Returning from Niuzhuang
7 Oct. 1900	No. 768 of the *Zhongwai Ribao*		Sailing to Yantai
2 May 1901	No. 975 of the *Zhongwai Ribao*		Returning from Niuzhuang
28 Jun. 1901	No. 1,032 of the *Zhongwai Ribao*		Returning from Niuzhuang
4 Sep. 1901	No. 1,100 of the *Zhongwai Ribao*	156 days	Returning from Niuzhuang
23 Dec. 1901	No. 1,209 of the *Zhongwai Ribao*		Suffered sea disaster when returning from Niuzhuang
4 Jan. 1902	No. 1,221 of the *Zhongwai Ribao*		Drifting on the sea near Fuzhou
28 Apr. 1902	No. 1,335 of the *Zhongwai Ribao*		Returning from Niuzhuang

as Taixie, dispatched most of the sand junks to Nanshi. In 1899, this firm sent 33 junks to Shanghai, of which 29 were sand junks. Four ships came from Niuzhuang. Other ships were from Qingkou, Jiacang, Jiaozhou, Laiyang and Wendeng. They also conducted shipping between Shanghai and the seaports in north-eastern Jiangsu province and the Shandong Peninsula.

The trading firm Tongkang dispatched 31 ships to Shanghai, of which 14 were sand junks. One junk each departed from Pizihe and Qishan; the other 29 ships were all involved in transportation between Niuzhuang and Nanshi. The trading firm Shenji sent 25 ships to Shanghai, of which seven were sand junks sailing between Niuzhuang and Nanshi. **Table 5** provides us with the information on the voyages by the *Qianzengyu*, a sand junk dispatched by Shenji.

The trading firm, Taihe, dispatched 21 ships, of which 15 were sand junks employed solely in transportation between Shanghai and Qingkou, a port located on the north-eastern coast of Jiangsu province. And the trading firm Zhenkang used three sand junks, which sailed ten times to Shanghai. According to **Table 6** below, this firm used two sand junks named *Hufuxing* and *Jinwan-*

Table 6 Transportation activities of Sand Junks dispatched by Zhenkang in 1899 according to *Zhongwai Ribao*

Issue	Issue date	Trading firm	Name of the sand junk	Port of departure
177	16 Feb	Zhenkang	Hufuxing	Niuzhuang
228	8 April	Zhenkang	Jinwannian	Niuzhuang
243	23 April	Zhenkang	Hufuxing	Niuzhuang
266	16 May	Zhenkang	Jinwannian	Niuzhuang
297	16 June	Zhenkang	Hufuxing	Niuzhuang
320	9 July	Zhenkang	Jinwannian	Niuzhuang
357	15 Aug	Zhenkang	Hufuxing	Niuzhuang
381	8 Sept	Zhenkang	Jinwannian	Niuzhuang
426	23 Oct	Zhenkang	Huyuxing	Niuzhuang
439	5 Nov	Zhenkang	Jinwannian	Niuzhuang

nian respectively. Together they sailed ten times to Shanghai. After it had called on the port of Nanshi in Shanghai in early April, the sand junk *Jinwannian* visited Nanshi five times in the same year in May, July, September, and November. Similarly, the sand junk *Hufuxing*, which was later renamed *Huyuxing*, also visited Nanshi five times in February, April, June, August and October. These records indicate that it was possible for a sand junk to sail five times a year between Nanshi and Niuzhuang. Detailed and quite rare, these late-Qing records concerning the shipping activities of sand junks published in Shanghai newspapers make it easier for us to understand that transportation by sand junks remained active well after its peak during the Jiaqing and the Daoguang reign periods.

4 Transportation by Bird Junks on East Asian Seas

According to the *Jianwen xubi* compiled in 1825 by Qi Xueqiu, more than 3,000 sand junks visited Shanghai. So did some 40 to 50 bird junks from Fujian betweenMay and June. These bird junks were twice as large in size as the sand junks. The bigger ones had a capacity of 3,000 Chinese bushels, and the smaller ones of 1,600 bushels. They sailed along the Chinese coasts and in the open sea. In the late eighteenth century, they maintained trade between China and Japan, and were the only type of vessel sailing between Zhapu (in Jiaxing Prefecture,

Zhejiang Province) and Nagasaki.[12]

In 1897, Ueno Senichi, First Consul of the Japanese Consulate in Xiamen, wrote a report on 'Transportation by sailing ships in South China'. This report, based on his investigations at the Fuzhou Customs, deserves attention. According to the report, every year Fuzhou Customs recorded about 2,000 ships that conducted trade between the port of Fuzhou and various places along the Chinese coast. Depending on their place of registration, these ships were classified into four groups. A specific colour of paint was applied to the stem of a ship to indicate its place of origin. Ships from Fujian had green stems, and were thus called *lütou*; ships from Ningbo were called *wucao* for their black stems, ships from Guangdong were referred to as *hongtou* for their red stems; and ships from Taiwan were known as *baidi* for their white stems. The Ningbo ships were usually employed in trade among Jiaozhou (in Shandong province), Ningbo, and Fuzhou. They sailed three times a year, carrying cotton cloth, rice, oil and salted fish to Fuzhou. When leaving Fuzhou, they were loaded with such local products as fir logs, paper and dried bamboo shoots. The Fujian ships shuttled once a year between Fuzhou and places as far as Tianjin in northern China. They left Fuzhou with paper, bamboo poles and dried bamboo shoots on board; on their return voyage, they brought back such products as fruits, soya beans and medicines from northern China. Sailing vessels from Quanzhou also belonged to the *lütou* group. They sailed mainly between Fuzhou and Taiwan, bringing daily supplies to Taiwan, and granulated sugar and salt back to Fuzhou. The Guangdong ships competed with the Fujian ships in North China. The former used to dominate the shipping business in the region. In later years, however, the appearance of steamships resulted in a drastic reduction in the number of Guandong ships voyaging to North China. The Taiwan ships were used in shipping between Fuzhou and Taibei. They carried rice and granulated sugar to Fuzhou, and fir and daily supplies back to Taiwan. The number of crew on a Chinese sailing vessel ranged from twenty to thirty persons, depending on the size of the ship. A seaman received two to three dollars as his monthly salary. The salary for the captain was decided by an agreement between him and the ship owner. The common practice was to link his salary with the net profits made from each voyage. The total value of the cargoes that a ship transported annually could range from 20,000 to 30,000 dollars. In a year of active trading, profit from the operation could reach as much as 20 per cent of the operating capital.[13]

On 3 January 1880, no. 2400 of the *Shenbao*, a newspaper in Shanghai, published an article about shipwrecks, reporting what had happened to a bird

---

12 Akira, *Shindai kaigai bōeki shi no kenkyū* (Kyoto, 2002), 98-117.
13 *Kampō*, 4148, 4 May 1897, 45.

junk named *Jinqianxing*. Owned by a Ningbo merchant, this junk encountered a storm near the Zhoushan Archipelagos. The ship lost its rudder and sails placing the 30 people on board in grave danger. It was fortunate, however, that a steamship *Yuankai* was in the same area and was able to rescue the sailors from the junk. However, a large amount of the cargo on board was lost.

As for the shipping activities of the Fujian merchants, the *Guomin Riri Bao*, also a newspaper published in Shanghai, carried an article on 21 August 1903 concerning the 'bankrupt Fujian merchants'. It reported that in Nantai, which was adjacent to the Min River in Fuzhou, Fujian province, a wealthy merchant, Zhang Li, owned several sailing ships, which he used for shipping between Fuzhou, Jiaozhou, and Niuzhuang. Zhang, however, ran into trouble with the local government when his seamen illegally loaded the ships with weapons. The Zhang family fled to Hong Kong; and the local government confiscated the family's assets. The reporter lamented, 'in Fujian only a few merchants possess capital that amounts to hundreds of thousands of dollars. Now another one of them has fallen into bankruptcy'. A record in volume six of the *Zhapu beizhi*, compiled during the Daoguang period, shows that Nantai, home town of the Zhang family in Fuzhou, flourished as a major distribution centre of timber. From Nantai, ships transported timber to Suzhou, a commercial centre during the Qing dynasty, and to Zhapu on the coast of northeastern Zhejiang province.

In the 'local news' section of no. 555 of the *Xiamen Ribao*, published on 8 December 1909, there is another article about a Fujian ship that had suffered shipwreck. Printed in Xiamen, Fujian province, during the late Qing dynasty, this newspaper reported that a ship from the Fuqing County was carrying rice from Hong Kong to Shantou, Guangdong province, when a gale capsized the vessel. Fortunately, another ship came to rescue the thirty people on board. But one person had already been washed away. This story provides an example of Fujian ships transporting rice to Guangdong province.

The *Minbao* was a newspaper published in Fuzhou, Fujian province, during the late Qing dynasty. On 7 May 1910, no. 1424 of this newspaper carried news of pirates in its section entitled 'Major News of the Provincial Capital'. On its way from Fuzhou to Shanghai, *Jinshunyi*, a merchant ship loaded with timber and other items, was attacked by ten pirate boats. On 26 November 1910, no. 1511 of the same newspaper reported a shipwreck: 'Having completed a voyage from Fuzhou to Jiaozhou, *Xinyuancheng*, a large merchant ship loaded with bean cakes and other items, was on its way back to Fujian. Soon after its departure from Jiaozhou, however, the ship encountered strong winds and consequently sank. The total loss amounted to 30,000 dollars.'

Shipping between China and Taiwan was also active during the late-Qing dynasty. Ships regularly voyaged between Xiamen and Tainan, and between Fuzhou and Danshui.[14] Since the Qing court had exerted control over Taiwan, many junks shuttled across the Taiwan Straits transporting people as well as goods. These roundbottomed vessels were known as *hengyangchuan*, *tangchuan*, and *toubeichuan* respectively.[15] It was, however, unclear where these ships were registered.[16] When Japan began to rule Taiwan in 1895; all the ships in Taiwan that had been registered as Chinese ships were requested to register as Japanese ships. Ship owners needed to present, through respective local authorities, two documents to the Government-General in Taiwan: a 'Request for the certificate of ship registration', and a 'Report on a Chinese-style ship'. The relevant local governments would carefully examine the documents. If they had questions about any details in the documents, they compiled a 'Report concerning the request for a certificate of ship registration', and submitted it with the two documents to the Government-General. The Government-General would eventually issue a certificate to the applicant. These application materials, the 'Report on a Chinese-style ship', in particular, provide us with valuable information on the ships in Taiwan. Depending on the individual applicant, the format of this report varied. In general, the report contained the following information: name of the ship, place of registration, the local government that exercised jurisdiction over the ship, the former name of the ship (in the case of a new ship, a remark 'newly built' inserted), its number of masts, the length, width, and depth of the ship, the place and time of its construction, the name of the ship's owner, the name of its boatswain, the capacity of the ship, the price of the ship, its place of purchase, and the name of the ship's former owner, if applicable. This information therefore sheds much light on the nature of ships in Taiwan as well as on their places of construction.[17]

No. 436 of the *Guowen Bao*, a newspaper published in Tianjin on 12 January 1899 revealed in its section on 'Yingkou news' that in 1898 as many as 450 steamships had called at Yingkou, a port located near the mouth of the Liao River in eastern Liaodong, before the river froze in winter. Besides steamships, 516 sailing ships also called at Yingkou. Of these ships, 187 came from areas

---

14 Matsuura Akira, *Qingdai Taiwan haiyun fazhanshi* (Taipei, 2002), 1-152; 'Rizhi shidai Taiwan yu Fuzhou zhijian rongke maoyi shiliao Tongshang huizuan jieshao'. *Taibei wenxian (zhizi)*, 152 (2005), 269-324, 153 (Taipei, 2006), 206-66.
15 See *Xiamen zhi* (*Zhongguo fangzhi congshu* edition. (Taipei, 1967), 108.
16 For regulations concerning ship registration by the Qing court, see Matsuura Akira, *Shindai kaigai bōeki shi no kenkyū* (Kyoto, 2002), 583-98. However, there are no detailed records of individual ships.
17 Matsuura Akira, 'Rizhi shiqi Taiwan he Zhongguo dalu zhijian de fanchuan hangyun', *Taibei wenxian (zhizi)*, 150 (Taipei, 2004), 51-82.

near the mouth of the Yangtze River in southern China, 72 from Ningbo, 42 from Fujian, and 29 from Shandong. Of these ships 36 per cent were sand junks, 14 per cent Ningbo ships, 8 per cent bird junks and 6 per cent Shandong ships. Sailing ships from eastern and southern China numbered 310, about 58 per cent of all the vessels that had visited Yingkou. These figures reflect the activities of the sailing ships from eastern and southern China at the port of Yingkou when steamships were already being used in shipping. One can infer that these figures would have been much higher before steamships were employed in transportation.

5 Conclusion

To conclude, Chinese ships dominated transportation in Chinese coastal waters; in the East China Sea, and the South China Sea from the seventeenth century onwards. A major factor contributing to this situation was the adoption of the 'national isolationist' policy by the governments of Korea and Tokugawa Japan that forbade their ships from sailing abroad. During this era, Chinese ships also proved best in terms of cruising capacity among East Asian ships. Thus shipping activities of Chinese sailing vessels flourished from the latter part of the seventeenth century – and continued to enjoy a dominant role in marine transportation until steamships appeared in the mid-nineteenth century.

CHAPTER 4

Junks ownen Yu Songnian 郁松年 and His Rare Book Collection

1 Introduction

Shanghai and Chongming-dao 崇明島 near the estuary of the Yangtze River during the Qing Dynasty, especially in these areas it had been used many ship, the flat bottom of the sailing ship that was called Sha-chuan 沙船, Sand ship. These owners had dominated the marine transport of the continent coastal Liaodong 遼寧 and North China coastal areas. Some of ship-owners owns from several Sha-chuan vessels to several dozen vessels, and loading and cotton, cotton cloth and tea leaves, daily of goods and such as Gangnam 江南 of products.

By the maritime route, Their vessels went to the Dongbei 東北 region and the Shandong Peninsula coastal, northeast production and Shandong production of soybeans and soybean oil, it had contributed greatly to the marine transport to bring such as the Gangnam meal. The one of the owners of Sha-chuan was family of Yu 郁, that family, In the middle of the Qing Dynasty, had been prosperous owns a 60-70 vessels of Sha-chuan, at the same time and Yu Sung-nien 郁松年 of this family was also in at the same time book collectors of Song and Yuan era with the owner of the ship.

In this paper, I would like to describe with respect to collection of Yu Sung-nien.

2 Yi-jia tang cong-shu

During the Daoguang 道光 reign period (1821-1850) of late Qing 清 times, the Collection from the Yi-jia Hall (*Yi-jia tang cong-shu* 宜稼堂叢書) was published in Shanghai. Included in this important collectanea are seven works by Song and Yuan authors, totaling 256 jiuan 卷. Two of them are histories of the state of Shu-Han 蜀漢 (A.D. 221-263) during the Three Kingdoms period (220-280). These two works have the same title: A Continuation of the Dynastic History of the Later Han (Xu-Han shu 續漢書), compiled by Xiao Chang 蕭常 of the Southern Song dynasty and Hao Jing 郝經 (1223-1275) of the Yuan dynasty respectively. There are also three works on mathematics, A Mathematical Work of Nine Chapters (Shu-shu jiu-zhang 數書九章) by Qin Jiu-shao 秦九韶 (1202-1261),[1] the Expositions of the Nine Chapters of Mathematical Arts (Hsiang-chieh chiu-chang suan-fo), and The Mathematical Arts by Yang Hui 楊輝 (Yang Hui suan-fa 楊輝算法), both by Yang Hui.[2] Works of two eminent Yuan literary figures also appear in the collection: the Complete Work of Yen-Yuan (Yen-Yuan chi) by Dai Biao-yuan 戴表元 (1244-1311) and the Complete Work of Recluse Qing-jung (Qing-jung chii-shih chi) by Yuan Jue 袁桷 (1266-1327), which was the first of these seven works to be printed. The editor of the collection wrote a preface for each work. The earliest preface dates from the fourth month of the twentieth year of the Daoguang reign period (1840), and the last one from the winter of the twenty-third year of the same reign period (1842). Judging from the date of the last preface, it seems that the collection was published about 1843.[3]

The outstanding feature of this collection is that works in the collection are transcribed from Yuan and Ming editions, which were very difficult to come by even during the editor's time. In particular, the two histories of the state of Shu-Han and the mathematical works are important and rare publications, giving particular significance to this collectanea.

Xiao Chang's A Continuation of the Dynastic History of the Later Han

---

1　The work appears under different titles in various places. In the Chih-chai shu-lu chieh-t'i (Shanghai: Shanghai ku-chi ch'u-pan-she, 1987), 12, p. 368, the title for this work is Shu-shu ta-liieh. In the Kuei-hsin tsa-chih (Peking:Chung-hua shu-chii, 1988), p.170, it is referred to as Shu-hsiieh taliieh, and in the Ssu-k'u ch'iian-shu tsung-mu (Peking: Chung-hua shuchii, 1965), 107, p. 905, as Shu-hsiieh chiu-chang. It is believed that the current title, Shu-shu chiu-chang, was given to it by Chao Ch'i-mei in about 1616, when he wrote the preface for a transcription of this mathematical work.

2　Besides the edition preserved in the Yi-jia 'ang cong-shu, the Hsiang-chiehchiu-chang suan-fo also exists in a Korean edition of 1482, which is now held by Beijing Library, China, and is considered a better edition than the Yi-jia 'ang cong-shu edition. The earliest extant edition of the Yang Hui suan-fo is a 1433 Korean edition.

3　In a newly published catalogue of the Chinese collection in Gest Library, there is a bibliographical entry for the Yi-jia 'ang cong-shu; see Ch'ang Pi-te, Wu Che-fu, P'u-lin-ssu-tun taihsiieh Ke ssu-te tung-fang t'u-shu-kuan chung-wen chiu-chi shu-mu (Taipei: Taiwan shang-wu yin-shu-kuan, 1990), p. 385. The Gest Library holds a copy of the original edition of this collection. But the catalogue dates it 1842.

comprises forty-seven jiuan 卷 and covers the period from A.D. 221 to 263. It took Hsiao twenty years to complete this work. He regarded Emperor Zhao lie 昭烈 (r. 221-223) of the state of Shu-Han as the legitimate successor of the Later Han dynasty (25-220) and his own work as a continuation of the Dynastic History of the Later Han (Hou-Han shu 後漢書). Hao Jing's work, as stated, also carries the title A Continuation of the Dynastic History of the Later Han, consists of ninety jiuan 卷, and covers roughly the same period as Xiao Chang's work. It was completed in 1272 and was first published in 1318 under the auspices of the Jiangxi 江西 Branch Secretariat (xing-sheng 行省) during the Yuan dynasty.

Qin Jiu-shao's work was a major contribution to the mathematics of his time. His process for numerical equations of higher degrees established him as the leader in this field, and he was at least three centuries ahead of his Western counterparts.[4] His work also deals with the application of mathematical approaches in a wide range of fields, such as astrology, surveying, taxation, construction, and business. This work, however, was not widely circulated even during Song times. So far, no printed Song edition of this work has ever been found.

Yang Hui was another mathematical giant in the thirteenth century. He and Qin Jiu-shao were credited with working out "full-blown decimal fractions applied to all operations." In China, the first occurrence of decimal fractions is to be found in a writing of the mid-third century A.D., whereas it was not until the sixteenth century that the Arabs and Europeans began to comprehend the significance of decimal fractions. In this field, Europe lagged behind China by over one thousand years.[5]

Works included in the Collection from the Yi-jia Hall are not only important and rare, but meticulously edited as well. In some cases, volumes of textual study of the works are attached to the original text. The person who collected, edited, and published these works in a collectanea is Yu song-nian, and the collectanea is a monument to his achievements as a scholarcollector.

---

4 Robert Temple points out that the mid-sixteenth century Western math-ematicians "considered that equations of higher degree were not relevant to the real world .... By and large, Europeans were far less willing to consider higher equations in the sixteenth century than the Chinese were in the thirteenth." See his The Genius of China, introduced by Joseph Needham (New York: Simon and Schuster, 1986), p. 142. For more detailed discussions of the Chinese contributions to mathematics in premodern times, see Joseph Needham, Science and Civilisation in China (Cambridge: Cambridge University Press, 1959),vol. 3.
5 Temple, The Genius of China, p. 143.

3   Yu Songnian and his Rare Book Collection

Yu song-nian was a celebrity in Shanghai County during the Tongzhi 同治 reign period (1862-1874). A biographical entry for him in the local gazet-teer describes him as the younger son of a successful local businessman and millionaire, Yu Run-nian 郁潤年. Song-nien had an older brother, Peng-nian 彭年, who is said to have been very resourceful and good at assigning his subordinates jobs commensurate with their abilities. Yü Peng-nian was also a businessman, perhaps spending much of his time helping his father with the family business. Yu song-nian was, however, different from his brother. He was both a scholar and book-lover and a businessman. During the Tongzhi reign period, he was a "tribute student by grace" (en kung-sheng 恩貢生), a designation used by the Directorate of Education (Guo-zi jian 國子監) to enable candidates, who were chosen through a specially arranged examination, to participate in the provincial civil service examination and be considered at least the equal of a national university student (jian-sheng 監生).

The family wealth enabled Song-nien to acquire a sizable private collection of books, said to have amounted to tens of thousands of jiuan 卷. He was an enthusiastic collector of Song-edition books, especially those that either had never been engraved or for which the wood printing blocks had been destroyed. His collection also included rare Yuan and Ming editions. To acquire these books, Song-nien spared no time or money. During the Daoguang reign period (1821-1850), Song-nien traveled all the way to Yangchou 揚州 to purchase from a local salt merchant a Yuan edition of the Sea of jade (Yü hai 玉海), a Southern Song encyclopedia of two hundred juan 卷. For this encyclopedia alone, Song-nien paid as much as six hundred liang 兩 of gold.[6]

The price that Yu song-nian paid for that one encyclopedia, and his expensive hobby of purchasing rare Chinese books over a long period, indicate that the Yü family must have been extremely wealthy. In a late Qing diary (fen Mo-shu t'ui-chih chaijih-chi), the Yu family was also referred to as "Yu Sen-sheng 郁森盛."[7] The term "Sen-sheng" seems to h ave been used as the name referring to the entire Yü family business, since it was also used by Song-nien's brother Peng-nian. The family had been in commercial shipping for at least two

---

6   "Shang-hai hsien-chih," in Chungkuo fong-chih ts'ung-shu (facsimile rpt. of 1871 edn.; Taipei: Ch'eng-wen ch'u-pan-she, 1975), 21, pp. 43b-44a; Ch'ing pai lei-ch'ao (Shanghai: Shangwu yin-shu-kuan, 1917), 72, p. 120.

7   See "Jen Mo-shu t'ui-chih chai jihchi," the twenty-fifth day of the twelfth month, 1855, in the Ch'ing-tai jih-chih hui-ch'ao (Shanghai: Shang-hai jen-min ch'u-pan-she, 1982), p. 240.

Yu songnian 郁松年 and His Rare Book Collection

Table 7　Yu Songnian Edit, "*Yijian-tan Congshu*" 郁松年編『宜稼堂叢書』

Title	Vol.	Author
Xu-Hou-Hanshu 續後漢書	48	Xiao-chang 蕭常
FuYin-yi xi-li Zhaji 附音義義例札記		Yu Songnian 郁松年
Xu-Hou Hanshu 續後漢書	94	Hao Jing 郝　經
Zhaji 札記		Yu Songnian 郁松年
Shushu jiuzhang 數書九章	22	Qin Jiushao 秦九韶
Zhaji 札記		Song Jingchang 宋景昌
Xiangjie Jiuzhan sunafa 詳解九章算法	3	Yang Hui 楊輝
Fu Zuankeu Zhaji 附篡類札記		Song Jingchang 宋景昌
Yang Hui Suanfa 楊輝算法	7	Yang Hui 楊輝
Fu Zhaji 附札記		Song Jingchang 宋景昌
Shanyuan-ji 剡源集	31	Dai Biaoyuan 戴表元
Fu Zhaji 附札記		Yu Songnian 郁松年
Qingrong jyushi-ji 清容居士集	51	Yuan Jie 袁　桷
Fu Zhaji 附札記		Yu Songnian 郁松年

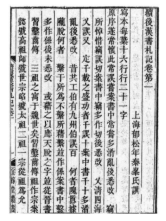

　　Figue 8　Xu-Hou-Hanshu Zhaji　　Figure 9　Xu-Hou-Hanshu Zhaji, Vol 1

generations. When Song-nien was in charge of the business, his fleet expanded to more than fifty ships.[8] And among the twenty-four shipping businesses in

---

8　These ships were referred to as "shach'uan." In G. R. C. Worcester's The junks and Sampans of the Yangtze (Annapolis: Naval Institute Press, 1911), pp. 162-167, the "sha-ch'uan" is illustrated and called a Kiangsu trader.

Shanghai, the Yü family's ranked number two. That business provided Song-nien with the funds to purchase his rare book collection.

4 Conclusion

The protective trading policy of the Qing court facilitated the Yü family's establishment of its dominant position in the lucrative coastal shipping business. This policy forbade foreign ships to sail or to transport goods along the Chinese coast and inland rivers, thus shielding the Yü family from foreign competition. The financial resources of the Yü family steadily increased. One measure of their unusual position in the business world is that in 1856 the family cast three types of silver coins.[9] Their privately issued silver dollars were among the earliest silver coins cast and circulated in Shanghai, or in China.[10] The casting and issuance of silver coins by the Yü family and other wealthy families in the commercial shipping business marked the apex of their economic strength.[11] But this strength was to be significantly weakened two years later, in 1858, when the Qing court signed a series of treaties with Western powers after its disastrous defeat in the Second Opium War, allowing foreigners various economic, political, and economic privileges in China. Four years later, in 1862, when the Qing court eventually lifted the ban on foreign ships engaging in transportation in China, the Yü family and other Chinese shipping business suffered great losses from foreign competition.[12] In the same year, Yüi Songnien died.

After the death of Yiü Song-nien, perhaps out of economic pressure or lack of interest in collecting traditional Chinese books, members of the Yü family began to sell Song-nien's rare book collection. It was the kind of opportunity other collectors are always waiting for. Some of his Song and Yuan rare books were purchased by Ding Ri-chang 丁日昌 (1823-1882), governor of Jiangsu 江蘇, but the majority of Yu song-nian's collection, which totaled forty-eight thou-

---

9 For a description of the inscriptions on these coins, see Chiang Chungch'uan, Chung-kuo chin-yin nieh-pi t'ushuo (rpt.; Hong Kong: Lung-men shu-tien, 1966), pp. 37-39 .
10 For a discussion of these silver coins, see L. S. Yang, Money and Credit in China (Cambridge, Mass.: Harvard University Press, 1962), paragraph 5.31, p. 49.
11 For a discussion of other families engaged in the casting and issuance of silver coins, see Kato Shigeshi, Shina keizaishi kosho (Tokyo: T6y6 bunko, 1952), vol. b, p. 455. The Chinese central government did not mint silver coins until after the Revolution of 1911.
12 Akira Matsuura, "Shindai makki no shasengyo ni tsuite," Kansai daigaku bungaku ronshu 39:3 (1990), pp. 1-71.

sand jiuan 卷, was sold to Lu Xin-yuan 陸心源, salt distribution commissioner in Fujian 福建 and a famed late Qing book collector. Yiü's rare book collection, however, was not to remain in Lu Xin-yuan 's private library.

In 1907, the collection was again sold, this time to Japan; it became the major holding of the Seikado bunko 靜嘉堂文庫,[13] originally a private library but now a branch of the Japan Diet Library in Tokyo.

---

13   Arthur W. Hummel, ed., Eminent Chinese of the Ch'ing Period (1644-1912) (Washington, D.C.: U.S. Government Printing Office, 1943), pp. 545-546.

CHAPTER 5

The Maritime Trade of Chinese Junks with Vietnam Hue (Huế) during 16-19 century

1 Introduction

The trade between China and Vietnam has a long history. In the *Zhu Fan Zhi* (诸蕃志) which is a Song Dynasty work by Zhao Rugua (趙汝适), have a record about this trade: "the east coast of Champa is connected to Guangzhou, ... a tailwind distance from Quanzhou (泉州) to Champa is more than 20 days".[1] In the Ming dynasty,the *Ying Ya Sheng Lan* (瀛涯胜覽), written by Ma Huan, a book about the countries visited by Ma Huan over the course of Zheng He's treasure voyages, also have a record about the trade between China and Champa: "From the Wuhumen (五虎門) of Fujian province, Sailing in the southwest, with a tailwind 10 days will be arrived to Champa".[2]

Even in the 19th century, the Hainan Island (海南島) which is located in the South China Sea, also have a prosperous trade with Vietnam. Specific examples can be written in 1832, Charles Gutzlaff Journal of a residence in Siam, and of a voyage along the coast of China to Mantchou Tartary seen. His diary wrote:

> Hainan is, on the whole, a barren country; and, with the exception of timber, rice, and sugar (the latter of which is principally carried to the north China), there are no articles of export. The inhabitants carry on some trade abroad; they visit Tungking, Cochin-china, Siam, and also Singapore. On their voyagers to Siam, they cut timber along the coasts of Tsiompa and Cambojia; and when they arrive at Bankok buy an additional quantity, with which they build junks. In two months a junk is finished, — the sails, ropes,

---

1 FENG Chengjun (annotation), *Zhu Fan Zhi Jiao Zhu annotation*, Peking, The Commercial Press,1940, pp3.
2 FENG Chengjun (annotation), *Ying Ya Sheng Lan annotation,* Peking: The Commercial Press, 1940, pp1.

79

ancor, and all the other work, being done by their own hands. These junks are then loaded with cargoes, saleable at Canton or on their native island, and both junk and cargo being sold, the profits are divided and cargo being sold, the profits are divided among the builders. Other junks, loaded with rice, and bones for manure, are usually dispatched for Hainan.[3]

This research is based on the maritime trade of Chinese Junks with Vietnam Hue (Huế) during 16-19 century, in order to elaborate the trade patterns at that time.

2 Sino Vietnam maritime trade in the late Ming Dynasty

Chinese Ming government had a sea policy called Haijin (海禁), which was a imposed ban on merchants' maritime shipping.[4] But by the late Ming Dynasty, Ming government relaxed Haijin policy, therefore, the trade scale between China and Southeast Asia were gradually increasing.

The Xu Fuyuan (許孚远), a high government official of Fujian province, had a description about the trade scale at that time of late Ming Dynasty in his work *Jing He Tang Ji* (敬和堂集). "In 1589 year, 88 ships had obtained government's permission to go overseas. among the 88 ships, 10 ships were sailing towards Vietnam. In particular, 4 ships were sailing towards Cochinchina (交阯), 3 ships were sailing towards Champa (占城), 2 ships were sailing towards Huế (順化)".

According to the description which was recorded by Ming dynastry merchants in Huế, merchants' actual activities can be understand.

Zhu Junwang (朱均旺), a merchant of Jiangxi province, doing business from 1574 year. In 1577 year, he set off from Jiangxi province to Zhangzhou port of Fujian province, in order to sell the cloth. After that, he went to Huế to sell porcelain by ship.

There were 30 Fujian ships in Huế. because of Too many goods, merchants employed some Cochinchina ships sailing to Quảng Nam which

---

3 *The Chinese Repository,* Vol. I, pp.90-91.
4 Sakuma, A Study of Relations between Japan and the Ming Dynasty, Tokyo, 1992.

was a province in the South Central Coast region of Vietnam, to sell goods.[5]

From this description, we could know that with the relaxed Haijin policy, some merchants such as ZHU Junwang could sailed for Vietnam to do business.

3 Sino Vietnam maritime trade in the Qing Dynasty

In the Qing dynastry, Kangxi Emperor drew up a policy called Great Clearance in 1661year. It required the evacuation of the coastal areas in order to fight the Taiwan-based anti-Qing loyalist movement of the Zheng Chenggong (鄭成功). But with the conquest of Taiwan, Great Clearance was lifted in 1669 year. Private overseas trade also Gradually flourishing from 1669 year.[6]

In 1726 year,the Mao Wenquan (毛文铨), a high government official of Fujian province, had a description in his memorial to the throne.

The merchant ship had been forbidden to go to Southeast Asia by Kangxi Emperor. But the Vietnam was the exception.[7]

In the same year, Yang Wenqian (楊文乾), a high government official of Guangdong province, also had a description in his memorial to the throne.

All of The customs duties of Guangdong customs were from foreign merchant ships and native merchant ships which were doing business with Southeast Asia. The main goods of native merchant ships were undurable goods such as charcoal betelnut and so on.[8]

---

5   HOU Jigao, *Quan Zhe Bing Zhi Kao* (全浙兵制考), National Archives of Japan, volume 2, *Fu Lu Jin Bao Wo Jing* (附録近報倭警).
6   MATSUURA Akira, *Studies in the History of Qing Period Maritime Trade*, Kyoto, 2002.
MATSUURA Akira, *the sailing ship of Qing Dynasty in East Asia and maritime commerce and pirate* (清代帆船東亞航運與南商海盜), Shanghai Lexicographical Publishing House,2009.
7   *Gong Zhong Dang Yong Zheng Chao Zou Zhe* (宮中檔雍正朝奏摺), Taipei: National Palace Museum,1978, volume 5,pp 688-68.
8   *Gong Zhong Dang Yong Zheng Chao Zou Zhe* (宮中檔雍正朝奏摺), Taipei: National Palace Museum,1978, volume 5,pp 613.

Part 1: The Activities of Chinese Junks on the East Asian Sea in Early Modern Ages

In 1727 year, another high government official called Chang Lai (常賚) had the following record about the trade between Qing dynasty and Vietnam.

Because Guangdong province was lack of arable land, masses of coastal residents had to go abroad to do business. Since the 1717 year, do business with Southeast Asia was only Limited to Vietnam, the trade with other Southeast Asia nations was been forbidden by Kangxi Emperor.... Most merchants were from Fujian and Guangdong province, doing business with other countries can make up the lack of arable land of Fujian and Guangdong province.[9]

Above were Chinese records bout Vietnam trade. The following records were from the Vietnam book *Fu bian za lu (撫邊雜錄)* which was compiled in 1776 year.

Huế (順化) was connect to Guangzhou and Fujian by waterway. From Huế to Guangzhou and Fujian was about 3 or 4 days by waterway. Therefore, most Chinese merchants came to Huế. Vietnam government had set up a institution called Shi bo ti ju si (市舶提舉司), in order to manage the merchant ships and collect taxes in Yong Le (永樂) period.[10]

This book also recorded the rate of customs duties against various countries merchant ships.

Japan merchant ships' first entry customs duties was 4000 cash; return trip customs duties was 400 cash. Siam merchant ships' first entry customs duties was 2000 cash; return trip customs duties was 500 cash; Luzon merchant ships' first entry customs duties was 2000 cash; return trip customs duties was 200 cash;...the first entry customs duties of China merchant ships like Guangzhou merchant ships, Zhejiang merchant ships, Hainan merchant ships and Shanghai merchant ships was 2100 cash...[11]

According to this record, most of the merchant ships coming to Vietnam were from Shanghai Zhejiang Hainan and Guangzhou.
Fu BianZzaLlu (撫邊雜錄) also had a record about Guangdong merchants.

---

9 *Gong Zhong Dang Yong Zheng Chao Zou Zhe* (宮中檔雍正朝奏摺), Taipei: National Palace Museum,1978,volume 8, pp 26.
10 *Le Quy Don tuyen tap tap* 3, PHU BIEN TAP LUC (Phan2), 2008, pp323.
11 *PHU BIEN TAP LUC* (Phan2), pp325.

The Maritime Trade of Chinese Junks with Vietnam Hue (Huế) during 16-19 century

A Guangdong merchant surnamed Chen, he took a ship from Guangzhou to Huế in 6 days with a tailwind way…. He Sold peppers in Huế …. Many merchants gathered in Quảng Nam, therefore, Quảng Nam was very prosperity.[12]

Li Guichun made some records especially of the Cantonese merchants in Shunhua[13]. According to his records, a Cantonese merchant surnamed Chan came to Shunhua by sea. It cost him only 6 days with the windward sailing and the shipping route has also be recorded.

On July 16, 1767, a merchant ship arrived at Nagasaki with several Japanese refugees who had wandered to Hui'an before[14]. Among those refugees who survived shipwrecks in the early November of 1759, four of them used to be the sailors of Himemiya-maru 姫宮丸 of Mito feudal clan 水戸藩号 and another three used to be the sailors of Sumiyoshi-maru 住吉丸 of Ohshu 奥州[15]. They wandered among the main ports in Hui'an and their experience was recorded in a book *Drifting in Hui'an*[16]. In the book, they wrote "there are 17 or 18 merchant ships coming from China in Hui'an". In order to go back to Japan, those refuges asked the merchant ships for help. After 27-days's sailing from Hui'an, they finally reached Nagasaki[17]. It could be estimated from the records that there were 17 ships or so coming to Hui'an for trades, which also proves the authenticity of next reference material written by the British in the 19th century.

In 1821, John Crawford, under the order from the British government, went to Siam and Cochin, and recorded the maritime trades between China and Vietnam in a book named "Journal of an Embassy to the Courts of Siam and

---

12 *PHU BIEN TAP LUC* (Phan2), pp330.
13 "廣東船商客、有姓陳者、慣販賣、伊言、自廣州府、由海道往順化。得順風只六日、夜入填海門、至富春河清庸、入大占海門、到廣南會安、亦無自廣州往山南只四日夜餘一更、只山南回帆點、惟ประฆ禹餘粮一物、順化亦只胡椒一味、若廣南則百貨無、所不有諸番邦、不及升華・尊盤・帰仁・廣義・平康等府及弟荘營、所出貨物。水陸船馬、咸湊於會安・庸州、……", PHU BIEN TAP LUC (Phan2), p.330.
14 Chen Jinghe 陈荆和, *Qing-chu Hua-bo zhi Changqi maoyi ji rinan yunhang* 清初华舶之长崎贸易及日南运航, Nanyang xueba o, 南洋学报, vol. 13, no.1,1957, pp.1-52.
15 〈安南船ヨリ外國漂着之者七人送來事〉,《長崎実録大成》卷十二,《長崎文献叢書第一集・第二卷, 長崎實録大成正編》長崎文献社、1973年12月、307〜311頁。
16 "この時、南京船十七、八艘、会安に逗留いたし候。なにとぞ便舟にて日本へは叶はず候とも、せめて南京までも渡り申したく願ひ候"〈安南国漂流物語〉,《石井研堂コレクション江戸漂流記総集》第二卷、日本評論社、1992年5月、263頁。
17 "安南より長崎まで、丑寅［北東］の方に向ひて、昼夜やすまず日数二十七日にて着仕り候"〈安南国漂流物語〉,《石井研堂コレクション江戸漂流記総集》第二卷、266頁。

Cochin China"[18].

The amount of the Chinese trade of Saigun yearly has been commonly as follows: —from fifteen to twenty-five junks of Hai-nan, measuring from 2,000 to 2,500 piculs each; two junks of Canton, one measuring five, and the other 8,000 piclus ; one junk of Amoy, measuring 7,000 piculs ; and six junks of Saocheu, measuring from 6 to 7,000 piculs each. The total number of junks may be reckoned at about thirty, and their total burthen about six thousand five hundred tons. The most valuable cargoes are imported from Amoy, consisting principally of wrought silks and teas, and the least valuable, form Hai-nan. The Canton junks, before a direct intercourse was established between the British possessions and Cochin China, used import all the opium consumed in the country, and the whole of the broadcloths and other woolens with which the King's troops were clothed, and they still continue to import a considerable quantity of both. The exports by these vessels are generally of the same description as from Siam, and the principal of them are cardamums, the areca-nut, sugar, fancy woods, eagle-wood, ebony, cotton, rice, stic-lac, ivory, pelty, hides, and horns, deers'sinews, ornamental feathers, particularly those of a species of kingfisher, &c. &c.

The Chinese trade of Fai-fo is with the same ports, and may be taken annually at the following amounts: —with Hainan, three junks, measuring about 2,500 piculs each; with Canton, six junks, averaging 3,000 each; with Amoy, four junks, averaging also 3,000 each; and with Saocheu, three junks, of about 2,500 piculs each. This gives about sizteen junks, giving a total burthen of near 3,000 tons. The small size of these vessels is accounted for by the shallowness of the river, or rather creek, of Fai-fo, which they must enter for shelter.

The trade of Hue, the capital, is also with the same ports, and amounts in all to about twelve junks, measuring from 2,500 to 4,000 piculs each, and to near 2,500 tons. None above 3,000 piculs can load with safety in the river, and those of larger size take in their cargoes in the Bay of Turan. The exports from Hue and Fai-fo are the same, and the principal articles consist of sugar, cotton, and cinnamon.

The Chinese trade of Tonquin by sea commonly consists of the following number of junks: —eighteen from Hai-nan, of 2,000 piculs each; six from Canton, from 2,000 to 2,500; seven from Amoy, of the same

---

18   John Crawfurd, *Journal of an Embassy to the Courts of Siam and Cochin China*, 1828, pp.511-513.

burthen as the least; and seven from Saoucheu, averaging 2,500 each. This gives a total of thirty-eight junks, and a tonnage of about 5,000 tons. By the statement of the Chinese traders, it appears that a junk of 3,000 piculs, or about one hundred and eighty-seven tons, is the largest which can enter the river of Tonquin with safety. The exports consist of areca-nut, cardamums, cotton, salt-fish, salt, rice, varnish, and a variety of other dyeing drugs, with gold and silver bullion.

The Chinese trade with the minor ports of Cochin China amounts, in all, to about twenty junks not measuring above 2,000 piculs each; and therefore giving a total tonnage of 2,300 tons. The usual exports are rice and cinnamon. The exportation of the first-named commodity being forbidden without a special licence, many of these junks do not enter the ports of Cochin China at all, but, lying off the coast, smuggle their cargoes on board.[19]

In light of that book, as part of the Sino-Vietnamese Trades, about 15 to 25 Chinese ship came to Saigun from Hainan Island, 2 ships from Guangdong, 1 ship from Amoy and 6 ships from Chaozhou every year. Besides, 16 ships went to Fai-fo among which 3 ships from Hainan, 6 from Guandong, 4 from Amoy and 3 from Chaozhou. As for Hue, Chinese Junks there amounted to 12 and the tonnage of every ship could reach 2,500 ton.

The number of Chinese Junks to Hue was 12, almost as same as the number of other ports. The cargo capacity of the ships varied from 2,500 piculs to 4,000 piculs and the cargo weight was about 2,500 ton. Due to the limitation of the rivers in Hue, it was impossible for large vessels to sail. Thus, the load limit of a ship was 3,000 piculs. Most cargoes were granulated sugar, cotton and cinnamon from China.

Crawford also recorded the Chinese Junks to Tonkin. It reads, "6 ships from Guangdong, 7 from Amoy, 7 from Chaozhou and the total number was 18".

In March 1830, under the calling of the British Parliament, Crawford adopted his dairy in the report relating to "East Asian Trades of Chinese sailings"[20]. In this sense, his testimony was included in the report called "First Report from the Select Committee on the Affairs of the East India Company (China Trade), 1830".

19　John Crawfurd, *Journal of an Embassy to the Courts of Siam and Cochin China*, 1828, pp.511-513.
20　Sasaki Masaya 佐々木正哉, 19seiki-shoki chuugoku jyanku no kaigaiboueki ni kansuru shiryou 十九世紀初期中国戎克の海外貿易に関する資料、Kindai Chugoku 近代中国, Vol. 3, 1978 May, pp. 56-74.

3.1 Native foreign Trade of China

The principal part of the junk-trade is carried on by the four contiguous provinces of Canton, Fokien, Cheliang and Kiannan. .... The ports of China at which this trade is conducted are Canton, Tchao-tcheou, Nomhong, Hoei-tcheon, Su-heng, Kongmoon, Changlim and Hainan, in the province of Canton; Amoy and Chinchew, in the prpvince of Fokien; Ningpo and Siang-hai, in the province of Tchekian; and Soutcheon, in the province of Kiannan. The following may be looked upon as a spproximation to the number of junks carrying on trade with the different places already enumerated; viz.

Japan, 10 junks, two voyages	20	Junks
Phillippine Islands	13	
Soo-loo Islands	4	
Celebes	2	
Borneo	13	
Java	7	
Sumatra	10	
Sincapore	8	
Rhio	1	
East Coast of Malay Peninsula	6	
Siam	89	
Cochin China	20	
Cambodia	9	
Tonquin	20	
Total	222	

This statement does not include a great number of small junks belonging to the island of Hainan, which carry on trade with Tonquin, Cochin China, Cambodia, Siam, and sincapore. Those for Siam amount yearly to about 50, and for the Cochin Chinese dominions to about 43; these alone would bring the total number of vessels carrying on a direct trade between China and foreign countries to 307. ...... With the exception of this branch of trade the foreign intercourse of the two provinces of Chekian and Kiannan, which are famous for the production of raw silk, teas and nankeens, is confined to the Philippine Islands, Tonquin, Cochin China, Cambodia and Siam, and none of this class of vessels, that I am aware of, have ever found their way to the western parts of Indian Archipelago. The number of these trading with Siam is 24, all of considerable size; those trading with Phillippines, 5, making in all 45, of which the average burden does not fall short of 17,000 tons.[21]

It was stated in the report that Siam was the first trading market of Chinese merchant ships and Vietnam came the second. Focusing on the Sino-Vietnamese Trades, Crawford wrote another report, finding that Chinese sailing-based trades were mainly proceeds by four provinces: Guangdong, Fujian, Zhejiang and Jiangsu and moreover, Canton, Tchao-tcheou, Nomhong, Hoei-Tcheon, Su-heng, Kongmoon, Changlim and Hainan of Guangdong, Amoy and Chinchew of Fujian, Ningpo of Zhejiang, Siang-hai and Sou-tcheon of Jiangsu were the center ports of the trades.

Based on the above materials, it is presumed that the trade scale with Chinese Junks of Vietnam ranked only second to Siam. Most of the Chinese sailings to Vietnam came from Hainan Island, Guangdong, Amoy and regions south of the Yangtze River. Every year, 46 to 71 ships from Hainan Island, 14 ships from Guangdong, 16 ships from Amoy, 16 ships from Sou-tcheon came to Vietnam. The average number of the ships to Saigon every year was 30, to Hai Phong 海防 of Vietnam was 16, to Tonkin was 38 and to Hue was 12. As mentioned before, in order to sail into the rivers in Vietnam, most of the ships were small sailboats.

The statement of Crawford was confirmed by the *Amoy Chorography* of 1839. It was described in the *Amoy Chorography* that the large Chinese sailings could carry more than 10,000 Shi of goods and those ships with silk fabrics, raw silk, porcelain, umbrellas, cottons, paper products, tea and iron, were permitted to sail to Singapore, Vietnam, Philippines and other Southeast Asia regions for trades.

According to Vol.1 of the *Amoy Chorography*, Vietnam used to be called Annam. There are 5 ports in Vietnam: Qinghua, Shunhua, Guangnan, Xinzhou and Tiyi. Besides, the specialties of Vietnam were gold, pearl, coral reefs, rhinoceros horn, ivory, shellfish, hawksbill, bronze drums, pomade, fragrance, wax, cubilose, logwood, cinnamon, etc.

Another customs report named "China. Imperial Maritime Customs, Decennial Reports, 1881-91, Kiungchow （瓊州）" in *Amoy Chorography*[22], proves full list of the goods exported to Vietnam from Hainan Island at the end of the 19th century.

---

21 Report from the Select Committee on the affairs of the East India Company and the trade between Great Britain, the East Indies and China, 1830, Irish University Press Area Studies Series British Parliamentary Papers, China 37, Irish University Press, 1971, pp. 298-299.
22 *China. Imperial Maritime Customs, Decennial Reports,* 1881-91, Kiungchow, p.623.

The bulk of our Exports goes to Hongkong, but there is a trifling coast trade to Pakoho, limited almost exclusively to Betel-nuts. With Tonkin, Annam, and the Straits Settlements our trade is still insignificant, and restricted to Leaf Tobacco, Opium Bowls, Fishing Nets, and Leather Trunks.

As stated in the custom report, although the port trade began to move from Hainan Island to Hong Kong, betel-nuts from Pakoho were still exported to overseas market. The trade scale between Tonkin, Annam and other British colonies around Malacca kept falling and the trade goods were limited to tobacco, opium, fishing net and leather goods.

Thus, it can be seen that, the sailing-based trades between China and Vietnam significantly decreased at the end of the 19th century.

4 Conclusion

Above all, the Nha Le 黎朝 and the Nha Nguen 阮朝 Dynasty in Vietnam were the heydays of the seaborne trade with China. From China's perspective, the sea trade came back to vogue in the late Ming Dynasty as the ban on maritime trade had been relaxed to some extent. Every year, nearly 100 Chinese Junks set sail from Fujian and Guangdong. In the 18th century, merchants of Chinchew went to Hoi An 會安, and made a lot of relevant records of the merchant ships, especially of the ships coming from Hainan Island[23]. Those ships exported Chinese products to Vietnam and carry back Vietnam specialties, mainly granulated sugar, cotton, rice and cinnamon in the return journey.

The late period of sailing-based trade, according to Crawford's reports, started from the Emperor Gia Long 嘉隆帝 of Nha Nguen Dynasty 阮朝 of the first emperor to the early half of the 19th century. During this period, a large number of Chinese Junks sailed to Hue for trades. However, with the conclusion of the Treaty of Nanjing following the Opium War in 1840, Canton, Amoy, Fuzhou, Ningpo and Siang-hai were forced to open. Thus, the number of ships, especially the steamboats, from western countries increased greatly, which shook the dominance of the Chinese Junks in Southeast Asia and impacted the maritime trade between China and Vietnam.

---

23 松浦章 Matsuura Akira, Shindai Senshu Shinko Hansen niyoru kaiyou bunnka koushou 清代泉州晋江帆船による海洋文化交渉, Higashi Ajia Bunka kousho kennkyu 東アジア文化交渉研究, Kansai University, No. 2, 2009 March, pp.145-164.

CHAPTER 6

Maritime Rescue & Salvage in Early Modern East Asia and Its Modern Transfiguration

1 Introduction

When Commodore Perry and his American fleet sailed into Uraga at Edo Bay in July 1853, he presented a letter to the Tokugawa Shogun on July 7th, requesting the opening of Japan and the conclusion of a treaty of friendship. In this letter, he wrote:

> The government of the United States wishes to obtain positive assurance from the Japanese government that henceforward people who suffer shipwreck along the Japanese coasts, or flee into Japanese ports to escape bad weather, shall be treated with humanity.[1]

Perry's request shows that due to the expansion of such maritime activities as whaling on the Pacific Ocean, the granting of humanitarian aid to Americans who had suffered perils of the sea had become an important issue.[2] Perry's attitude toward this issue remained unchanged. In his conversation with Hayashi Akira on March 8th, 1854, Perry pointed out that Japan's treatment of people on wrecked ships was inhuman. But Hayashi Akira categorically rejected Perry's assertion, and maintained that Japan had always rescued people from such distressed ships.[3]

---

1 *Narrative of The Expedition of American Squadron to the China Seas and Japan. Performed in the Years 1852, 1853, and 1854, Under the Command of Commodore M. C. Perry* (United States Navy, Washington, 1856), vol. 1, p. 244.
2 Yamashita Shōto, *Hogei (Whaling)* (Tokyo: Hosei Daigaku Shuppankai, 2004), vol. 2, pp. 104-123.
3 *Dainippon komonjo bakumatsu gaikoku kankei monjo furoku no ichi* (*Ancient documents of Japan: Documents concerning foreign relations during the latter days of the Tokugawa Bakufu, supplement one*) (Tokyo: Teikoku Daigaku, 1913), pp. 538-540.

Part 1: The Activities of Chinese Junks on the East Asian Sea in Early Modern Ages

Before the invention of aircraft, one important issue in negotiating an international treaty was whether the involved countries should rescue each other's people from sea disasters out of respect for human life. This, in fact, remains an issue today. In this article, I shall examine human rescue and salvage in East Asia before Perry's visit to Japan.

The sea route that links the Yellow Sea, the Donghai (Tōkai), the Korean Peninsula, the Japanese archipelagos, the Southwest Islands (the Ryūkyū Islands), and Taiwan played an important role in the history of exchange among East Asian countries. When sailing on the sea, however, there was no guarantee for safety. And bad weather often led to sea disasters. In many cases, when a ship, its crew and passengers had been rescued in Japan, local authorities would conduct an investigation into the circumstance of the incident, and compile a report in Chinese *kanji* in order to convey the information to other countries in the Chinese cultural sphere.[4] We therefore have detailed *kanji* records of sea disasters. Becoming interested in sea disasters in East Asia, and the ways in which they were handled by the various governments in the region, I have recently examined these records.

In early modern times, Chinese sailboats were most active on the East Asian seas.[5] But very few source materials cast light on their activities. However, if we pay attention to records concerning maritime disasters, the activities of Chinese sailboats, which have so far not been fully researched by scholars, become clearer. In this way we can further advance our research into Chinese coastal as well as overseas shipping activities.

China had long been the center for salvage of wrecked ships along Chinese coasts and in East Asian waters. During the Kangxi period (1662-1722), the Qing court legalized a salvage system, which further developed and reached maturity during the Yongzheng (1723-1735) and the Qianlong (1736-1795) periods respectively. Salvage in China was conducted basically according to imperial orders. So far, the best work on salvage in East Asia has been done by Kanazashi Shōzō. This work, entitled *Research into the Salvage System during*

---

4 For records about Chinese ships that suffered sea disasters, see the works published by the Kansai University Press in the bibliography.

5 Tian Rukang, *Zhonguo fanchuan maoyi yu duiwai guanxi shi lunji* (*Collected essays on the history of China's junk trade and foreign relations.* Hangzhou: Zhejiang Renmin Chubanshe, 1987), pp. 1-99. Matsuura Akira, *Shindai kaigai bōekishi no kenkyū* (*Studies in the overseas trade during the Qing dynasty*) (Kyoto: Hōyūshoten, 2002), pp. 264-306.

Matsuura Akira, *Shindai Shanghai sasen kōunshi no kenkyū* (*Studies in the history of sand boat transportation during the Qing dynasty*) (Suida: Kansai Daigaku Shuppankai, 2004), pp. 63-75.

Early Modern Times, is a detailed study of the statutes, and some specific cases, concerning salvage.[6] Tang Xiyong, of Academia Sinica (Taiwan), has examined Chinese salvage during the Qing Dynasty, with a focus on the methods of salvage in such countries as China, Korea, and Vietnam before the early modern time.[7] In this article, I shall examine the forms of rescue and salvage in various East Asian countries in early modern times when diplomatic treaties were not yet employed in international relations, and, for comparison, some specific cases of salvage from a later era when such treaties came into use between countries.

2 Salvage and maritime rescue in East Asia during early modern times

2.1 The case of the Qing Dynasty

The basic materials for the study of maritime relations between China and foreign countries during the Ming and the Qing dynasties are the regulations concerning tribute in the *Da Ming huidian* (大明會典 *Statutory precedents of the Ming dynasty*), the *Da Qing huidian* (大清會典 *Statutory precedents of the Qing dynasty*), and the *Da Qing huidian shili* (大清會典事例 *Statutory precedents of the Qing dynasty with cases*). In the *Da Ming huidian* published during the Wanli period (1573-1620), the related matters are listed country by country; but in the *Da Qing huidian*, these matters are recorded with the names of countries attached to specific events. This is also the practice for records in the *Da Qing huidian shili* of the Jiaqing period (1796-1820). Volumes 392 to 401 in the *Jiaqing Da Qing huidian shili* (*Statutory precedents of the Qing dynasty with cases of the Jiaqing reign period*) carry the title "Tributes, Ministry of Rites," under which there are fourteen categories: imperial ordinances, time of a tributary mission's arrival, the routes it took, tributary items, ceremonies, imperial gifts for foreign visitors, arrangements for greeting and farewell, trading activi-

---

6 Kanazashi Shōzō, *Kinsei kainan kyūjo no kenkyū* (*Studies in maritime disaster relief in recent times*) (Tokyo: Yoshikawa kōbunkan, 1968), p. 757.

7 Tang Xiyong, "Shindai zenki chūgoku ni okeru Chōsenkoku no kainansen to hyōryūmin kyūjo ni tuite (*The salvage of shipwrecks and the rescue of castaways from Korea during early Qing China*)," *Nantou Shigaku*, no.59 (2002), pp. 18-43. See also his "Shindai Chūgoku ni okeru Betonamu kainansen no kyūjo hōhō ni tuite (*The practices of salvaging Vietnamese shipwrecks during Qing China*)," *Nantou Shigaku*, no.60 (2002), pp. 38-56.

ties, obituary gifts, salvage, members of the mission, foreign students, accommodations, and interpreters.[8] Records in these volumes thus include many details concerning the tributary relations between China and its neighbors. When we examine the records in volume 400 of the *Jiaqing Da Qing huidian shili*, the practices that the Qing court adopted in rescuing people from sea disasters in East Asia become obvious.

These records show that starting from the early Qing dynasty, the court adopted a basic policy of extending help to all ships, Chinese or foreign, that had suffered disaster at sea. In 1737, Emperor Qianlong issued an ordinance to reiterate this policy, which remained in force until the end of the Qing. When it came to maritime rescue, the court would use public funds to purchase clothes and food for the crew and the passengers from a damaged vessel, to repair the vessel, and to send them, as well as their cargo, home. This practice was applicable to the Japanese as well, even though Japan did not pay tribute to China. As a result, not only the Japanese washed up on Chinese shores received help; some, when washed ashore in Cebu of the Philippines, were also saved by nearby Chinese ships. They were brought back to Fujian, and consequently sent back to Japan from Ningbo in 1767. As a token of gratitude, the Governor of Nagasaki presented 70 bags of rice to the Chinese shipper, 30 bags to the ship owner, 30 bags to the sub shipper, and 30 bags to the interpreter. And there are many such cases.[9]

2.2 The case of the Korean Kingdom

Records in volume 70 of the *Dongmun hwigo* (同文彙考 *Documents on foreign relations*) reveal how Korea, as a tribute-paying country to Qing China, treated Chinese ships when they were washed up on Korean shores. These records show that when a Chinese ship drifted into Korean waters, the ship, if undamaged, was allowed to return home when there was tailwind. If the ship was badly damaged, its crew would be sent to the capital Seoul. If the crew members were from northeast China, they would be sent to Fengcheng. But they would be taken to Beijing if they were from areas south of the Great Wall. In either case, the Korean court would submit a report to the Ministry of Rites in

---

8 *Qinding Da Qing huidian (Jiaqing chao)* (*Statutory precedents of the Qing dynasty approved by His Majesty (The Jiaqing reign period)* (*Jindai Zhongguo ziliao congkan sanbian* edition. Taibei: Wenhai Chubanshe, 1992), vol. 64, p. 8135, pp. 8137-8138, p. 8139, p. 8143.

9 Soda Hiroshi, "Kinsei hyōryūmin to Chūgoku (The castaways and China in recent times)," *Fukuoka Kyōiku Daigaku shakaika kiyō*, 31:2 (1982), pp. 1-20.

Beijing.[10] When Japanese ships drifted to Torai 東萊 on the Korean coast, their crew members were provided with water and firewood. For Japanese ships that were washed ashore in other places in Korea, they were also given grains, food and drinks.[11]

Document no. 835 preserved in the Korean archives, Academia Sinica (Taiwan), records that in late Qing Yu Xing 于興, the helmsman of a ship owned by Yao Fuqing 姚福慶 from Xiaochangdao 小長島, Jinzhou prefecture in southern Liaodong peninsula, reported that the captain and his crew, altogether seven people, had loaded the ship with lumber from Fengtian and sailed toward the Wuli Island of the Wendeng county 文登縣 on the Shandong peninsula. On their way back, however, they encountered a storm and drifted toward Korea, where they were rescued and returned home.[12] These cases indicate that it was a basic policy of both China and Korea to make efforts to save lives no matter if it was a Chinese or a Japanese ship that had suffered a disaster on the seas.

2.3 The case of the Ryūkyū Kingdom

According to the *Chūzan Seikan* (中山世鑑 *Official history of the Ryūkyū Kingdom*), in the early Qing there were cases of Chinese and Koreans who were repatriated by the Ryūkyū Kingdom, which was a tribute-paying country to China.[13] Chinese who had drifted onto the shores of the Ryūkyū Islands were sent home by Ryūkyū tribute-paying ships to China. Koreans, whose country was similarly a tribute-paying country to China and who had drifted ashore to Ryūkyū, were not sent home directly from Ryūkyū. Instead, they would board Ryūkyū tribute-paying ships to Fuzhou first. From there they would return home via Beijing.

Wei Yuanlang 魏元烺, Governor of Fujian, presented the court with a memorial on the twenty-seventh day of the fourth month, 1837. In this memorial he reported that a Ryūkyū ambassador had sent back some Chinese from Guangdong who had suffered shipwreck in the Ryūkyū Islands. They were Chen Facai 陳發材, the helmsman of the ship, and forty-eight crew members. They sailed to

---

10 *Dongmun hwigo* (Seoul: Daikan Minkoku Bunkyōbu Kokushi Hensan Iinkai, 1978), vol. 2, p. 1329.

11 *Zōsei kōrin shi* (*Enlarged and revised records on foreign relations*) (Soul: Ajia Bunka Sha, 1974), p.199.

12 *Qingji Zhong Ri Han guanxi shiliao* (*Historical materials concerning China, Jana, and Korea during the late Qing dynasty*) (Taipe: Zhongyang Yanjiuyuan Jindaishi Yanjiusuo, 1972), vol. 3, pp. 1350-1353.

13 *Ryūkyū shiryō sōsho (4)* (*Historical materials on Ryūkyū Series*) (First published in 1940. Reprint, Hōbun shokan, 1990), p. 127, p. 133, p. 141, p. 143.

Tianjin on a ship loaded with sugar. On their way back, they and ten merchants traveled to Shandong province to purchase soybeans. However, their ship was blown off course when sailing homeward. And they ended in the Ryūkyūs. Later, a Ryūkyū ship took them back to Fuzhou.[14] The memorial of Wei Yuanlang also reported how the Qing court treated the Ryūkyū ambassador in question. During their stay in China, the ambassador and his entourage received money to purchase food. On the day of their departure, they again received fees sufficient to purchase food for consumption during the following month. Moreover, officials on the mission also received silk fabrics as well as reimbursement for repairing the damaged Chinese ship. Wei Yuanlang permitted members of the mission to sell the goods they brought to China at the Ryūkyū Guesthouse in Fuzhou. But he also instructed them to leave Fuzhou for home as soon as they had completed their trading. On the other hand, the Chinese who had been rescued in Ryūkyū received travel documents. They were then escorted home via the land route, and were allowed to resume their former occupations.

Although many Ryūkyū ships drifted to China, some were in fact owned by private merchants who came to trade under the pretext that their ships had drifted to China, since trade with Qing China was economically very important to the Ryūkyū Kingdom.

2.4 The case of Tokugawa Japan

Japan was not a tributary country to Qing China. The Tokugawa Shogunate promulgated statutes to govern the rescue of foreign ships that suffered sea disasters. Vol. 35 of the *Ofuregaki Kampo shūsei* (*Collection of laws and ordinances issued during the Kampo period*) contains a record from the seventh month of 1641. It reads:

> When foreign ships approach the [Japanese] shores, [officials of] various domains should, as the statutes promulgated previously specified, survey the ships and the people on board, and not allow any of them to land. They should instead be sent to Nagasaki.[15]

In fact, as early as 1639, the Shogunate had already made it an ironclad rule that when foreign ships were washed onto Japanese shores, local authorities

---

14 *Gongzhongdang Daoguang chao zouzhe* (*Memorials of the Daoguang reign period preserved at the Imperial Archives)*, no.2 (3) (Taibei: Palace Museum, unpublished documents), pp.749-750.

15 *Ofuregaki Kampo shūsei* (Tokyo: Iwanami Shoten, 1934; reprint 1989), vol. 35, p. 969.

should first investigate the number of people on the ships, but should not allow anyone to land. These people had to stay aboard when receiving assistance. Then they would be sent to Nagasaki. A few years later in 1671, a similar regulation was issued in the seventh month that required local authorities to send people on Chinese ships to Nagasaki.[16]

In the fifth month of 1680, a ship carrying eighteen Padan 波丹 people arrived at Miyazaki. They were sent to Nagasaki in the sixth month, but twelve of them consequently died. The six survivors received an instruction from the Shogunate: they should leave Japan on board a Dutch ship to Batavia in the ninth month. From there they would return home.[17]

In general, when foreigners were shipwrecked and drifted ashore in Japan, after necessary investigations they were sent home on either Chinese or Dutch ships.

3 Evolution of maritime disaster relief and salvage practices in modern East Asia

In modern times, countries have concluded diplomatic treaties; they have also signed treaties to handle sea disasters. I shall examine some cases of salvage and rescue preserved in the documents of the Meiji government. In the *Dajō ruiten* (太政類典 *Classified Statutory precedents of the State Council*), a record dated the tenth month of 1876 reports that the British government presented gifts to officials of Shizuoka prefecture in appreciation of their efforts to rescue a British ship that was wrecked on the 25th of the tenth month, 1876. On the other hand, in the *Dajō ruiten*, there is also a case of persons from Okinawa who were rescued by an English ship in 1877.

In 1871, the Meiji government adopted the policy of abolishing the feudal domain system and establishing prefectures (*haihan chiken*). As a result, the Ryūkyū Kingdom was put under the jurisdiction of Kagoshima prefecture. The following year, the government transformed the Ryūkyū kingdom into a clan and assumed control of its diplomacy. In 1879, the government abolished the Ryūkyū clan by force, and set up Okinawa prefecture. The case of the rescue in 1877, discussed above, occurred when Ryūkyū was treated as a clan. An English

---

16 *Ofuregaki Kampo shūsei*, vol. 42, p. 1142.
17 *Nagasaki jitsuroku taisei* (*A compilation of veritable records on Nagasaki*) (Nagasaki: Nagasaki Bunkensha, 1973), pp. 289-290.

ship was heading toward Hong Kong from Yokohama when it rescued some Japanese from Okinawa. They were brought to Hong Kong, and handed over to the Japanese consulate. To express its gratitude, the Japanese government presented the captain with thirty *yen* and a considerable amount of goods.

According to the *Dajō ruiten*, the Meiji government issued document no. 282 on the 3rd day of the eighth month, 1873 to handle Korean vessels which had drifted to Japan. This document was in fact an amended bill. Previously in 1868, the government had already issued a relevant document, which was then revised in 1873. These documents specified that Koreans who had drifted to Japan should be taken to either the Nagasaki prefectural office, or its branch office in Tsushima, according to their place of landing. They should then be sent home.

According to document no. 283, since many of the Korean ships were damaged beyond repair and were not seaworthy, the Japanese government adopted the following method of repatriating people on these ships. They did not have to pay a fee for repatriation. The fee was to be paid by the prefectural office with jurisdiction over the place of their landing.

Subsequently, Japan and Korea concluded a treaty regarding the relief and the repatriation of the castaways. The related documents have been preserved in the diplomatic archives, the Ministry of Foreign Affairs. One of these documents was dated the 24th day of the eighth month, 1876, part of which reads:

> When people of one country unfortunately drift ashore in another country, the local authorities and people should at once render them help and provide them with clothes, food and other necessary goods. They should not be confined or imprisoned.[18]

This document shows that although the treaty of 1876 between Japan and Korea was the first unequal treaty that Japan imposed on its neighbors, this treaty nevertheless contains certain regulations that guaranteed the rescue and repatriation of the castaways of both countries. Furthermore, the document states that both the Japanese and the Korean governments would provide the castaways with clothes and money to purchase food. Each of them would receive 10 *sen* while staying in Japan, or 50 *mon* while in Korea.

In the seventh month of 1871, Japan and Qing China signed a treaty. The twenty-ninth section of the chapter on commerce stipulated: "If merchant ships of one country have suffered sea disasters and drifted to another country's

---

18 *Nisshin ryōkokukan sōnanmin kyūjo hiyō shōkan yakuyō ikken (2-6-1-9)* (*An agreement on payment for the fees incurred in rescuing the castaways from Japan and China*) (preserved at the diplomatic archives, Ministry of Foreign Affairs).

shores, local officials should received them and send them to officials at a port open to foreigners."[19] As one section of the chapter on commerce, this regulation applied mainly to merchant ships. But it also guaranteed that in case of a sea disaster, all the castaways would be rescued and returned home.

Later on, treaties between Japan and Qing China contained even more detailed regulations concerning the rescue of wrecked ships. In 1901, for example, the two countries signed an "Agreement on repayment for the cost of rescuing wrecked ships," which contains the following articles.

Article One
When either country is involved in the rescue of castaways along its coasts and incurs expenditure on clothes, food, travel, medicine, retrieval or burial of corps for them, the government of the castaways shall repay [its counterpart] all the fees.
Article Two
When either country is involved in the rescue of castaways and incurs expenditure on travel by officials, escort, telegraphic communication, or dispatch of official correspondence, the government of the castaways shall repay [its counterpart] all the fees.
Article Three
When the rescue and storage of cargoes from a wrecked ship incurs fees, the person who receives the cargoes shall repay the fees.[20]

4 Conclusion

As discussed above, salvage and rescue had conducted along the Chinese coasts and on the East Asian seas from early times; but the center of such activities had been China. More specifically, the salvage system of Qing China started from the Kangxi period; it evolved during the Yongzheng period, and was fully established during the Qianlong period. The system functioned according to imperial ordinances.

The Qing government based its salvage policy on humanitarian and other policy considerations. The aim was to establish authority over coastal waters and to project a positive image for the Qing Empire. For this purpose, salvage and rescue during the Qing was extended not only to ships from countries that

---

19 Ibid.
20 Ibid.

had tributary relations with China, such as Korea and Ryūkyū, but also to those from Japan and various Western countries. In the case of Korea and Ryūkyū, repatriation of their castaways was conducted through tributary channels. For example, when Korean envoys dispatched to China returned home, they would bring back Korean castaways. Similarly, tribute-paying ships from Ryūkyū arrived in Fuzhou every year. They would also sail home with Ryūkyū castaways on board. As for the Chinese who had drifted to the Korean peninsula, they would return home by themselves if their vessels were seaworthy. If their ships had been damaged, they would come home with a Korean tribute-paying mission to Beijing.

In the case of Japan, which was not a tributary country to China, all the Japanese castaways in China would travel home on ships trading with Japan. Chinese castaways in Japan, on the other hand, if their ships were in good shape, would sail to Nagasaki first, accompanied by Japanese ships. There they were questioned again by local officials and then allowed to return home by themselves. If their ships had been damaged, they would return home with ships coming to Nagasaki to trade.

Although the method of repatriation used by East Asian countries varied from one to another, Japan, Korea, and Ryūkyū employed a method that was basically the same as that of China: people who had suffered a sea disaster were rescued and sent home. Records concerning the salvage and rescue activities have been preserved in official documents of these countries. In most cases, a country extended help to castaways and repatriated them out of considerations for its own prestige in the international community. Lifesaving and repatriation thus coexisted with the prestige of a country.

From the mid-nineteenth century, international treaties came to be used around the world. Along with this development, diplomatic treaties also stipulated how rescue and repatriation of people who had met with disaster at sea should be conducted. However, it now became a controversial issue: which country should shoulder the expenditures incurred when saving the castaways and sending them home. As a result, diplomatic treaties often contained specific articles to handle this issue.

(Translated by Wang Zhenping, Nanyang Technological University, Singapore)

Supplement I   Cases of maritime disaster in modern East Asia

From the cases of the sea disaster recorded during the Ming dynasty, we know that Korean ships sometimes drifted ashore on China's coasts.[21] And in Korean and Ryūkyūan records dating from the Quing dynasty, there are many entries concerning Chinese ships that had been wrecked or washed ashore on the coasts of these two countries.[22] I have examined these records. The results are shown in the following table. The records concerning sailboats washed ashore in the Ryūkyū are based on the *Rekidai hōan* (歴代宝案 *Treasure archives of the successive dynasties*), and those to Korea, on the *Dongmun hwigo*. Of the records in these two works, I have selected only those that specified the cargos on the Chinese sailboats.

Table 8   Cases of Qing sailboats drifting to Ryūkyū, Korea and their cargos

A.D.	Chinese calendar Year /Month	Place of departure	Port of call	cargo	Source
1705	Kangxi 44/05	Minanzhen, Fuzhou	Haizhou	Cedar	Rekidai hōan
1705	Kangxi 44/11	Qingzhou, Shandong	Fujian	soybeans, red Chinese dates, seaweed, melon seeds, walnuts	Rekidai hōan
1723	Yongzheng 01/06	Jinzhou	Fujian	Melon seeds	Dongmun hwigo
1723	Yongzheng 01/06	Jinjiang	Jinzhou	Bowls, cloth, pepper, sapanwood	Dongmun hwigo
1727	Yongzheng 05/11	Shandong	Fujian	dried persimmon cakes, walnuts, seaweeds, wheat flour, green beans	Rekidai hōan
1732	Yongzheng 10/06	Liuhe	Shandong	Groceries	Rekidai hōan
1739	Qianlong 04/10	Tianjin	Suzhou	red Chinese dates, black Chinese dates	Dongmun hwigo

21   Matsuura Akira, "Mindai ni okeru Chōsensen no Chūgoku hyōchaku ni tuite (*The encounters of Korean ships in Ming China*)," *Kansai Daigaku Bungaku Ronshū*, 51:3 (2002), pp.25-45.

22   Matsuura Akira, "18~19 seki ni okeru nansei shotō hyōchaku Chūgoku hansen yorimita Shindai kōungyo no ichisokumen (A view of the shipping business during the Qing dynasty as seen from the Chinese junks drifted to the Southwestern Islands from the eighteenth to the nineteenth centuries)," *Kansai Daigaku Tōzai Gakujyutsu kenkyūsho Kiyō*, no. 16 (1983), pp. 17-75. See also my "Richō hyōchaku Chūgoku hansen no 'monjō bettan' nituite (On the *monjō bettan* concerning Chinese ships cast ashore to Korea during the Yi dynasty)," *Kansai Daigaku Tōzai Gakujyutsu kenkyūsho Kiyō*, no.17 (1984), pp. 25-83; no. 18 (1985), pp. 33-96.

Part 1: The Activities of Chinese Junks on the East Asian Sea in Early Modern Ages

1740	Qianlong 05/06	Zhangshou	Jinzhou	yellow tea, wide cotton cloth	*Dongmun hwigo*
1740	Qianlong 05/06	Xiamen	Ningbo	Sugar	*Rekidai hōan*
1741	Qianlong 05	Jinzhou	Ningbo	Melon seeds	*Dongmun hwigo*
1746	Qianlong 11/04	Gaiping	Longxi	Beans	*Dongmun hwigo*
1746	Qianlong 11	Fujian	Tianjin	Sugar	*Dongmun hwigo*
1746	Qianlong 11	Laizhou	Putian, Fujian	Beans, bean cakes, rice	*Dongmun hwigo*
1746	Qianlong 11	Laizhou, Shandong	Fujian	soybean oil, noodles made from bean starch, bean cakes, seaweeds	*Dongmun hwigo*
1749	Qianlong 14/05	Xiamen	Shanghai	Sugar	*Rekidai hōan*
1749	Qianlong 14/07	Shanghai	Jinzhou	Tea	*Rekidai hōan*
1749	Qianlong 14/10	Jinzhou	Jiangnan	Melon seeds, soybeans	*Rekidai hōan*
1749	Qianlong 14 /11	Jinzhou	Fujian	soybeans, melon seeds	*Rekidai hōan*
1749	Qianlong 14/11	Jiaozhou	Zhapu	Green soybeans, white beans, green beans, walnuts, dried persimmon cakes	*Rekidai hōan*
1749	Qianlong 14 /11	Jiaozhou	Zhenyang, Jiangnan	Beans, seaweed, soybean oil	*Rekidai hōan*
1749	Qianlong 14/11	Shandong	Fujian	Green beans, walnuts	*Rekidai hōan*
1749	Qianlong 14/11	Shandong	Fujian	Green beans, wheat flour, seaweeds, Chinese medicine	*Rekidai hōan*
1749	Qianlong 14	Dazhuang-hekou	Dengzhou	Soybeans	*Rekidai hōan*
1749	Qianlong 14	Jinzhou	Jiangnan	soybeans, melon seeds	*Rekidai hōan*
1749	Qianlong 14	Jinzhou	Jiaozhou	Beans, melon seeds	*Rekidai hōan*
1749	Qianlong 14	Jiangnan	Tianjin	Ginger	*Rekidai hōan*
1749	Qianlong 14	Jiangnan	Jinzhou	black carp	*Rekidai hōan*
1749	Qianlong 14	Xiamen	Shandong	sapanwood, bowls, sugar	*Rekidai hōan*
1749	Qianlong 14	Jinzhou	Jiangnan	Beans	*Rekidai hōan*

Maritime Rescue & Salvage in Early Modern East Asia and Its Modern Transfiguration

1749	Qianlong 14	Shandong	Jiangnan	Beans, salted pork, seaweeds	Rekidai hōan
1749	Qianlong 14	Jiaozhou	Suzhou	Beans, salted pork, seaweeds	Rekidai hōan
1749	Qianlong 14	Jiaozhou	Jiangnan	beans, pork, soybean oil, seaweeds	Rekidai hōan
1749	Qianlong 14	Shandong	Jiangnan	White beans, pigs	Rekidai hōan
1749	Qianlong 14	Jiaozhou	Xiamen	green beans, wheat flour, seaweeds	Rekidai hōan
1760	Qianlong 25/05	Guangdong	Tianjin	Cargoes	Rekidai hōan
1760	Qianlong 25/05	Quanzhou	Tianjin	Sundries	Rekidai hōan
1760	Qianlong 25/10	Tianjin	Guangdong	red Chinese dates	Rekidai hōan
1760	Qianlong 25/11	Daishan, Shandong	Ningbo	red Chinese dates	Rekidai hōan
1765	Qianlong 30/05	Zhangshou	Jiangnan	Cargoes	Rekidai hōan
1765	Qianlong 30/05	Jiangnan	Jinzhou	Tea	Rekidai hōan
1766	Qianlong 31/10	Jinzhou	Zhangshou	Beans	Rekidai hōan
1768	Qianlong 33/10	Guangdong	Fujian	melon seeds, beans, soybean cakes, cocoons	Dongmun hwigo
1769	Qianlong 34/10	Zhenyang	Jiaozhou	delicacies from South China	Rekidai hōan
1769	Qianlong 34/12	Jiaozhou	Zhenyang	Salted pork	Rekidai hōan
1777	Qianlong 42/06	Jinzhou	Xiamen	Soybeans, melon seeds, wheat flour, roots of Chinese thorowax, cotton, coins	Dongmun hwigo
1777	Qianlong 42/06	Xiamen	Jinzhou	Sugars	Dongmun hwigo
1777	Qianlong 42/09	Gaizhou	Soybeans	soybeans, cotton, Chinese medicine, fungus, cocoons of wild silkworm, dry clams, whitebait	Dobun iko
1777	Qianlong 42/10	Fuzhou (復州)	Fujian	yellow beans, green beans, green soybeans	Dongmun hwigo
1777	Qianlong 42/10	Soybeans	Jiangnan	a variety of sugar	Dongmun hwigo
1777	Qianlong 42/10	Jiangnan	Tianjin	Tea	Dongmun hwigo

Part 1: The Activities of Chinese Junks on the East Asian Sea in Early Modern Ages

1779	Qianlong 44/06	Fuzhou	Jinzhou	Paper products	*Rekidai hōan*
1779	Qianlong 44/10	Jinzhou	Fuzhou	Melon seeds	*Rekidai hōan*
1785	Qianlong 50/03	Jinzhou	Soybeans	soybeans, melon seeds, sesame	*Rekidai hōan*
1785	Qianlong 50/03	Soybeans	Shanghai	red sugar	*Rekidai hōan*
1785	Qianlong 50/06	Ninghai, Fengtian	Chenghai, Guangdong	Soybeans	*Rekidai hōan*
1785	Qianlong 50/06	Chenghai	Tianjin	betel-nuts	*Rekidai hōan*
1785	Qianlong 50	Jiangnan	Shandong	Paper products	*Rekidai hōan*
1785	Qianlong 50	Jinzhou	Xiamen	Beans	*Rekidai hōan*
1797	Jiaqing 02/07	Fuzhou	Tianjin	Cartons	*Dongmun hwigo*
1797	Jiaqing 02/11	Jinzhou (金州)	Soybeans	Soybeans	*Dongmun hwigo*
1801	Jiaqing 06/06	Tongan	Tianjin	Groceries	*Dongmun hwigo*
1801	Jiaqing 06/10	Tianjin	Tongan, Fujian	red Chinese dates, black Chinese dates, walnuts, pears	*Rekidai hōan*
1801	Jiaqing 06	Wusongkou	Qingkou, Shandong	Paper, lumber	*Rekidai hōan*
1801	Jiaqing 06/06	Guangdong	Tianjin	red sugar, white sugar	*Rekidai hōan*
1801	Jiaqing 06/10	Gaizhou	Quanzhou	Beans, cotton, cocoon, *yucai*, leather goods	*Dongmun hwigo*
1808	Jiaqing 13/10	Piziwo, Guandong	Jiangnan	Chinese sorghum	*Rekidai hōan*
1808	Jiaqing 13/10	Donglong	Tianjin	red sugar, white sugar	*Rekidai hōan*
1810	Jiaqing 15/05	Fuzhou	Gaizhou	Paper	*Dongmun hwigo*
1810	Jiaqing 15/10	Gaizhou	Tongan	Green beans, beans	*Dongmun hwigo*
1813	Jiaqing 18/05	Taiwan	Tianjin	black sugar, white sugar	*Dongmun hwigo*
1813	Jiaqing 18/05	Taiwan	Shanghai	red sugar	*Dongmun hwigo*
1813	Jiaqing 18/06	Soybeans	Tianjin	granulated sugar, pepper, sapanwood	*Dongmun hwigo*

1813	Jiaqing 18/10	Jinzhou	Tongan	soybeans, rice, Chinese medicine, melon seed, venison, cakes, dried cattle tendons	*Dobun iko*
1813	Jiaqing 18/10	Tianjin	Fujian	black Chinese dates, red Chinese dates, raisins, rice, white spirit, white dried fish	*Dongmun hwigo*
1813	Jiaqing 18/11	Tianjin	Fujian	red Chinese dates	*Dongmun hwigo*
1816	Jiaqing 21/09	Liaodong	Shanghai	soybeans, lamp oil from *perilla ocimoides*, soybean cakes	*Rekidai hōan*
1819	Jiaqing 24/09	Soybeans	Gaiping	Sugars	*Dongmun hwigo*
1821	Daoguang 01/04	Chenghai	Shanghai	yellow sugar, sapanwood	*Rekidai hōan*
1821	Daoguang 01/05	Shanghai	Chenghai	cotton, soybean cakes, cotton cloth	*Rekidai hōan*
1821	Daoguang 01	Taiwan	Tianjin	Rice	*Rekidai hōan*
1824	Daoguang 04/06	Taiwan	Tianjin	Grains and rice	*Rekidai hōan*
1824	Daoguang 04/09	Chenghai	Tianjin	Sugars	*Rekidai hōan*
1824	Daoguang 04/10	Tianjin, Shandong	Tongan, Fujian	black Chinese dates, bean cakes	*Rekidai hōan*
1824	Daoguang 04/10	Gaiping	Zhangzhou	soybeans, green beans, beans, noodles made from bean starch, dried cattle tendons, dried clams, spirit	*Dongmun hwigo*
1824	Daoguang 04/10	Tianjin, Ningyuan	Chenghai, Guangdong	Chinese sorghums, black Chinese dates, beans	*Rekidai hōan*
1824	Daoguang 04/10	Jinzhou (金州)	Tongan	Beans	*Rekidai hōan*
1830	Daoguang 10/08	Lingshui, Guangdong	Tianjin	yellow sugar, white sugar	*Rekidai hōan*
1830	Daoguang 10/09	Ningyuan, Fengtian	Chenghai	Soybeans	*Rekidai hōan*
1830	Daoguang 10/11	Fushan, Shandong	Chenghai	soybeans, wheat, soybean cakes	*Rekidai hōan*
1830	Daoguang 10/08	Chenghai	Tianjin	Sugars	*Rekidai hōan*
1830	Daoguang 10/09	Guandong	Quanzhou	soybeans, green beans, melon seeds, roots of *fangfeng*	*Dongmun hwigo*
1830	Daoguang 10/ leap 04	Taiwan	Tianjin	Sugars	*Dongmun hwigo*

1830	Daoguang 10/11	Shanghai	Chaozhou	Cotton, rice, beans	*Rekidai hōan*
1836	Daoguang 16/05	Raoping, Guangdong	Tianjin	Sugars	*Dongmun hwigo*
1836	Daoguang 16/09	Tianjin, Ningyuan	Zhangzhou	Beans, Chinese dates	*Dongmun hwigo*
1844	Daoguang 24/04	Taiwan		portable cooking stove	*Rekidai hōan*
1845	Daoguang 25/10	Zhejiang	Qingkou, Haizhou	peanuts, green cakes	*Rekidai hōan*
1854	Xianfeng 04/10	Jiangnan	Laiyang, Shandong	Cotton, cotton cloth	*Rekidai hōan*
1854	Xianfeng 04/11	Laiyang, Shandong	Jiangnan	rapeseed oil, peanut, noodles	*Rekidai hōan*
1861	Xianfeng 11/07	Yingkou	Shanghai	Green beans, bean cakes	*Rekidai hōan*
1861	Xianfeng11/07	Tianjin	Fujian	soybean cakes, white beans, wheat flour, fur hats, spirit, tobacco, black Chinese dates	*Rekidai hoan*
1861	Xianfeng 11/07	Jinjiang, Fujian	Tianjin	lumber, white sugar	*Rekidai hōan*
1861	Xianfeng 11/08	Shanghai	Shandong	yellow paper, carpet, paulownia oil	*Rekidai hōan*

Cases in this table show that Qing sailing ships were active along the entire Chinese coastal area, from Guangdong in the south to Liaoning in the north. Conversely, it can be argued that transportation along the Chinese coasts was the underlying factor that contributed to sea disasters.

Supplement II   A selected bibliography for further reading
Works on Chinese ships cast ashore to Japan
Oba Osamu ed., "Materials concerning Chinese ships cast ashore to Hachijo-jima Island in 1753." 大庭脩編著『宝暦三年八丈島漂着南京船資料』関西大学出版部、1985年3月、476頁。

Tanaka Kenji & Matsuura Akira eds., "Materials concerning Chinese ships cast ashore to Enshū (Shizuoka) in 1826." 田中謙二・松浦章編著『文政九年遠州漂着得泰船資料』関西大学出版部、1986年3月、650頁。

Matsuura Akira ed., "Materials concerning Chinese ships cast ashore to Kōchi prefecture in 1789." 松浦章編著『寛政元年土佐漂着安利船資料』関西大学出版部、1989年3月、416頁。

Matsuura Akira ed., "Materials concerning Chinese ships cast ashore to Kōchi prefecture in 1808." 松浦章編著『文化五年土佐漂着江南商船郁長發資料』

関西大学出版部、1989年3月、134頁。
Oba Osamu ed., "Materials concerning Chinese ships cast ashore to Chikura (Awa) in 1780." 大庭脩編著『安永九年安房千倉漂着南京船元順號資料』関西大学出版部、1990年3月、248頁。
Yabuta Yutaka ed., "Materials concerning Chinese ships cast ashore to Enshū (Shizuoka) in 1800." 藪田貫編著『寛政十二年遠州漂着唐船萬勝號資料』関西大学出版部、1997年3月、278頁。
Matsuura Akira, "Materials concerning Chinese ships cast ashore to Wakayama prefecture in 1871." 松浦章「文政四年「清人漂着譚」―紀州漂着中国商船―」『関西大学東西学術研究所紀要』第38輯、2005年4月、11〜29頁
Matsuura Akira, "On the Qing merchant ships cast ashore to Kishū prefecture." 松浦章「清代沿海商船の紀州漂着について」『関西大学東西学術研究所紀要』第20輯、1987年1月、39〜62頁。
Matsuura Akira, "Materials concerning to The Chinese Ship casted away on the coast of Koichi Prefecture in 1827 (Bunsei 10)." 松浦章「文政十年土佐漂着江南商船蔣元利資料」関西大学出版部、2006年11月、231頁。
Matsuura Akira, "Materials Concerning to The Chinese Ship casted away on the cast of Japan in 1855, 1856 (Ansei 2, 3)" 松浦章「安政二・三年漂流小唐船資料」関西大学出版部、2008年3月、560頁。
Matsuura Akira, "Materials concerning to The Chinese Ship casted away on the coast of Shizuoka Prefecture in 1815 (Bunka 12)" 松浦章「文化十二年豆州漂着南京永茂船資料」関西大学出版部、2011年2月、385頁。

Works on Chinese ships cast ashore to Korea
Matsuura Akira, "A record concerning Chinese ships cast ashore to Korea during the Yi dynasty." 松浦章「李朝時代における漂着中国船の一資料―顕宗八年（1667）の明船漂着と「漂人問答を中心に―」『関西大学東西学術研究所紀要』第15輯、1982年1月、53〜101頁。
Symposium, "Castaways and the state in recent times" シンポジウム「近世東アジアの漂流民と国家」『史学雑誌』第108編第9号、1999年9月, 120〜123頁。
The following are the articles included in this issue:
春名徹「歴史学における〈漂流〉の現在」、
荒野泰典「近世東アジア漂流民送還体制の総括的特質」、
松浦章「環黄海・東海沿海漂着中国帆船について」、
池内敏「近世日朝間の漂流・漂着事件」、
小林茂「朝鮮―琉球間の漂流民の送還と自力回航」、
真栄平房昭「漂着記録に探る海外情報―土佐藩領に漂着した琉球船を中心に」、
生田美智子「漂流民と異文化コミュニケーション（ロシアへの漂流民の場合）」。

Part 1: The Activities of Chinese Junks on the East Asian Sea in Early Modern Ages

Works on Korean ships cast ashore to Japan
Ikeuchi Hitoshi, *Japan and Korean castaways in recent times*. 池内敏『近世日本と朝鮮漂流民』臨川書店、1998年6月、294頁、附録173頁。

Works on Ryūkyū ships cast ashore to China
Dana Masayuki, "Drifting and drifting ashore of the Ryūkyū ships." 田名真之「琉球船の漂流・漂着―乾隆期の事例を中心に―」『第八回琉中歴史関係国際学術会議論文集』琉球中国関係国際会議、2001年3月、119～139頁)
Akamine Mamoru, "Relief provided for Ryūkyū castaways in Fuzhou during the Qing dynasty." 赤嶺 守「清代福州における琉球漂着民の撫恤について―加賞を中心に―」『第七回琉球・中国交渉史に関するシンポジウム論文集』沖縄県教育委員会、2004年10月、65～78頁。

Works on handling sea disasters in East Asia.
Tang Xiyong, "The handling of foreign shipwreck in Taiwan and its impact during the Qing dynasty." 湯熙勇「清代台湾的外籍船難的處理方法及其影響」台湾・国科會研究計画成果報告（編號：NSC85-2411-001-012)、1995年9月。
Tang Xiyong, "Foreign shipwreck and its rescue in Taiwan during the Qing dynasty."湯熙勇「清代台湾的外籍難船與救助」、湯熙勇主編『中國海洋發展史論文集)』第七輯、台北・中央研究院中山人文社會科學研究所、1999年3月。
Tang Xiyong, "Practices of rescuing Korean shipwrecks and providing relief for Korean castaways during the Shunzhi and the Qianlong reign periods in China." 湯熙勇「清順治至乾隆時期中國救助朝鮮海難船及漂流民的方法」、朱德蘭主編『中國海洋發展史論文集』第八輯、2002年5月、105～172頁。

Historical materials related to sea disasters
Tang Xiyong, Liu Xufen, and Matsuura Akira eds., *A collection of materials concerning shipwrecks around the China Sea in recent times*. 湯熙勇・劉序楓・松浦章主編『近世環中国海の海難資料集成：以中国・日本・朝鮮・琉球為中心』中央研究院中山人文社會科學研究所、1999年8月。

Part 2:

Sino-Japanese Interaction based on Chinese Junks in the Edo period

CHAPTER 7

Sino-Japanese Interaction based on Chinese Junks in the Edo period

1 Introduction

Cultural interaction between Japan and China in the Edo period was characterized by the policy of national isolation adopted by the Tokugawa *Bakufu*, which prevented Japanese from sailing to China. For the most part, this was an era in which Sino-Japanese interaction was maintained through the arrival of vessels from China to Nagasaki, Japan. It is for this reason that Chinese sailing vessels, which were called *Tō-sen* by the people of Edo, were a major channel of cultural trade between China and Japan.

The term, *Tō-sen*, derives from the word that people in the Edo period generally used for China—Tang, after the Tang dynasty. Likewise, people who sailed to Japan were called *Tōjin* (people from Tang). Chinese were already aware by the end of the Ming dynasty that China was called Tang in Japan. In the 5th year of Tianqi (1625), Nan Juyi, the governor (*xuanfu*) of Fujian, reported to Emperor Tianqi on the *To-sen*. The 58th volume of the *Xizong Shilu* (Authentic Records of Xizong), states that on the first day of the 4th month of the 5th year of Tianqi:

> The governor of Fujian, Nan Juyi, wrote that peoples on land and sea use the ocean for rice fields; the powerful use it for trade, buying and selling in Japan and Europe; the officials use it to extract fees; the national military, moreover, uses it as a system for dividing the wealth. None of this is forbidden. How could we know that merchant junks would go to Japan and other countries?.... I've heard that people from Fujian, Suzhou, and Zhejiang live in the Japanese archipelago. I don't know how many hundreds of thousands of families are there. Or how many have married Japanese, and have sons and grandsons. They call the locale Tang City. These hundreds of thousands of clans, and the families of the married

couples, are aware of who is secretly taking part in this trade. Many people are involved. The junks that frequent the port are called Tang junks. All the big ones carry goods from China, which they sell directly to the Japanese, or through joint ventures with the Japanese. Nan Juyi (1625)

At the beginning of the Ming dynasty, the court adopted a policy of gradually restricting sea trade, but this policy was relaxed from the latter half of the 16th century, after which the number of merchant junks sailing clandestinely to Japan increased. Thus, from before the Tokugawa *Bakufu* was established, Sino-Japanese cultural trade had already been established through Chinese shipping.

The Tokugawa *Bakufu* prohibited Japanese plebeians from engaging in trade abroad in order to restrict policies toward foreign countries. Active promotion of relations with foreign countries was limited to the efforts of the Satsuma clan towards the Ryukyu Islands, and of the Sō clan of Tsushima towards the Korean court. Trade was the focus of these efforts, through the relationship via Nagasaki between Japan and Holland, and between Japan and China. Though China typically required tributary status of its neighbors, Japan was able to maintain a constant trade relationship with the Ming and the Qing courts on an equitable basis. Sino-Japanese cultural interaction continued to take the remarkable form of cultural exchange via Chinese merchant ships and junks arriving in Nagasaki throughout most of the Edo period.

In this paper I will be examining the role of the *Tō-sen* that frequented the port of Nagasaki in cultivating an environment for Sino-Japanese cultural interaction.

2 Review of Research on Sino-Japanese Cultural Interaction in the Edo Period

Research on Sino-Japanese cultural interaction in the Edo period dates back to eight issues of *Kinsei Shina no Nihon bunka ni oyoboshitaru seiryoku eikyō— kinsei shina o haikei to shitaru Nihon bunkashi* (The Powerful Influence Exerted by Pre-Modern China on Japanese Culture—the Cultural History of Japan against the Backdrop of Pre-Modern China) in Number 2, Volume 25 (February 1914) through Number 2, Volume 26 (February 1915) of *Shigaku Zasshi* (History Journal) by Nakamura (Nakayama) Kyūshirō. In his seminal work, Nakayama considered Sino-Japanese cultural relations from a variety of perspectives: Confucianism, history, literature, linguistics, art, religion, medicine, natural history, receptivity to new knowledge of Western learning and political law through Chinese texts, Japanese and Chinese products, food and drink, music, martial arts, customs, and games. Nakayama emphasized the necessity of using a variety of theories to research the influence on Japan of the Qing dynasty, which had collapsed just two years earlier. About the influence of the culture of Qing China, he concluded that "the influence of pre-modern China on Japan is exceedingly great, and hardly inferior to that extended by Tang dynasty documents."[1] Nakamura thus stressed the importance of the culture of the Ming and Qing dynasties for Edo Japan.

Nakamura's research was followed by work done by Yano Jinichi from the perspective of trade, specifically, with Nagasaki. In the early summer of 1923 (Taisho 12) Yano was asked to compile a Nagasaki city history, and in the following year he gave the lecture, "On Trade with Nagasaki as Seen in Chinese Annals."[2] In 1915 (Taisho 14), Yano published his first paper, "Nagasaki Trade As Seen in the Chinese Annals" in Numbers 1-3, Volume 9 of *Tōa Keizai Kenkyū* (Studies in Asian Economics). The opening paragraph of Yano's paper states:

> The role of Nagasaki in trade resembles that played by the only foreign port in China: Canton. When we compare the influence from overseas trade at Nagasaki with that of Canton, however, we can see that trade via Nagasaki cannot be put into the same category. The influence from abroad on Japan through the port of Nagasaki is far greater, indicating just how different in scale are the cultures of China and Japan. Nakamura (1938)[3]

He concludes:
> When we speak of foreign trade at Nagasaki we are really only talking about Dutch-Japanese and Sino-Japanese trade, but it was Sino-Japanese trade that was especially important. The size of trading vessels between Japan and Holland was large, and the cargo many, but the number of Dutch ships was far fewer, and such trading vessels visited the port of Nagasaki only once a year.
> The frequency cannot compare with Chinese junks, which arrived at the Japanese port three times a year—in the spring, summer, and autumn. Yano

---

1 *Shigaku Zasshi*, No. 2, Volume 26 (February 1915), p. 4.
2 Speech given at the symposium of the Society of Historical Research, June 14, 1914. Article column on bulletins, *Society of Historical Research*, vol. 9, number 4, October, 1924; pp. 149-150.
3 *Nagasaki-shi shi tsūkō bōeki-hen tōyō shokokubu* (The History of Marine Trade in Nagasaki City with Far Eastern Nations), Nagasaki City Office, April, 1938, p. 462.

(1938)[4]

As Yano points out, the amount of Chinese trade was two to three times that of the Dutch, a fact that underscores the influence of Chinese trade on Japan. Thereafter, Yano continued his research of pre-modern Chinese history in conjunction with Chinese trade with Nagasaki, and published the results of his research in November, 1938 (Showa 13) in *Nagasaki-shi shi, tsūkō bōeki hen toyō shokokubu, Nagasaki shi* (The History of Maritime Trade in Nagasaki City with Far Eastern Nations, Nagasaki City). In the foreword to his history of Nagasaki Yano states:

> Simply narrating the trajectory of trade development is insufficient to describe the history of Nagasaki trade. The passage of trade via the gateway of Nagasaki has exerted an immeasurable influence on the culture of our country through the influx of culture from China. This has greatly helped in the development of our own culture, while the impact of China's textiles and the import of silk thread has been tremendous. Import of textiles has contributed greatly to the development of our country's silk industry. The important issues of cultural and industrial history must be examined through the data on Nagasaki trade. Yano (1938)[5]

In his history, Yano proposes that areas he did not cover therein be researched in the future. Yet even now after nearly eighty years have passed, we still cannot say that the issues he raised have been sufficiently resolved.

Research in this field was subsequently published by Yamawaki Teijirō in his *Nagasaki no Tōjin bōeki* (Chinese Trade with Nagasaki) (Yoshikawa Hirofumikan, 1964). The field was further developed in new directions by Ōba Osamu in his *Edo jidai ni okeru tōsen mochiwatashisho no kenkyū* (Research on Chinese Trading Vessel Cargo Lists in the Edo Period) (Kansai University Institute of Oriental and Occidental Studies, 1967), and *Edo jidai ni okeru Chūgoku bunka juyō no kenkyū* (Research on Receptivity to Chinese Culture in the Edo Period) (Dōhōsha Pub., 1984). Research on Nagasaki trade from the Japanese perspective was subsequently published by Nakamura Tadashi in *Kinsei Nagasaki bōekishi no kenkyū* (Research on the History of Trade in Nagasaki) (Dōhōsha Pub., 1988), and by Ōta Katsunari in *Sakoku jidai Nagasaki bōekishi no kenkyū* (Research on Nagasaki Trade During the Period of National Isolation) (Shibunkaku Pub., 1992). Research that has provided details about the

---

4 Ibid., p.463.
5 Ibid., preface, p.5.

Chinese side of the trade include Matsuura Akira's *Shindai kaigai bōekishi no kenkyū* (Research on the History of Overseas Trade in the Qing Period) (Dōhōsha Pub., 2002). The task of researching the cultural aspects of Sino-Japanese trade, as proposed first by Nakayama Kyūshirō in his 1915 magnum opus, however, continues to be widely overlooked.

3 Sino-Japanese Commercial Interaction Via *Tō-sen* in the Edo Period

During the Kan'ei era of the Edo Period (1624-1643), when the Tokugawa *Bakufu* enacted *sakoku* (period of national isolation), Chinese junks that had heretofore visited several ports in Kyushu were now restricted to the port of Nagasaki.

From the first half of the seventeenth century to the first half of the eighteenth century at the end of the Ming through the beginning of the Qing periods, Chinese junks that frequented Nagasaki sailed from nearly the entire length of the Chinese coast to Southeast Asia. In addition, trade was also carried out by Koxinga (Zheng Chenggong, 1624-1662), who used Taiwan as a base to support the collapsing Ming government, and by the countervailing Qing court forces.

In the 22nd year of Kangxi (1683), Koxinga's grandson, Zheng Keshuang, still based in Taiwan, surrendered to the Qing government. The Qing court issued the *zhanhailing* (edict for development of the seas) the following year, which lifted the ban against maritime shipping. Consequently, there was a sudden increase in the number of trading junks visiting the port of Nagasaki from the coastal regions of China, and in particular from the Yangtze River Delta and the Jiangnan region. Examples of trading ships from that era are the Ningbo junks numbered 84 and 85 that arrived in Nagasaki in October, 1685 (Jōkyō 2).

> In the case of our junks, there is a shortage of transport goods from Zhangzhou in our country so we are petitioning for goods to be sent. This spring they will be coming from Zhangzhou to the area of Zhejiang, and to Ningbo Prefecture. For some time, we have been asking for goods for shipping abroad, and are petitioning again for some now. *Kai hentai* (1981)[6]

---

6   *Kai hentai* (Chinese Metamorphosis), Vol. 1, Tōyō Bunko, Nonprofit Corporation, March, 1958; Reprinted by Tōhō Shoten, Nov. 1981, p.536.

These two Ningbo junks originally were based in Zhangzhou, Fujian. It is quite possible that because there weren't enough sailors or cargo to go to Japan, the merchants trading in Zhangzhou went north of Amoy to Ningbo and then procured goods for Japan before sailing to Nagasaki.

From the above it is clear that when the ban was lifted on shipping, there were many merchants desirous of trading with Japan, but there was a shortage of commodities to trade.

Chinese junks arrived in Nagasaki every year. The ships arriving to conduct trade were numbered chronologically according to the twelve branches of the Chinese sexagenary cycle (*jia yi, jia er*, etc.).

The number of Chinese junks that visited Nagasaki in 1687 (Genroku 1) climbed to 194. The following chart presents the data, organized by month.[7]

Table 9   No. of Crew and Arrival of 194 Chinese Junks in Nagasaki by Month;1687

Month	March	April	May	**June**	July	August	Sept.	Oct.	Total
Junks(#)	6	7	20	**98**	41	15	4	3	194
%	3.1	3.6	10.3	**50.5**	21.2	7.7	2.1	1.5	100%
Crew	246	291	946	**4,432**	2,037	894	225	220	9,291
%	2.6	3.2	10.2	**47.7**	21.9	9.6	2.4	2.4	100%

In response to the rapid rise in the number of junks arriving in Japan in 1687, the government began restricting the number of trading vessels allowed to visit ports, so that only 70 junks came to Nagasaki in 1688 (Genroku 2), and 80 junks came in 1698 (Genroku 11). From 1709 (Hōei 6) the number of trading vessels visiting ports was restricted to 59.

The main products transported by Chinese junks from Japan to China were Japanese copper and marine delicacies. From the beginning of the Edo period, the Qing court began actively seeking the purchase of Japanese copper. As China's monetary economy developed, there was a shortage of silver and copper coins in circulation. The Chinese relied on Japan as an important source of copper for minting copper coins used as currency throughout the Kangxi era (1661-1772), a need that resulted in the arrival of many Chinese merchants in Nagasaki. Japan became a major source of supply of these metals.

Copper was also produced in the Yunnan region of China, but in 1716 (Kangxi 55), the amount of copper supplied to the Qing court from Yunnan was only 1,663,000 catties in comparison with approximately 2,772,000 catties from

---

7   Matsuura Akira, *Edo jidai tōsen ni yoru nitchū bunka kōryū* (Sino-Japanese Cultural Interaction via Chinese Junk in the Edo Period), Shibunkaku Press, July 2007, p.248.

Japan. In other words, Japanese copper contributed a significant 62.5% of the total amount of copper used to supply the Qing dynasty's monetary economy.[8]

Japanese copper production decreased after the 18th century, however, and the amount of copper supplied to China correspondingly also fell. China next sought Japan's marine products, such as dried abalone (*baoyu* or *fuyu* in Chinese); sea cucumber; and shark's fin (*shayu* or *yuchi* in Chinese).[9] These items were used in Chinese cooking and gave a unique flavor to dishes. Dried abalone and shark's fin appeared as major ingredients in seafood dishes in China during the Qing period, when such dishes began to grow in popularity even among average people. Dried sea cucumber, literally, "ocean ginseng" (*haishen*) was also highly prized for its medicinal value, and rivaled the agriculturally-grown variety. Dried marine products thus developed into a major trade commodity between the two countries as Japan became an important source of supply,[10] perhaps indicating a significant impact of Japanese foodstuffs on the culinary traditions of China's masses.

In Japan as well, increased production of these three products—dried sea cucumber, dried abalone, and shark's fin—called collectively *tawaramono* or *hyōmotsu* (goods in straw bags), was actively promoted. At the beginning of the Guangxu years (1875-1908), He Ruzhang, who was appointed as plenipotentiary to Japan, wrote in his *Shidong zaji* (Miscellany of an Envoy in Japan): "Many Chinese merchants take raw cotton and white sugar, and return with various marine products such as *haishen* (sea cucumber) and *fuyu* (dried abalone)."[11] He Ruzhang's entry clearly underscores the importance of these products in China even after the Edo period.

In 1715 (Shōtoku 5), the Japanese government promulgated the *Shōtoku Shinrei* (New Edict of the Shōtoku Era), which restricted the outflow of gold, silver, and copper through Nagasaki trade. In comparison with the constraints on the number of junks allowed to trade at Nagasaki until this time, the *Shōtoku Shinrei* allowed for new issuing of trading licenses (*shinpai*) mainly to junks docking in Nagasaki.

After promulgation of the *Shōtoku Shinrei* edict on sea trade, possession of

---

8 Matsuura Akira, *Edo jidai tōsen ni yoru nitchū bunka kōryū* (Sino-Japanese Cultural Interaction via Chinese Junk in the Edo Period), p. 111.
9 See: Matsuura Akira, *Shindai kaigai bōekishi no kenkyū* (Research on the History of Foreign Trade in the Qing Period).
10 Matsuura Akira, *Shindai kaigai bōekishi no kenkyū* (Research on the History of Foreign Trade in the Qing Period, pp 382-402.
11 He Ruzhang, *Shidong zaji* (Miscellany of an Envoy in Japan), *Xiaofanghu zhai yudi congshao, dishizhi suoshou* (Geographical Essays from the Xiaofanghu Studio, Collection Bound in the Tenth Volume).

a *shinpai,* granted by the Japanese government to conduct trade in Nagasaki, became imperative for trade. If captains of Chinese ships did not have this license, they were not allowed to dock in Nagasaki the next time they sailed to Japan. Further, any Chinese captain or merchant caught violating this law would not be allowed a second chance to obtain the license and it would be impossible for that person ever to come to Japan again. This system ensured that junks coming to Nagasaki without a license would thereafter not be allowed to engage in trade. The licenses thus constituted a limitation on trade as well as a system for designating merchants.

Subsequently, the policy was gradually tightened. In 1717 (Kyōhō 2) 40 junks were allowed to enter the port of Nagasaki; in 1765 (Meiwa 2), 13 junks were permitted to dock; and in 1791 (Kansei 3), only 10 junks were allowed, a situation that continued until the end of the Tokugawa period. The Muromachi *Bakufu's* control of shipping from China indicates that the relationship between the Muromachi government and the Ming court was strictly commercial, and although the two governments were allied politically, Japan did not have tributary status.[12]

After promulgation of the *Shōtoku Shinrei,* junks entering the port of Nagasaki were mainly restricted to those from the Jiangnan delta region of China, immediately south of the lower reaches of the Yangtze River, as I will discuss shortly. *Kairo sarani kazu narabi ni kokin Karakuniwatari minato no setsu* (Explanation of Shipping Routes and Numbers as well as Ports Old and New in Crossing to China) in Volume 10 of the *Nagasaki jitsuroku taisei* (Compilation of the Authentic Account of Nagasaki), states:

> In that era, there were two convenient ports: Shanghai and Zhapu. All of the junks would travel back and forth to, and congregate in, these two ports to conduct trade. These two ports, however, restricted their trade to textiles, various medicines, low-quality goods, and a variety of containers and tools produced in several places. Several hundreds of traders would bring goods, whereupon merchants from Jiangnan, Zhejiang, and Fujian would check the silver purchasing price and ship the goods from these two ports. Even if there are junks sailing over from Ningbo, Zhoushan, Putuoshan, Fuzhou, Amoy, and Guangdong, most of the junks come from Shanghai and Zhapu.[13]

---

12 Matsuura Akira, *Edo jidai tōsen ni yoru nitchū bunka kōryū* (Sino-Japanese Cultural Interaction via Chinese Junk in the Edo Period), vol. 3; See: *Shinchō Chūgoku to Nihon* (Qing China and Japan).

13 *Nagasaki bunken sōsho daiisshū 1, daiinimaki, Nagasaki jitsuroku taisei seihen* (Nagasaki Documents Series, Series 1, vol. 2, Principal Compilation of the Authentic

From the above we can conclude that the most important ports for conducting trade via Chinese junks with Japan were Shanghai and Zhapu. The seventy-second volume of the *Shizong Shilu* (Authentic Account of the Emperor Yongzheng), written on the seventeenth day of the eighth month of 1728 (Yongzheng 6), states:

It is known that there is an area called Zhapu in Pinghu County. It is an eminent seaport for Jiangsu and Zhejiang. Trade from Zhapu reaches the countries across the sea. Moreover, it is only a little over 200 *li* (approximately 129,000 meters) from Hangzhou.

Zhapu was closely guarded as an area that required defending. The importance of Zhapu as a port for trade with foreign countries was noted as follows in 1730 (Yongzheng 8) by the provincial governor of Zhejiang, Liwei, in a report to the emperor dated the sixth day of the first month of 1730 (Yongzheng 8): "Zhapu is an important port for conducting marine trade with Japan in the East."[14] Acknowledged as an important seaport for trade with Japan, the village of Zhapu received attention as a base under jurisdiction of Pinghu County, Jiaxing Prefecture, Zhejiang Province.

Zhapu continued to maintain its position as a major trading port with Japan until well into the middle of the nineteenth century. The British said of Zhapu in the mid-nineteenth century:

Chapoo, on the Gulf of Hang-chow, owes all its commercial importance to the exclusive trade which it enjoys with Japan, monopolized by six imperial junks.[15]

Why did Zhapu receive such attention? One of the most important reasons was that Suzhou was in its hinterland. In the Qing period, Suzhou was an important hub for Chinese commerce. The reason trade was restricted mainly to the Jiangnan delta region, as mentioned above, was that it was a convenient location for collecting together fine silks and other handicrafts that were ideal for shipping, as well as for selling products imported from Japan.[16]

Account of Nagasaki), Nagasaki Bunkensha, December 12, 1973, p.241.
14 *Gongzhongdang Yongzhengchao zuozhe, diyiwu ji* (Report to the Yongzheng Court, Inner Palace Files, Compilation No. 15), *Gongli gugong bowuyuan* (National Palace Museum), January 1979, p. 424.
15 Thomas Allom & G, N. Wright, *China, in a Series of Views, Displaying the Scenery, Architecture, and Social Habits, of that Ancient Empire*, 1843, Vol. III, p. 49.
16 Matsuura Akira, *Shindai kaigai bōekishi no kenkyū* (Research on the History of

Part 2: Sino-Japanese Interaction based on Chinese Junks in the Edo period

The geographic location of Zhapu fostered a close relationship with the major commercial center of Suzhou. In addition, situated on the coast of the continent, Zhapu was a port of call for coastal trading ships from Fujian and Guangdong in China's southeastern region. Sugar, for example, which was produced along China's southeastern coastal region, was transported by coastal sailing ships to Zhapu, transferred to trading ships heading for Japan, and then taken to Nagasaki. Of the goods transported by Chinese junks to Nagasaki, sugar produced in southeastern China was important as an inexpensive cargo.

Changes in political policies in the Qing period and trading policies in Japan greatly influenced trends in Chinese trade in Nagasaki. Economic exchange was the focus of Sino-Japanese relations during the Edo period, a focus that was profoundly influenced politically by policies of the Qing court and the Tokugawa *Bakufu*.

4 Sino-Japanese Cultural and Scholarly Interaction

The nearly constant Chinese trade that occurred in Nagasaki throughout the Edo period provided a basis for the cultural interaction that occurred between Japan and China in the pre-modern era.

It is well known that Japan was the recipient of Chinese learning, but the role of captains of junks in this transmission of culture has not been widely explored. Beginning in the first half of the 18th century, Chinese merchants who engaged in trade with Japan were mainly organized into shippers (*caidong*), captains of ships visiting Nagasaki (*chuanshu*), boat owners (*chuanhu*), and crew (*huochang, zongguan, shuishou*, etc). The central figure in Nagasaki trade among Chinese merchants was the *chuanshu*, or captain (*sentō* in Japanese).[17]

The Chinese who sailed to Nagasaki stayed in the foreign settlement known as *Tōkan* or *Tōjin yashiki* (Chinese Residence). The residential area built for the Chinese was called *Tōjin yashiki* in Japanese and *Tangguan* in Chinese. During the early stages of Nagasaki trading, a portion of the district called Yadochō was designated for lodging for Chinese, but after a variety of problems arose with the arrangement, a separate "Chinese Residence" was built in 1689

Foreign Trade in the Qing Period), Hōyū Shoten, January 2002, pp 382-402.
17 Matsuura Akira, *Shindai kaigai bōekishi no kenkyū* (Research on the History of Foreign Trade in the Qing Period, pp. 73-90.

(Genroku 2), and Chinese coming by sea to Nagasaki were ordered to stay in the housing provided there. This was the case until 1868 (Keiō 4), when the residences began to be dismantled.

Many Chinese captains, who had been sailing to Nagasaki for a long time, included intellectuals with whom Japanese men of letters sought to interact. One such person, Wang Shengwu, was the first to introduce the entire *Gujin tushu jicheng* (Complete Collection of Illustrations and Writings Past and Present) to Japan. Nagasaki became a desired location for Japanese men of letters in the Edo period who sought out Chinese scholar merchants. Interaction between the geographer, Nagakubo Sekisui (1717-1801), from Mito, and shipping merchant, Ming Heqi, for example, is depicted in Nagakubo's *Shinsa shōwashū* (Collection of Qing Raft Prayers) (See illustration below). In addition to these cases, Shiba Kōkan (1747-1818), a famous Japanese painter and printmaker, met the Chinese merchant, Tian Mingqi.[18]

Some of the individuals who came from China to Nagasaki as traders also sought documents that had already been lost in China, the best example being Wang Peng (Wang Zhuli). Wang Peng came to Japan to look for the lost book, *Guwen xiaojing* (Classic Book of Filial Piety). After locating the book, he took it back with him to China and it was later reprinted by Bao Yanbo in his *Zhibuzu zhai congshu* (Collected Reprints from the Studio of Insufficient Knowledge). Even now it is possible to find the name of Wang Peng in the preface of the *Guwen xiaojing* (The Ancient Script Version of the *Classic of Filial Piety*).[19] Since Wang Peng used the alternate name of Wang Zhuli when he came to Nagasaki as a merchant, little attention was paid to his presence. If his name had been recorded in the trade annals under Wang Peng, he would not have been overlooked until recently. Considering that Wang Peng was restricted during his sojourn in Japan to the Chinese Residence in Nagasaki, in all probability he was compelled to retrieve the lost document by securing the cooperation of Japanese merchants. His contributions to the development of scholarship at the Qing court are all the more impressive considering the lengths to which he was driven to recover the *Guwen xiaojing*. A well-known case of a Chinese merchant scholar in the Meiji era was Yang Shoujing (1839-1915), the son of a wealthy Chinese merchant who became famous as a calligrapher, epigraphist, geographer, and bibliophile, and who came to Japan to take back documents pertaining to China. What has been less known is that Yang Shoujing was preceded by over

---

18 Matsuura Akira, *Edo jidai tōsen ni yoru nitchū bunka kōryū* (Sino-Japanese Cultural Interaction via Chinese Junk in the Edo Period), vol.3; See: *Chūgoku shōnin to Nihon* (Chinese Merchants and Japan).
19 Matsuura Akira, *Edo jidai tōsen ni yoru nitchū bunka kōryū* (Sino-Japanese Cultural Interaction via Chinese Junk in the Edo Period), pp. 202-216.

a century by a merchant scholar with the same intentions.

Other Chinese intellectuals who sailed to Japan included men with scientific knowledge. On a plaque in the Shrine of Mazu at Sōfukuji Temple in Nagasaki, for example, is engraved the name of a Yang Sixiong (Yang Xiting), who was known as having had the knowledge of a medical doctor.[20]

Sino-Japanese cultural interactions during the Edo period were not limited to cases of successfully-conducted trade. Unexpected relationships arose when storms at sea caused shipwrecks and the problem of castaways. Examples of castaways in China during the Edo period have already been enumerated by the Japanese scholar, Sōda Hiroshi.[21] Some of the records of castaways during the Edo period remain even now in possession of established families. There are also examples of classical Chinese poems sent from Chinese to Japanese castaways embellishing *fusuma* Japanese sliding paper doors of such family homes.[22]

Pre-modern Sino-Japanese relations were also influenced by world events. In particular, when the Tokugawa *Bakufu* abandoned the isolationist policy it had maintained since its inception, Japanese began actively going abroad. The *Bakufu* dispatched official ships to Shanghai with the intention of expanding trade. The first such ship, which left Nagasaki for Shanghai in April, 1862 (Bunkyū 2; Zhiyuan 1), was the *Senzai-maru*. Takasugi Shinsaku and Godai Tomoatsu were aboard the *Senzai-maru*; they brought back to Japan a new image of a prospering Shanghai and of Qing China. During the era they were traveling to Shanghai a newspaper written in literary Chinese and called the *Shanghai Xinbao* was being published in the city. The first issue of the newspaper was published in November, 1861 (Xianfeng 10) in Shanghai by the British merchant newspaper company, *Zilin Yanghang*. Most of the articles were translated from foreign newspapers, but there were also extremely useful stories carried in the paper concerning the Taiping Rebellion, the large-scale revolt that lasted from 1850 to 1864 and affected significant portions of southern China. The *Shanghai Xinbao* also carried information on the crew of the *Senzai-maru* and their stay in Shanghai from the beginning of June 1862 through the end of July. Another influential newspaper published in Shanghai at the time, the *North-China Herald*, said in its July 7 issue (No. 619):

---

20 Matsuura Akira, *Shindai kaigai bōekishi no kenkyū* (Research on the History of Foreign Trade in the Qing Period, pp 247-251.

21 Sōda Hiroshi, *Kinsei Hyōyūmin to Chūgoku* (Castaways in the Pre-modern Period and China) in *Fukuoka Kyōiku Daigaku Kiyō*, (Fukuoka University of Education Bulletin), vol. 31, Booklet 2, February 1982.

22 Matsuura Akira, *Edo jidai tōsen ni yoru nitchū bunka kōryū* (Sino-Japanese Cultural Interaction via Chinese Junk in the Edo Period), vol.3; pp. 301-324.

The arrival at the port of Shanghai, during the past few days, of a British-built vessel sailing under the Japanese flag is in itself an event worthy of notice. When we learn further that this ship has not only been purchased by the native [Japanese] government, but that she is laden with the produce and manufactures of the country for trading purposes abroad, it throws an entirely new light upon the exclusive policy of that peculiar people. Hitherto we have been led to understand that the Tycoon and his Yaconins, and the Damios who rule with despotic sway over the subjects of the empire, were not only averse to the encouragement of foreign commerce, but held in contempt those who pursued the vocations of merchants and ship-traders....[23]

The foregoing article indicates strong interest in the *Senzai-maru* then docked in Shanghai. Mention of the dispatching of the *Senzai-maru* informed Westerners residing in Asia that the Tokugawa *Bakufu* was abandoning its policy of seclusion to begin foreign trade. This new development in Japan was of major interest to Westerners in Asia.

The group in China that most influenced the many years of Nagasaki trade was the Taipings, which were expanding their power on the Chinese mainland in the mid-1800s. The Taiping Rebellion devastated the economy of Jiangnan, the base of Chinese merchants who traded with Nagasaki. Subsequently, it became difficult to continue trade via Chinese junks to Nagasaki; some merchants even tried to maintain trade by chartering British ships. Other Chinese trading merchants were compelled to resort to making a living by residing in Japan.

Mutual political influence is apparent in the relationship between the two countries. If we consider only the Japanese perspective, however, the Nagasaki trade conducted by Chinese merchants was not merely an economic exchange; it was also a cultural and scholarly interaction that became an important foundation for furthering modernization in Japan from the latter half of the 19th century.

5 Conclusion

The nature of Chinese trading in Nagasaki toward the end of the Qing era changed greatly with shifting world trends. First, the attack by the Taipings on

---

23   *Gaikoku Shinbun ni Miru Nihon,* (Japan As Seen in Foreign Newspapers),Volume 1, 1851-1873, *Mainichi Komyunikeshonzu* (Mainichi Communications), September 1989, p. 186.

Zhapu, which had served as a base for trade with Nagasaki and the Chinese hinterland of Suzhou, caused a collapse in the merchants' trade organization. Later, when Japan opened to the world after its years of isolation, fast new clipper ships and steamships from the West began frequenting Japanese ports in great numbers for trade. As a result, Chinese junks that had been sailing to Nagasaki quickly lost their competitiveness in the new international setting.

Sino-Japanese cultural and intellectual interchange during the Edo era was a unique interlude in world history, one that depended on the efforts of Chinese shipping merchants whose junks dominated marine transportation in Asia in the seventeenth and eighteenth centuries. The relationship also depended on the adoption by the Tokugawa *Bakufu* of a national isolationist policy that prohibited Japanese ships from sailing abroad. Further inquiries into Sino-Japanese relations in this period should delve more deeply into the remarkable cultural exchange that resulted from this unique state of affairs.

References

Allom, Thomas & G, N. Wright, *China, in a Series of Views, Displaying the Scenery,*
Architecture, and Social Habits, of that Ancient Empire, vol. 3, 1843.
Gaikoku Shinbun ni Miru Nihon, (Japan As Seen in Foreign Newspapers) 外国新聞に見る日本1851-1873. In vol. 1 of *Mainichi Komyunikeshonzu* (Mainichi Communications), 毎日コミュニケーションズ. September 1989.
Gongzhongdang Yongzhengchao zuozhe, diyiwu ji (Report to the Yongzheng Court, Inner Palace Files, *Gongli gugong bowuyuan* 宮中档雍正朝奏摺. (National Palace Museum), 国立故宮博物院 Compilation No. 15. January 1979.
He Ruzhang, 何如璋. *Shidong zaji* (Miscellany of an Envoy in Japan), 使東雑記. *Xiaofanghu zhai yudi congshao, dishizhi suoshou* (Geographical Essays from the Xiaofanghu Studio, Collection Bound in the Tenth Volume) 小方壺齋輿地叢鈔第十帙所収.
Kai hentai (Chinese Metamorphosis) 華夷変態, vol. 1. Tōyō Bunkō, Nonprofit Corporation, 財団法人東洋文庫. March, 1958; Reprinted by Tōhō Shoten, Nov. 1981.
Matsuura Akira 松浦章. *Shindai kaigai bōekishi no kenkyū* (Research on the History of Foreign Trade in the Qing Period), 清代海外貿易史の研究. Hōyū Shoten, January 2002.
Matsuura Akira, 松浦章. *Edo jidai tōsen ni yoru nitchū bunka kōryū* (Sino-Japanese Cultural Interaction via Chinese Junk in the Edo Period), 江戸時代唐船による日中文化交流. Shibunkaku Press, July 2007.

Nagasaki bunken sōsho daiisshū 1, daiinimaki, Nagasaki jitsuroku taisei seihen (Nagasaki Documents Series, Series 1, vol. 2, Principal Compilation of the Authentic Account of Nagasaki), 長崎文献叢書第一集第二巻 長崎実録大成正編. Nagasaki Bunkensha, December 12, 1973.

Nakamura Kyūshirō, 中村久四郎. *Kinsei Shina no Nihon bunka ni oyoboshitaru seiryoku eikyō—kinsei shina o haikei to shitaru Nihon bunkashi* (The Powerful Influence Exerted by Pre-Modern China on Japanese Culture—the Cultural History of Japan against the Backdrop of Pre-Modern China) 近世支那の日本文化に及ぼしたる勢力影響—近世支那を背景としたる日本文化史—. *Shigaku Zasshi,* 史学雑誌. vol. 26,no.2, February 1915.

Nakamura Kyūshirō, 中村久四郎. Speech given at the symposium of the Society of Historical Research, June 14, 1914. Article column on bulletins, *Society of Historical Research,* 日開催の史学研究会例会における講演. 史林. vol. 9, number 4, October, 1924.

Sōda Hiroshi, 相田洋. *Kinsei Hyōyūmin to Chūgoku* (Castaways in the Pre-modern Period and China) 近世漂流民と中国. In *Fukuoka Kyōiku Daigaku Kiyō,* (Fukuoka University of Education Bulletin), 福岡教育大学紀要. vol. 31, booklet 2, February 1982.

Yano, Jinichi, 矢野仁一. "Shina no Kiroku kara mita Nagasaki bōeki" 支那ノ記録カラ見夕長崎貿易, Tōakeizai Kenkyū 東亜経済研究 9, nos1-3, 1925.

Yano, Jinichi, 矢野仁一. *Nagasaki-shi shi tsūkō bōeki-hen tōyō shokokubu* (The History of Marine Trade in Nagasaki City with Far Eastern Nations), 長崎市史 通交貿易編東洋諸国部. Nagasaki City Office, April, 1938.

Part 2: Sino-Japanese Interaction based on Chinese Junks in the Edo period

Figure 10   Chinese Junk from *Tokan Rankan to emaki* (Picture Scroll of the Chinese and Dutch Residences) Painted by Ishizaki Yushi

Figure 11   Nagasaki Woodblock Print: Illustration of a Chinese Junk Entering at Harbor (Nagasaki Yamatoya Print)

Figure 12   Scene inside the Chinese Residential Area from *Tokan Rankan to emaki* (Picture Scroll of the Chinese and Dutch Residences) Painted by Ishizaki Yushi

Figure 14   Dried sea cucumber (*Haishen*)

Figure 13   Illustration of Chinese in *Shinsa showashu* (Collection of Qing Raft Prayers)

CHAPTER 8

The Trade in Dried Marine Products from Nagasaki to China during the Edo Period

1 Introduction

The Chinese intellectual Wang Tao 王韜 (1828-1897), who visited Japan at the end of the Qing Dynasty, described the restricted nature of contact between Japan and the Qing Empire in the fourth volume of *Wengyou yutan* 甕牖餘談, under the title "Tongshang Riben shuo 通商日本説 [Tales of Trade with Japan]". The relationship between China and Japan during most of the Qing Dynasty, he observed, was limited to trade conducted by Chinese junks at Nagasaki 長崎.[1] The most important goal of Chinese traders bound for Nagasaki was to acquire copper for Chinese coinage. In exchange for this copper, Chinese merchants

---

* Translator's note: I use "dried goods" for *tawaramono* 俵物, goods that were traditionally-transported and stored in straw bags. The precise goods varied, but in this context generally were understood to be dried marine products, and above all the three discussed here.
** Paper translated by Michael Thornton.
1 日本一國、密邇中土、⋯⋯國朝順治以後、惟通市、不遣使、其市亦惟中國商船往、無倭船來也。其與中國貿易在長崎島、百貨所聚、商旅通焉。國饒銅、中土鼓鑄所資、自滇銅而外、兼市洋銅、⋯⋯每年採購定額、四百四十三萬餘斤、設官商船十六艘、皆以內地綢緞・絲棉・糖・薬往易、商辦銅斤、必藉倭照以爲憑驗。The country of Japan is very close to China. . . . Once the country's government established control, only trade occurred, with no diplomatic envoys. Trade only took place with Chinese merchant ships, with no Japanese ships coming [to China]. Their trade with China took place on the island [sic] of Nagasaki where all manner of goods were gathered and traded by companies of travelling merchants. The country was abundant in copper, and supplied the coin minting needs of China: in addition to copper from Dian (Yunnan 雲南), foreign [Japanese] copper) was purchased. . . . Every year a set amount was acquired—some 4,430,000 *jin* 斤. The position of state merchant was established, and sixteen vessels carrying domestically produced silk brocade, cotton, sugar and medicines travelled to trade, acquiring copper ingots. This trade depended upon the required Japanese Trade Licence. *Biji xiaoshuo daguan*, 258.

125

transported Chinese silk products and raw silk, as well as sugar and Chinese medicines. In order to legally trade at Nagasaki, merchants required a seal issued by the Japanese authorities, the so-called 'Japanese seal' or 'Japanese Trade License (*shinpai* 信牌)'.

Wang's account lists several characteristic products traded between China and Japan during the Edo period (1603-1867). The largest Japanese export to China was Japanese-mined copper. Additionally, in 1875 He Ruzhang 何如璋 (1838-1891), then Chinese envoy to Japan, noted in his *Shidong zaji* 使東雜記 [Miscellany of an Envoy to Japan] that "many Chinese merchants take raw cotton and white sugar, and return with various marine products such as sea cucumber (*iriko* 煎海鼠) and dried abalone (*hoshiawabi* 干鮑)."[2] His description indicates that Japan's primary exports to China at the beginning of the Meiji period (1868-1912) were also copper and various dried marine products.

The 1828 woodblock book *Zhapu beizhi* 乍浦備志 [Supplementary Gazetteer of Zhapu] recounts the history of the market town of Zhapu in Pinghu district of Jiaxing prefecture in Zhejiang (浙江省嘉興府平湖縣乍浦鎮). Volume 14, which records events of the mid-Qianlong years (1736-1795) when Zhapu was the base of trade with Japan, describes how merchants were organized: The Chinese side comprised two groups of merchants, one of state offfficials and one of private citizens. Each had three ships, for a total of six sent to Japan every year between the summer solstice 夏至 and the minor heat 小暑 of the old calendar (corresponding roughly to late June and early July in the Gregorian calendar). Those ships carried sugar from Fujian 福建 and Guangdong 廣東, as well as Chinese goods highly desired by Japanese, and set out eastwards for Japan.[3] Then, in the ninth month the Chinese ships were loaded with copper, kelp, dried sea cucumber and various marine plants before returning to Zhapu, revealing that, in addition to copper, marine products such as kelp and sea cucumber formed an important component of the trade with Japan.[4]

During the Edo period, the quantity of dried sea cucumber, dried abalone and shark fin (*fukahire* 鱶鰭), exported from Nagasaki to China grew considerably. Particularly during the Qing Dynasty, the growing popularity of seafood produced a taste for sea cucumber (*haishen* 海參), dried abalone (*fuyu* 鰒魚) and shark fin (*yuchi* 魚翅) in China. As a result, export of these marine products increased steadily during the Genroku period 元禄時代 (1688-1703; Kangxi 康熙 27-42). Consumption was greatest in the Lower Yangzi delta region, but by the

---

2 Wang, *Xiaofanghuzhai yudi congchao*, 8001.
3 *Zhongguo difangzhi jicheng xiangzhenzhi zhuanji*, 229.
4 In the middle of the ninth month, the ships were loaded with copper ingots, kelp, sea cucumber and other marine plants before returning to Zhapu. Ibid., 230.

late Qing Dynasty consumption increased as dried sea cucumber, dried abalone and shark fin made their way into the interior, enlivening dining tables around China.[5]

Qing China's most sought-after product from Japan was Japanese copper, known in China as 'foreign copper'.[6] The amount of copper supplied to the Qing government in 1716 totaled 4,130,000 *jin* 斤, of which 'foreign copper' comprised some 2,770,000 *jin* and domestically produced Yunnan copper some 1,660,000 *jin*.[7] Proportionally, Japanese copper represented 62.5 percent of Qing China's supply, compared to 37.5 percent from Yunnan 雲南, demonstrating that Chinese domestic production could by no means satisfy the needs of Qing society. Therefore the import trade from Nagasaki, which was also relatively convenient, held considerable value for Qing society.

The vessels operating that trade were junks, Chinese merchant sailing ships that Edo period Japanese referred to as *Tōsen* 唐船. In order for these ships to sail safely and smoothly across the open ocean, they required large quantities of cheap and portable material for ballast. Sugar fulfilled the criteria of cost and quantity, and moreover proved popular in Japanese society.[8] In return went the 'foreign copper,' the Japanese copper sought by the Qing court. However, as Japanese copper production gradually declined, export of dried marine products increased to supplement the metal trade.

In this essay, I wish to investigate historical changes in the Edo period trade in copper and dried marine products at Nagasaki using the logs and cargo inventories of ships returning from Nagasaki to China.

2 Trade in Dried Marine Products with China during the Genroku, Hōei 宝永 and Shōtoku 正徳 Periods

After pacifying the Ming loyalist Zheng 鄭 clan of Taiwan, the Qing proclaimed the 'Order of the Open Seas' (*zhanhailing* 展海令) in 1684,

---

5 Matsuura, "Nisshin bōeki ni yoru tawaramono no Chūgoku ryūnyū ni tsuite", 19-38; Matsuura, *Shindai kaigai bōekishi no kenkyū*, 382-402.
6 Yan, *Qingdai Yunnan tongzheng kao*, 3. The treasury of the Board of Finances and the mint of the Board of Works in Beijing required over 4,400,000 *jin* of copper every year to mint coins. Ibid., 4.
7 *Shangyu Tiaoli*, hubu, "bantong tiaoli" 上諭條例 戶部、辦銅條例 [*Edicts and Regulations*, Finances Section, "Regulations for the procurement of copper"], 1736; Matsuura, *Edo jidai Tōsen ni yoru nitchū bunka kōryū*, 111.
8 Matsuura, "Edo jidai Tōsen ni yoru satō yu'nyū to kokunai shōhi no tenkai," 335-59.

prompting large numbers of Chinese coastal merchants to set sail overseas. They focused particularly on Japan. As a result, Nagasaki hosted several thousand Chinese residents year round, leading to restrictions on Chinese settlement in the city proper and the development of so-called Chinese quarters (*Tōjin yashiki* 唐人屋敷, known by the Chinese as *Tang-guan* 唐館) where the Chinese were forced to reside.[9] This period also saw the start of a steady increase in exports of dried marine products to China.[10]

On that note, let us look at the *Tō tsūji kaisho nichiroku* 唐通事會所日錄 [Daily Record of the House of Chinese Interpreters] for a sense of the state of dried marine product exports in the Genroku, Hōei and Shōtoku periods (1688-1716), when some seventy to eighty trade junks arrived in Nagasaki from China every year.

2.1 Dried Abalone and Shark Fin

Sea cucumber and abalone figured prominently in the request for goods by the Chinese residing in Nagasaki's Chinese quarters on 1689/4/3. Merchants planned to dry sea cucumbers and abalone every day in order to return to China with them.[11]

A passage dated 1698/9/2 records that the twenty-eighth ship[12] returning to China carried a large amount of copper, which had made the ship too heavy to sail, forcing it to return to Nagasaki.[13] The ship carried "about 1,500 crates of copper, along with dried goods, together forming a large load."[14] On 1702/6/8, the twenty-third Ningbo 寧波 ship of 1701 was sent to Nagasaki after drifting ashore on Amakusa 天草. The Ningbo ship was loaded with dried marine prod-

---

9   Matsuura, *Kinsei Higashi Ajia kaiiki no bunka kōshō*, 31-50.
10 Matsuura, *Shindai kaigai bōeki shi no kenkyū*, 382-402.
11 いりこ・あわび類毎日干候て連ゝ買渡ル儀二御座候而、蔵に入置候而ハ、尤時々干可申候。 [Sea cucumbers and abalone are dried daily, and sold seemingly without end. They are in warehouses, and it must be said that an impressive amount is always dried.] *Tō tsūji kaisho nichiroku*, 1: 244.
12 Chinese ships entering Nagasaki were assigned numbers according to the order of their arrival. In principle, this numbering system (known as *banzuke* 番付) included the zodiac sign of the lunar calendar year; for example, ships arriving in the year of the dragon would receive appellations such as "Year of the Dragon, first ship, Year of the Dragon, second ship," and so forth. Extraordinary ships, such as those shipwrecked on Japanese shores, were not numbered. Instead, they were listed as extras (*bangai* 番外), thus "Year of the Dragon, Extra." [Translator's note: I have omitted the zodiacal year in the ship's numbers below, relying instead on the Western year approximation.]
13 *Tō tsūji kaisho nichiroku*, 2: 330.
14 Ibid., 2: 331.

Figure 15   Dried abalone.

ucts, but bad weather delaying its departure from Nagasaki had caused the sea cucumber and abalone to go damp.[15] In 1706/7, the twenty-second Nanjing 南京 ship of 1705, which had become stranded in Satsuma 薩摩, was towed to Nagasaki, where it was dismantled and sold. The crew and cargo were split between the thirty-first, thirty-second, thirty-sixth and fortieth Nanjing ships, as well as the thirty-third Nanjing ship,[16] and returned to China. In addition to the 53 crew members and 640 crates of copper, the ship had carried 31 *maru* 丸 of sea cucumber and abalone.[17]

In 1706/7, Fukuda Dennoshin 福田傳之進 and other city elders (*machi toshiyori* 町年寄) of Nagasaki received a pheasant from the ninety-first Taiwan ship. As a return gift, "Dennoshin offfered thirty *kin* of sea cucumber and thirty *kin* of dried abalone."[18]

In 1707/8 the eighty-first Taiwan ship received permission to acquire supplies of "thirteen *maru* (390 kg) of sea cucumber and dried abalone, and five barrels (*oke* 桶) of soy sauce."[19] On the other hand, in the same month the seventy-sixth Nanjing ship was denied a request to return to China with "seven hundred *kin* of sea cucumber; abalone; dried cuttlefish; shark fin; ceramic ware; rice bowls; mushrooms; all together seven types of goods."[20] Also in the same

---

15 本船ニ積込申候いりこ・あわひ等、永〻日和悪敷候に付、殊外しめり申候。[This ship's load of dried sea cucumber and abalone had, due to many days of poor conditions, become exceedingly damp.] Ibid., 3: 263.
16 Occasionally the number assigned to ships did not strictly conform to the order in which they arrived in port. Therefore, the numbers are not always continuous. The reasons for this irregularity are not clear, but it likely was due to the situation of the ship owner or circumstances in Nagasaki.
17 Ibid., 4: 144, 147-48.
18 Ibid., 4: 152.
19 Ibid., 4: 243.
20 Ibid., 4: 244.

Figure 16   Dried shark fin

month, the eighty-first ship had loaded for its return voyage "thirteen *maru* of dried abalone. Yet these did not please the Chinese, and they sought to return them, submitting a request indicating their desire to unload the goods onto land."[21] Finally, in 1707/9 money from the sale of goods from a damaged ship was used to "purchase sea cucumber and abalone, which the Chinese requested to carry with them onto the thirty-ninth [Taiwan] ship."[22]

In 1708/6 a returning cargo vessel requested "these four items: sea cucumber, abalone, dried cuttlefish, and *tengusa* てん草 seaweed," and was given permission to take them on as cargo.[23] In the same month, Cheng Yi Fan 程益凡, owner of the sixty-first ship, received permission "to load the following dried goods the next morning: four hundred *kin* of sea cucumber, one hundred *kin* of dried abalone, and two hundred *kin* of dried cuttlefish."[24]

Liu Huaqian 劉華謙, owner of the forty-seventh ship, which returned on 1709/6/19, submitted a request to exchange his cargo of one hundred baskets (*kago* 籠) of sugar for sea cucumber, dried abalone and kelp.[25] In 1709/11, the fiftysixth Ningbo ship asked to see "samples of dried goods" (*tawaramono tehon* 俵物手本).[26] After being shown kelp, dried cuttlefish, dried sea cucumber, shark fin and dried abalone, they decided to take the goods for their return cargo.

On 1710/9/2, the twenty-eighth Taiwan ship and the thirty-fifth Xiamen 厦

---

21   Ibid., 4: 246.
22   Ibid., 4: 261.
23   Ibid., 5: 45.
24   Ibid., 5: 48-49.
25   砂糖類百かこ餘口へ牛皮有之候を、何卒いりこ・あわひ・昆布類ニ替させ被下候様。 [Would it somehow be possible to exchange our more than one hundred crates (かこ) of sugar, as well as our leather, for sea cucumber, dried abalone, and kelp?] Ibid., 5: 160.
26   Ibid., 5: 198.

門 ship "purchased various goods such as dried cuttlefish, dried abalone and soy sauce."²⁷ Around 1713/1, the Ningbo and Nanjing ships bought "sea cucumber and abalone" for their return cargo.²⁸ On 1713/11/27, the returning third Nanjing ship requested to exchange its 120 *maru* of kelp for sea cucumber and dried abalone.²⁹ On 1714/2/12, the forty-sixth ship requested for its return cargo "dried goods, including two hundred *kin* of sea cucumber, one hundred *kin* of abalone, and one hundred *kin* of shark fin."³⁰

2.2 Dried Sea Cucumber

The dried sea cucumber loaded as return cargo on Chinese junks was procured from regions surrounding Nagasaki.³¹ As discussed below, these goods probably originated in Ōmura 大村 and Hirado 平戸, both domains close to Nagasaki.

Figure 17   Dried sea cucumber

Of the various dried goods merchants³² and "five sea cucumber, dried cuttlefish, shark fin and bonito merchants"³³ active in Nagasaki in 1708/2, two people worked daily in the Chinese quarters, inspecting the goods purchased by Chinese ships for their return cargoes. The eighty-second Nanjing ship, returning on the third day of the sixth month, submitted a request to purchase two *maru* of dried sea cucumber.³⁴ On 1710/8/26, gifts of dried sea cucumber were distributed to nine ships as thanks for exotic birds sent as presents to Japa-

---

27   Ibid., 5: 297.
28   Ibid., 6: 107.
29   Ibid., 6: 210-11.
30   Ibid., 7: 22.
31   Ibid., 2: 387.
32   Ibid., 4: 302.
33   Ibid., 4: 304.
34   Ibid., 5: 30.

nese offficials.[35] The ships were given a total of 190 *kin* of dried sea cucumber in return for the birds they brought at the request of merchants in Nagasaki, which included parakeets, pheasants and mynah birds. On 1712/3/11, the fortyfirst ship sought dried sea cucumber, shark fin and kelp[36] for its return cargo, but due to disagreements over the price, the trade was unsuccessful.

2.3 Return Cargo of Chinese Junks during the Hōei 宝永 Period (1704-1711)

Chinese demand for marine products existed from the start of the Edo period. Despite this, marine products represented a smaller portion of the return cargoes of Chinese ships than copper. Not many records remain of the cargoes taken on by Chinese merchant ships for their return journeys after completing their trade in Nagasaki. The only known compilation is the *Tōban kamotsuchō* 唐蠻貨物帳 [Accounts of Trade with China and the Barbarians], held in the Naikaku Bunko collection of the Japanese National Archives.[37] I wish to look at the first account from that compilation, which records the seventh ship of 1709. The record is summarized in table 10, and figure 18 shows these values in the

---

35   Details for the nine ships are as follows:

Ship	Return gift	Amount	In exchange for
Second Ningbo ship	Sea cucumber	1 box, 15 *kin*	one blue parakeet (*qingyingge* 青鸚哥)
Sixth ship	Sea cucumber	1 box, 25 *kin*	one pheasant (*jinniao* 錦鳥)
Seventh ship	Sea cucumber	1 box, 15 *kin*	one blue parakeet
Ninth Ningbo ship	Sea cucumber	1 box, 15 *kin*	one meadow bunting (*huameiniao* 畫眉鳥)
Eleventh ship	Sea cucumber	2 boxes, 25 *kin*	two pheasants
Eleventh ship	Sea cucumber	1 box, 15 *kin*	one meadow bunting
Twelth Nanjing ship	Sea cucumber	1 box, 15 *kin*	one crested mynah (*bageniao* 八哥鳥)
Fifteenth Nanjing ship	Sea cucumber	1 box, 15 *kin*	one meadow bunting
Sixteenth Nanjing ship	Sea cucumber	1 box, 15 *kin*	four pheasants
Eighteenth Nanjing ship	Sea cucumber	1 box, 25 *kin*	two red-billed wrens (*sōshichō* 相思鳥)

Ibid., 5: 286-87.

36   Ibid., 6: 46.
37   *Tōban kamotsu chō* [Lists of cargoes from China and Europe], parts 1 and 2. Both parts are facsimiles, totaling 1,626 pages. The second part includes Yamawaki Teijiro's 山脇悌二郎 "*Tōban kamotsu chō kaidai*" 唐蠻貨物帳解題 ["Explanatory Notes on *Tōban kamotsu chō*"], 1-12.

form of a pie chart:

Table 10   Return cargo of the seventh Nanjing ship, 1709[38]

Goods and Expenditures	Trade value (*in monme* 匁 of silver)	Gold equivalent (in *ryō* 両)	Volume of cargo (in *kin*)
Silver	2,700.000	45.0	
Copper	40,739.060		35,673.4327
Recycled copper goods	1,850.160		1,587.7500
Sundry goods (*komamono iroiro* 小間物色々)	690.000		
Fox pelts	5,353.000		
Sea cucumber	20,780.970		6,164.0000
Shark fin	1,113.400		475.5000
Dried abalone	5,632.9700		1573.5000
Dried shellfish	70.200		108.0000
Kelp	1,255.815		5,841.0000
Total purchases	**77,485.575**	**1,291.5**	
Expenditures	29,614.430	493.5	
Total	**109,800.000**	**1,830.0**	**51,423.1827**

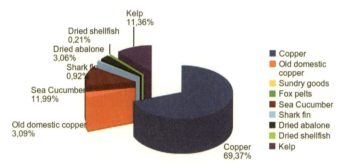

Figure 18   *Trade value of return cargo of the seventh Nanjing ship, 1709 (by value in silver).*

In comparison, the following figure 6.5 represents the same goods broken down by volume.

It is clear that in this period copper easily comprised more than half the

---

38   "寶永六丑年 七番南京船帰帆荷物買渡帳 船頭 沈秋堂 七月十日 [Sixth year of Hōei [1709], Year of the Ox: Record of the Purchase of Return Cargoes for the Seventh Nanjing Ship; Captain Shen Qiutang 沈秋堂. Tenth day of the seventh month]" in *Tōban kamotsu chō*, 1: 2-7.

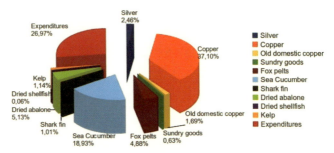

Figure 19   *Trade value of return cargo of the seventh Nanjing ship, 1709 (by volume).*

volume of exports from Nagasaki on Chinese junks.

3   Export of Marine Products to China in the Middle and Late Edo Periods

On 1741/12/8 (Kampō 寛保 1, Qianlong 乾隆 6), a Chinese ship returning from Nagasaki drifted ashore on the island of Ōshima 大島 in the Ryūkyū kingdom 琉球国. On board were fifty-three passengers, including Xu Weihuai 徐惟懐, all merchants from the county of Wu in Suzhou prefecture, Jiangnan 江南蘇州府吳縣. Their cargo included 77,499 *kin* of copper bars, 25,080 *kin* of sea cucumber and abalone, 4,200 *kin* of cockscomb algae (*hong cai* 紅菜) and squid, and 24,000 *kin* of kelp.[39] The proportions of copper, dried goods and kelp were roughly 61.2 percent for copper, 19.8 percent for dried goods, and 19.0 percent for kelp, revealing that the amount of copper was still a large proportion of the total cargo.

An example of a Chinese ship with an even larger cargo of copper may be found in a report by Fujian governor Zhong Yin 鐘音 dated 1756/12/4. Returning to Zhejiang province from Nagasaki, the ship unexpectedly encountered troubles at sea and became stranded in the seas near Fuqing 福清 county along the Fuzhou 福州 coast in Fujian. Damaged, the ship was unable to transport its cargo, and so asked the Fujian government to purchase its load of 172,500 *kin* worth of red copper.[40] Thus we see how in 1756, more than 170,000 *kin* of

---

39   *Rekidai hōan*, 4: 405.
40   浙江歸安縣商人高山輝、從乍浦出口、往販東洋置貨、回棹適遇颶風、於閏九月初五日、飄至閩省福清縣沙塢地方、船隻受傷、莫能駕駛回、帶有紅銅一十七萬二千五百

copper was exported from Nagasaki on returning Chinese merchant ships.

In 1762/4, the seventh ship of the previous year returned to China from Nagasaki. I would now like to take a look at its return cargo record. A work titled *Nagasaki hiroku* 長崎秘録 [Secret Records of Nagasaki] lies in the Murakami Collection of the Kariya Municipal Library in Aichi Prefecture. The second volume of that work contains copies of the Nagasaki trade records for the Hōreki years (1751-1764), including information about the return cargoes of three ships from 1762/4 and three ships from 1762/9, out of a total of twelve ships that arrived in Nagasaki in 1761 and fifteen that arrived in 1762.[41] I would like to look at the first record, of the seventh ship from 1762, which returned on 1762/4/22. The following tables summarize the goods purchased:

Table 11   *1762 Seventh Ningbo ship, value of return cargo*[42]

Item	Value in silver *monme*	Amount in *kin*
Silver	1,100.0	
Copper	118,576.0	102,750.7
Dried sea cucumber	90,586.4	280,201.3
Dried abalone	5,688.0	21,040.0
Dried shark fin	1,680.0	840.0
Dried cuttlefish	2,184.0	1,680.0
Cockscomb algae	6,300.0	6,000.0
Kelp	53,126.4	159,060.0
Sake	275.0	
Soy sauce	40.0	
Gold-leaf lacquer ware	330.0	
Expenditures in Nagasaki	50,570.9	
Total	330,456.7	

By this time the amount of copper as a proportion of the return cargo of the

---

舶、情願就閩収買、以供鼓鋳、⋯。 [Gaoshan Hui 高山輝, a merchant from Guian in Zhejiang 浙江帰安縣, set out from Zhapu to acquire goods in Japan. Upon turning his ship, he ran into a storm, and on the fifth day of the intercalary ninth month, washed ashore in Fuqing County, Min [Fujian] Province, in the Shawu region 閩省福清縣沙塢地方. His ship had sufffered damage, such that horses were not able to drag it free. He requested that the Min government purchase his cargo of 172,500 *jin* of red copper, which they used to mint coins.] *Gongzhongdang Qianlongchao zouzhe*, 16: 238.

41   *Nagasaki hiroku*, 2.

42   "巳年七番 寧波船買渡荷物帳 宝暦十二年 午四月廿二日帰帆 船頭曹體三 唐人数八拾三人 [Seventh Ningbo Ship: Record of Return Cargo, Returning on the twenty-second day of the fourth month, 1762, Captain: Cao Tisan 曹體三 Crew: 83 Chinese]." *Nagasaki hiroku*, 2: 10-12.

Part 2: Sino-Japanese Interaction based on Chinese Junks in the Edo period

Chinese merchant ships had decreased, offfset by a rise in the amount of marine products.

Wang Lujie 王履階, a representative of the Twelve Families 十二家 of quota merchants (and who later became a state merchant),[43] sought to export an additional three hundred thousand *kin* of goods, of which 70 percent would be copper and 30 percent dried goods. Yet due to a shortage of dried good imports into Nagasaki that year, he took the full three hundred thousand *kin* in copper.[44] As this example indicates, Chinese merchants valued dried goods as much as copper.

Table 12   *1761-1762 Chinese ships, return cargoes; volume of copper and marine products (in* kin*)*

Year	1761	1762	1762	1762	1762	1762	1762
Ship	Third Xiamen	Seventh Ningbo	Eighth Nanjing	Ninth Ningbo	Tenth Ningbo	Twelfth Nanjing	Sixth Ningbo
Captain	Cui Jingsan 崔景三	Cao Tisan 曹體三	Gong Zixing 龔子興	Wang Shengwu 汪繩武	Yuan Shenghuan 袁盛寰	Cheng Yutian 程玉田 & Zhao Zhuruo 趙主若	Fang Gongchen 方拱宸 & Shen Lunxi 沈綸溪
Crew	83	83	80	115	75	112	77
Copper	100,000	102,750.7	150,000	142,763.5	100,000	161,091.3	132,816
Sea cucumber	27,752.4	28,021.3	26,390.1	39,782.9	22,829	24,266.2	22,920
Abalone	2,258.9	2,040	2,123.3	7,836.6	5,181.8	3,840	5,038.7
Shark fin	1,080	840	1,080	1,080	420	420	600
Kelp	155,608.7	159,060.8	136,139.4	157,586.4	179,097.8	158,377.6	165,316.4
Leaf No.	7-8	10-11	17-18	21-22	25	28-29	34-35

Table 13 and figure 22 depict the amount of copper and dried marine products in the cargo of the third ship of 1764, as found in the records of the Dutch

---

43   Matsuura, *Shindai kaigai bōeki shi no kenkyū*, 151-53.
44   唐國ヨリ元絲銀三百貫目持渡ル。此代リ銅三拾萬斤、內正銅七分、俵物三分、可被相渡約條ニテ、二拾ヶ年可持渡憑文渡置ル。但今年俵物拂底ニ付、正銅三十萬斤相渡サル。[[Wang Lujie] carried three hundred thousand *monme* of silver currency from China. In exchange for this he sought goods valued at three hundred thousand *kin* of copper, 70 percent actual copper and 30 percent dried goods. He hoped to set up a contract for these conditions lasting twenty years. However due to a shortage of dried goods this year, he received 300,000 *kin* of copper.] *Nagasaki jitsuroku taisei* 11, 278, entry for Hōreki 13.

The Trade in Dried Marine Products from Nagasaki to China during the Edo Period

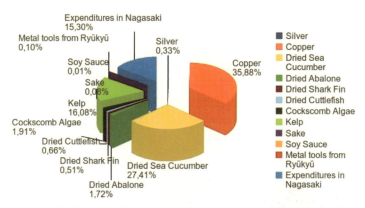

Figure 20   *1762 seventh Ningbo ship, value of return cargo (by value in silver).*

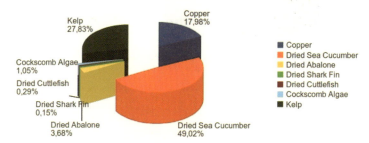

Figure 21   *1762 seventh Ningbo ship, value of return cargo (by volume).*

Trading House in Nagasaki.[45]

Accounts of how much copper was loaded onto returning Chinese vessels appear in the palace memorials of Qing court offificials. The first account, from Zhejiang governor Xiong Xuepeng 熊学鹏, dates from 1763/1/24: Under the command of merchant-offficial Fan Qingzhu 范清注[46] the ship *Yangshihe* 楊士合 entered Zhapu port on 1762/5/11. Thereafter we know that the *Weiyuansheng* arrived in Zhapu on 1762/5/17, and the *Shixinli* 施新利 on 1762/9/30. The *Yangshihe* carried "one thousand crates of copper ingots;" the *Weiyuansheng* 魏元盛, carried "one thousand crates of copper ingots;" and the *Shixinli* carried "one thousand crates of copper ingots" as well. These cargoes of copper, known as 'official copper'—that is, copper destined for government use—were transported on from Zhapu to Beijing, where they became raw material for minting

---

45   Nagazumi, *Tōsen yushutsunyūhin suryō ichiran* 1637-1833 *nen*, 265.
46   Matsuura, *Shindai kaigai bōeki shi no kenkyū*, 148.

copper coins.[47]

Table 13 *Volume of copper and dried marine products, return cargo of the third ship, 1764 (in* kin*)*

1764 Third ship	Copper rods	Dried sea cucumber	Dried abalone	Shark fin	Kelp	Dried cuttlefish
	172,550	20,000	6,360	540	174,545	1,080

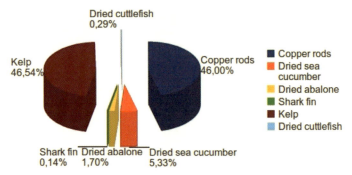

Figure 22 *Volume of copper and dried marine products, return cargo of the third ship, 1764.*

---

47   官商范清注、採辦銅斤、由乍（乍浦）起運、觧供蘇省、分觧五省官銅、該官商、乾隆二十七年、辦回船戸楊士合船、銅斤一千箱、於五月十一日、由乍進口、入境即於十二日、起運赴蘇、於本月二十三日出境、又船戸魏元盛船、銅斤一千箱、於閏五月十七日、由乍進口、入境即於二十六日、起運五百四十箱、又於二十九日、起運四百六十箱赴蘇、俱於六月初一日出境、又船戸施新利船、銅斤一千箱、於九月三十日、由乍進口、入境即於十月初六、七等日、起運赴蘇、於十月十三日出境、均経沿途各県、加謹稽查防護、並無偸盗・沈溺事。 [Merchant-offficial Fan Qingzhu obtained copper ingots. He set offf from Zhapu and supplied Suzhou and five other provincial governments with copper. Under that merchant-offficial [Fan], the ship *Yangshihe*, carrying one thousand crates of copper ingots, left Zhapu on the eleventh day of the fifth month. It entered our territory on the twelfth, and left again for Suzhou on the twenty-third of the same month. The *Weiyuansheng*, carrying one thousand crates of copper ingots, left Zhapu on the seventeenth day of the intercalary fifth month. It entered our territory on the twenty-sixth. It initially transported 540 crates, and then on the twenty-ninth transported another 460 crates to Suzhou, leaving our territory on the first day of the sixth month. The *Shixinli*, with one thousand crates of copper, left Zhapu on the thirtieth day of the ninth month. It entered our territory on the sixth or seventh day of the tenth month. It travelled onwards toward Suzhou, leaving our borders on the thirteenth day of the tenth month. It stopped at each prefecture along the way, and by taking great care and precautions, avoided both piracy and disaster.] *Gongzhongdang Qianlongchao zouzhe*, 16: 655-57.

Similar records exist through 1783, and, as shown in table 14, the majority of trade vessels returning to Zhapu from Nagasaki were laden with one thousand crates of copper.[48]

As the above table illustrates, each of the Chinese merchant ship sent to Nagasaki and commanded by merchant-offficials returned with one thousand crates—one hundred thousand *kin*—of copper.

Table 14   *Chinese Junks under the command of Qing merchant-offficials returning to Zhapu*

Western year	Chinese year	Date of entry to Zhapu	Name of vessel	Copper cargo (crates)	Source
1762	Qianlong 27	5/11	Yangshihe	1,000	G 28/1/24
	State merchant:	IC5/17	Weiyuansheng	1,000	
	Fan Qingzhu	9/30	Shixinli	1,000	
1763	Qianlong 28	3/7	He Yanbao 何延寶		G 28/1/6
	State merchant:				
	Fan Qingzhu	4/12	Yangshihe	1,000	
		9/10	Wangyongqing 王永慶	1,000	
1764	Qianlong 29	4/1	Shishunxing 史順興	1,000	G 30/1/22
	State merchant:				
	Fan Qinghong 范清洪	5/13	Jinyuntai 金允泰	900	
		9/27	Yangshihe	1,000	
		11/15	He Tingbao 何廷寶	1,000	
1765	Qianlong 30	3/6	Weiyuansheng	1,000	Z 31/1/7
	State merchant:	9/4	Linyongshun 林永順	500	
	Fan Qingji 范清濟		Wang Yongsheng* 王永順	721	
		9/8	Wan Youshun 萬友順	1,000	
		10/9	Weiyuansheng	1,000	
			Linyongshun*	500	
1766	Qianlong 31	2/12	Jinyuntai	1,000	Z 32/1/4
	State merchant:	2/24	Shishunxing	1,000	

---

48 Matsuura, *Shindai kaigai bōeki shi no kenkyū*, 354-56.

Part 2: Sino-Japanese Interaction based on Chinese Junks in the Edo period

Western year	Chinese year	Date of entry to Zhapu	Name of vessel	Copper cargo (crates)	Source
	Fan Qingji	5/12	Linyongshun	1,000	
		5/14	Weiyuansheng	1,000	
		9/24	He Tingbao	1,000	
		9/27	Yangshihe	1,000	
		10/1	Zhoushunxing 周順興	1,000	
		10/15	Shishunxing	1,000	
		10/19	Weiyuansheng	1,000	
1767	Qianlong 32	5/18	Jinyuntai	1,000	G 33/1/3
	State merchant: Fan Qingji	10/6	Xuxianchun 許咸春	1,000	
		10/24	Jinwanyu 金萬裕	1,000	
		11/20	Wanrixin 萬日新	1,000	
		11/20	Weiyuansheng	1,000	
1768	Qianlong 33	9/3	Wanrixin	1,000	Z 34/1/27
	State merchant: Fan Qingji	9/3	Linyongshun	1,000	
		9/3	He Tingbao	1,000	
		11/3	Jinwanyu	1,000	
		11/13	Xuxianchun	1,000	
1769	Qianlong 34	3/18	Yangshihe	1,000	Z 35/1/7
	State merchant: Fan Qingji	9/20	Shishunxing	1,000	
		9/26	Weiyuansheng	1,065	
		11/6	Jinwanyu	1,000	
		11/21	He Tingbao	1,000	
1770	Qianlong 35	5/5	Wanrixin	1,000	Z 36/1/11
	State merchant: Fan Qingji	5/7	Xuxianchun	1,000	
		9/19	Yangshihe	1,000	
		9/22	Linyongshun	1,000	
		9/22	Jinwanyu	1,000	
		10/8	He Tingbao	1,000	
1771	Qianlong 36	3/13	Wanrixin	1,000	Z 36/12/11
	State merchant: Fan Qingji	3/13	Shishunxing	1,000	
		9/9	Jinwanyu	1,000	
		9/10	Zhouyong'an 周永安	1,000	

The Trade in Dried Marine Products from Nagasaki to China during the Edo Period

Western year	Chinese year	Date of entry to Zhapu	Name of vessel	Copper cargo (crates)	Source
		9/10	Yueshunxing 岳順興	1,000	
		9/10	Fanjizong 范繼宗	1,000	
1772	Qianlong 37 State merchant: Fan Qingji	2/18	Linyongshun	1,000	Z 38/1/6
		4/22	He Tingbao	1,000	
		9/8	Weiyuansheng	1,000	
		9/19	Shishunxing	1,000	
		9/19	Wanrixin	1,000	
1773	Qianlong 38 State merchant: Fan Qingji	3/19	Zhouyong'an	1,000	G 38/12/1
		3/22	Jinwanyu	1,000	
		8/21	Linyongshun	1,000	
		10/11	Jiangxiangtai 江祥泰	1,000	
		10/18	He Tingbao	1,000	
		10/18	Wanrixin	1,000	
1774	Qianlong 39 State merchant: Fan Qingji	3/12	Weiyuansheng	1,000	G 39/12/6
		3/25	Shishunxing	1,000	
		3/26	Fanjizong	1,000	
		3/26	Jinyuanbao 金源寶	1,000	
		4/27	Zhoushunli 周順利	1,000	
		9/18	He Tingbao	1,000	
		9/30	Linyongshun	1,000	
1775	Qianlong 40 State merchant: Fan Qingji	2/2	Wanrixin	1,000	Z 40/12/27
		2/2	Weiyuansheng	1,000	
		4/5	Hongchengtai 洪成泰	1,000	
		5/6	Fanjizong	1,000	
		5/9	Jinyuanbao	1,000	
		9/28	Zhoushunli	1,000	
		10/24	He Tingbao	1,000	
		Int 10/8	Jinyuanbao	1,000	
1776	Qianlong 41 State merchant: Fan Qingji	5/1	Linyongshun	1,000	Z 41/12/12
		8/22	Weiyuansheng	1,000	
		9/19	Hongchengtai	1,000	

Part 2: Sino-Japanese Interaction based on Chinese Junks in the Edo period

Western year	Chinese year	Date of entry to Zhapu	Name of vessel	Copper cargo (crates)	Source
		9/19	Fanjizong	1,000	
		9/21	Wanrixin	1,000	
		10/11	Jinyuanbao	1,000	
1777	Qianlong 42	4/16	Shishunxing	1,000	G 42/11/24
		9/8	Zhoushunli	1,000	
		9/11	Wanrixin	1,000	
		10/3	Weiyuansheng	1,000	
		10/9	Linyongshun	1,000	
		10/9	He Tingbao	1,000	
1778	Qianlong 43	4/20	Hongchengtai	1,000	G 43/12/4
	State merchant:	5/6	Jinyuanbao	1,000	
	Fan Qingji	5/23	Wanrixin	1,000	
		9/27	Shishunxing	1,000	
		10/6	Fanjizong	1,000	
		10/8	Zhoushunli	1,000	
		10/8	Weiyuansheng	1,000	
1779	Qianlong 44	3/9	He Tingbao	1,000	Z 44/12/10
	State merchant:	4/7	Linyongshun	1,000	
	Fan Qingji	4/7	Fanjizong	1,000	
		4/7	Jinyuanbao	1,000	
		10/12	Zhouwanshun 周萬順	1,000	
		10/17	Wanrixin	1,000	
		11/4	Shishunxing	1,000	
1780	Qianlong 45	4/22	Weihongsheng 魏宏勝	1,000	Z 45/11/28
	State merchant: Fan Qingji	4/24	Fanjizong	1,000	
		5/8	Jinyuanbao	1,000	
		5/18	He Tingbao	1,000	
		10/12	Linyongshun	1,000	
		10/15	Zhouwanshun	1,000	
		10/18	Wanrixin	1,000	
1781	Qianlong 46 State merchant: Fan Qingji	262,533 *kin* of 'foreign copper': "A total of 262,533 *jin* of foreign copper left Suzhou on the seventh day of the sixth month of Qianlong 46."[49]			G 46/9/19

The Trade in Dried Marine Products from Nagasaki to China during the Edo Period

Western year	Chinese year	Date of entry to Zhapu	Name of vessel	Copper cargo (crates)	Source
1782	Qianlong 47	5/9	Zhouwanshun	1,000	G 47/11/27
	State merchant:	5/10	Weihongsheng	1,000	
	Fan Qingji	5/12	He Tingbao	1,000	
		10/19	Jinyuanbao	1,000	
		10/19	Wanrixin	1,000	
		10/25	Fanchangji 范常吉	1,000	
1783	Qianlong 48	4/12	Linyongshun (Fan)	1,000	G 48/12/5
	State merchants: Fan Qingji Wang Shirong 王世榮	11/1	Wanrixin (Wang)	1,000	

'Z' refers to the *Zhupi zouzhe* 硃批奏摺 in the Chinese Number One Historical Archives 中国第一歷史檔案館, while 'G' refers to the *Gongzhongdang Qianlongchao zouzhe* in the Taiwan Palace Museum. Arabic numerals denote the dates of memorials, and are given in the old calendar.
[*denotes ships that returned together with the preceding ship]

4 The Export of Marine Products to China in 1803 and 1804

According to the *Nagasaki kaisho gosatsumono* 長崎會所五冊物 [Fivevolume Record of the Nagasaki Trade Offfice],[50] which details the accounts of the Nagasaki clearing house for foreign trade accounts following the revised trade laws of 1791, "those responsible for selling copper to the Chinese ships sold a predetermined amount equivalent to 110,000 *monme* of silver."[51] Each ship "took on one hundred thousand *kin* of copper"[52] carried in one thousand boxes of one hundred *kin* each.[53]

The *Nagasaki kaisho gosatsumono* also mentions dried goods. In this

---

49 *Gongzhongdang Qianlongchao zouzhe*, 48: 837.
50 *Nagasaki kaisho gosatsumono*, 1-243.
51 Ibid., 39.
52 Ibid., 40.
53 唐人渡方之節ハ、壹箱宛正味百斤ニ掛改. [The regulations were revised so that each crate of the Chinese merchants contains 100 *kin*.] Ibid., 39. Also see Matsuura, "Shindai kanshō saiben yōdō benkai senseki", 38-45.

143

Part 2: Sino-Japanese Interaction based on Chinese Junks in the Edo period

Table 15   Value in silver of return cargoes for Chinese Junks, 1803-1804 (in kanme)[54]

Year	Ship No./Origin	Ship Name	Trader	Copper
1803	Seventh Nanjing*	Yongxing 永興	Twelve Families	115,000
1803	Eighth Ningbo*	Rixin 日新	Wang	115,000
1803	Tenth Nanjing*	Jieji 皆吉	Twelve Families	115,000
1803	First Nanjing	Jinquansheng 金全勝	Wang	115,000
1803	Second Nanjing	Yongtai 永泰	Twelve Families	115,000
1803	Fourth Ningbo	Yuansheng 源盛	Wang	115,000
1803	Third Ningbo	Yongbao 永寶	Twelve Families	115,000
1803	Fifth Ningbo	Yuanbao 源寶	Wang	115,000
1803	Seventh Nanjing	Dawan'an 大萬安	Wang	115,000
1803	Sixth Nanjing	Jieji	Twelve Families	115,000
1804	Eighth Ningbo*	Yongxiang 永祥	Twelve Families	115,000
1804	Ninth Ningbo*	Jinquansheng	Wang	115,000
1804	Tenth Nanjing*		Twelve Families	115,000
1804	Third Nanjing	Desheng 得勝	Wang	115,000
1804	Unnumbered*	Yuansheng	Wang	115,000
1804	First Ningbo	Yongtai	Twelve Families	115,000
1804	Second Ningbo	Dawan'an	Wang	115,000
1804	Fourth Ningbo	Rixin	Wang	115,000
1804	Seventh Nanjing	Yongxing		115,000
1804	Unnumbered	Yongbao	Twelve Families	115,000
	Totals			2,300,000
	Averages			115,000

[* indicates ships that left for Nagasaki the previous year; hence their numbers are not aligned with the year they returned to China]

period, when only ten ships were allowed to trade at Nagasaki every year, each Chinese vessel exported roughly 95,400 *monme* worth of dried goods, meaning the total volume reached 954,000 *monme* per year. Dried goods constituted dried sea cucumber, dried abalone and shark fin.[55]

The *Nagasaki kaisho gosatsumono* categorized all goods aside from copper and dried goods as miscellany (*shoshiki* 諸色). Such miscellany included not only kelp, which comprised a large chunk of the return cargoes of Chinese vessels, but also dried seaweed products such as *tengusa* seaweed, and other

---

54   This data was originally recorded in units of *kanme*, rather than the more common *monme*. 1 *kanme* is equal to 1,000 *monme*.
55   *Nagasaki kaisho gosatsumono*, 40.

Dried goods	Misc	Kelp	Total Cargo Value	Source (leaf no.)
91,177	60,785		266,962	8
89,455	59,537		264,091	18
101,760	67,840		284,600	27
98,048	65,365		278,413	38
100,370	66,913		282,283	48
100,560	67,040		282,600	58
86,654	57,770		259,424	87-88
90,247	60,164		265,411	100-01
93,178	62,119		270,297	113
134,160	89,440		338,600	124-25
107,414	71,609		294,023	23
131,284	87,523		333,807	35
124,542	83,028		322,570	45
98,419	65,613		279,032	55
58,218	58,218	25,300	256,736	65
90,526	60,350		265,876	89
89,381	59,587		263,968	99
97,690	65,126		277,816	109
98,024	65,350		278,374	137
59,350	59,350	25,300	259,000	141
1,940,457	1,332,727		5,623,883	
97,023	66,636		281,194	

dried marine products such as dried cuttlefish, dried shrimp and scallops.[56]

56　昆布・鰑・茯苓・鶏冠草・所天草・鰹節・千切レ砂食煎海鼠・千切レ蟲入干鮑・藤海鼠・刻昆布・干海老・五倍子・椎茸・干瀬貝・寒天・樟脳・いたら貝・獺皮・御種人参・會津・雲州和人参・銅器物・流金道具・蒔繪小間物・呉服、其外樽物等を諸色と唱、唐人共買渡申候、則壹船當時買渡平均六拾三貫六百目程之積リ、壹ケ年拾艘六百三拾六貫目程、出帆之時々荷造仕、唐人相好候品々買渡候儀ニ御座候。 [Kelp, cuttlefish, *fu ling* mushrooms, cockscomb algae, *tengusa* seaweed, dried bonito flakes, diced dried sea cucumber, diced dried abalone speckled with holes 千切レ蟲入干鮑, black sea cucumber, chopped kelp 刻昆布, dried shrimp, sumac gallnuts, *shiitake* mushrooms, dried sea snail 干瀬貝, seaweed-based gelatin, camphor, scallops, otter pelts, Korean ginseng 御種人参, Japanese ginseng from Aizu and Izumo, copperware, gold-leaf lacquer ware 流金道具, lacquer goods, kimono fabrics, and all other barreled goods are

The *Kyōwa sannen idoshichū shuppan hikiawasechō* 享和三年亥年中出帆引合帳,[57] and the *Bunka gannen nedoshichū shuppan hikiawasechō* 文化元子年中出帆引合帳,[58] both in the collection of the Nagasaki Museum of History and Culture, contain records and calculations of the value of return cargoes of Chinese ships arriving in Nagasaki in 1802, as well as records of the expenditures of their crews while in Nagasaki. The first record bears the title "The Twelve Families. Index of the Original Values in Silver of the Seventh Nanjing Ship, Year of the Dog: the *Yongxing* 十二家戌七番南京船元代銀引目録 永興." The 'Twelve Families' were a group of Chinese traders, a private [i.e. not court-afffiliated] group of merchants. The name Wang 王, which will appear below, denotes a state merchant designated by the Qing court.[59] *Yongxing* was the name of a Chinese vessel.[60] This record shows that, out of a total trade value of 266,962 *monme* of the *Yongxing*, 115,000 *monme* were spent on copper, slightly more than 91,177 *monme* on dried goods, and slightly more than 60,784 *monme* on miscellaneous items. Proportionally copper represents 43 percent, dried goods 34 percent and miscellaneous items 23 percent.[61]

If we compare these figures to the twenty ships of 1803 and 1804 (ten per year), looking at the average total cargo values and proportions, we see little change: copper averaged 115,000 *monme*, bagged goods just over 97,000 *kin*, and miscellany slightly more than 66,000 *kin*. Proportionally speaking copper was on average 41 percent, bagged goods 35 percent and miscellany 24 percent of the total cargo. We may imagine that the percentages by value for return cargoes throughout this period are similar.

---

called miscellany. These goods were purchased by the Chinese, and it was stipulated that one ship would purchase an average of 63,600 *monme* of goods. Thus the ten ships per year carried a total of 636,000 *monme*. At the time of the ships' departure, both wholesalers and Chinese merchants were happily engaged in the trade of goods.] Ibid., 41.

57 *Kyōwa sannen idoshichū shuppan hikiawasechō*.
58 *Bunka gannen nedoshichū shuppan hikiawasechō*.
59 Matsuura, *Shindai kaigai bōeki shi no kenkyū*, 144-46.
60 Ibid., 289.
61 The value of the seventh ship's cargo and a breakdown of its contents—copper, dried goods and miscellany—is as follows:
A total of 266,962.3587 *monme* was used to purchase goods:
– 115,000 *monme* for 100,000 *kin* of copper (100 *kin* cost 115 *monme*)
– 151,962.3587 *monme*
  ○ 91,177.4152 *monme* of dried goods
  ○ 60,784.9435 *monme* of miscellany
See *Kyōwa sannen idoshichū shuppan hikiawasechō*, leaf 8.

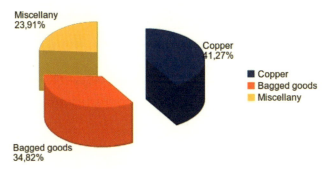

Figure 23   *Value in silver of return cargoes for Chinese Junks, 1803-1804 (in* monme*).*

5   Export of Marine Products to China in the Bakumatsu Period

The records of the Dutch Trading House in Nagasaki include the amounts of return cargo on Chinese ships in 1833.[62] These data appear in the following table.

Figure 6.10 represents the average return cargoes of copper, sea cucumber, dried abalone, kelp and gelatin from the fifth through ninth ship. It immediately becomes clear that the quantity of kelp was quadruple that of copper, indicating that from the 1830s onward kelp exports increased dramatically.

6   Cargo Sent to Shanghai on the Offficial Bakufu Ship *Senzai-maru* 千歳丸, 1862

After dismantling its policy of national seclusion in the 1850s, the Tokugawa *bakufu* sent its first offficial ship overseas. The *bakufu* relied on the history of the return cargoes of Chinese vessels calling at Nagasaki to determine what cargo to take on board this ship, the *Senzai-maru*.[63] The chosen goods are shown in the following table.

---

62   Nagazumi *Tōsen yushutsunyūhin sūryō ichiran 1637-1833nen*, 328.
63   Kawashima, "Saisho ni kokoromita Shanhai bōeki," 115-66.

Table 16 *Principle cargo of Chinese ships returning in 1833 (in kin)*[64]

Ship number	Date of arrival	Date of return	Copper	Sea cucumber	Dried abalone	Kelp	Seaweed gelatin (寒天 *kanten*)
5	1832 12/1	1833 4/6	105,000	20,000	25,000	490,000	12,000
6	12/4	4/6	105,000	21,000	25,000	394,000	12,000
7	12/4	4/6	105,000	21,000	25,000	442,000	12,000
8	12/6	4/6	105,000	21,000	25,000	418,000	12,000
9	1833 1/18	4/6	105,000	21,000	25,000	406,000	12,000
Average			105,000	20,800	25,000	430,000	12,000

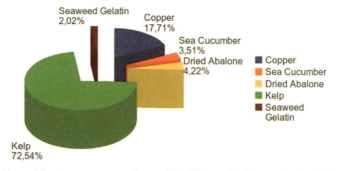

Figure 24 *Average cargo volume of five Chinese Junks returning in 1833.*

The above items were those carried in large quantities; an additional sixty or so goods were transported in lesser amounts. Although the cargoes of earlier Chinese junks returning from Nagasaki were ostensibly used as a reference, no copper was included in the *bakufu* ship's cargo. A new product replaced it: coal.

As Japan's domestic copper production declined over the course of the Edo period, so too did copper exports. By the time the Tokugawa *bakufu* dispatched the *Senzaimaru*, the system of copper exports was already collapsing. Anxious to dispatch the *Senzai-maru* to Shanghai, the *bakufu* selected coal from the Takashima Mine near Nagasaki to serve as the ship's ballast. In the last years of Tokugawa rule, Saga Domain and the Scottish merchant Thomas Blake Glover (1838-1911) excavated the Takashima Mine. Glover had travelled to Shanghai in

---

64 64 Dates of arrival and return are taken from the *Tōsen shinkō kaitōroku Shimabara bon Tōjin fūsetsu gaki wappu tome*, 208-9; figures for cargo are taken from Nagazumi, *Tōsen yushutsunyūhin sūryō ichiran* 1637-1833 *nen*, 328.

The Trade in Dried Marine Products from Nagasaki to China during the Edo Period

Table 17   *Cargo on the ship Senzaimaru in 1862*

Goods from Nagasaki clearing house for foreign trade accounts	
Sea cucumber	24,000 *kin*
Dried abalone	36,000 *kin*
Shark fin	1,800 *kin*
Tengusa seaweed	12,000 *kin*
Cockscomb seaweed	3,000 *kin*
Mitsuishi-kelp 三ツ石昆布[65]	3,600 *kin*
Goods from Nagasaki Market	
First grade dried cuttlefish	3,000 *kin*
Second grade dried cuttlefish	2,550 *kin*
Windmill palm leaf sheathes	5,687 *kin*
Japanese ginseng from Aizu	2,500 *kin*
Japanese ginseng from Izumo	2,500 *kin*
Coal[66]	250,000 *kin*
Goods from individual merchants	
Gelatin from *tengusa* seaweed	1,800 *kin*
Mitsuishi kelp[67]	26,424 *kin*

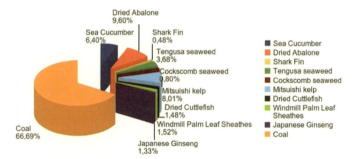

Figure 25   *Cargo on the ship Senza-imaru in 1862.*

1859, where he joined Jardine Matheson Holdings Ltd. (known as *Yihe yanghang* 怡和洋行 in Chinese). In 1859/9, he arrived in Nagasaki, which the *bakufu* had just opened as a treaty port. Glover became Jardine Matheson's representative in

---

65   Ibid., 124-25.
66   Ibid., 133-34, 138-39.
67   Ibid., 139.

Nagasaki, where he also started his own trading company, thus entering the trade industry. He probably helped mediate an increase in shipping at Shanghai: the coal needed to fuel those ships was not available near Shanghai, giving Glover an opportunity to make a profit by shipping coal from Japan. Thereafter foreign ships carried the coal trade between Nagasaki and Shanghai.

7 Sources of Japanese Marine Products

Records of the original production areas of the various dried marine products discussed above appear in the "Tawaramono shoshiki detokoro 俵物諸色出所 [Origins of Miscellaneous and Dried Goods]," contained in the *Kaban kōeki meisaiki* 華蠻交易明細記, which details the various places in Japan whence goods were imported to Nagasaki.[68] These accounts date from the mid-18th century to the early 19th century, and allow us to consider the production areas of each marine product in the mid to late Edo period.[69] Dried sea cucumber was produced in southern Hokkaido and wide areas of coastal Honshū. In particular, over fifty percent of sea cucumber was produced in present-day Hokkaido, Aomori, Kōchi, Yamaguchi and Ishikawa prefectures. Nearly 80 percent of dried abalone came from the Hirado, Gotō and Tsushima regions of present-day Nagasaki Prefecture. During the Edo period, coastal shipping transported these goods to Nagasaki, whence they were exported to China. The only origin of kelp recorded in the *Kaban kōeki meisaiki* is Matsumae, with "roughly 790,000 *kin*" produced,[70] suggesting that most kelp was produced in what is today southern Hokkaidō before being imported to Nagasaki via Shimonoseki on cargo ships plying the Sea of Japan coast.

---

68 *Kaban kōeki meisaiki*, 245-425.
69 Ogawa Kuniharu 小川国治 demonstrates how the Edo *bakufu* and individual domains controlled the production of dried goods through the Edo period in his *Edo bakufu yushutsu kaisanbutsu no kenkyū—tawaramono no seisan to shūka kikō* [*Studies on Marine Products Exported by the Edo Bakufu: Structures of Production and Collection of Dried Goods*]. For an account that draws upon Dutch documents to explain the state of marine products sent from Japan to China, see Arai, *Kinsei kaisanbutsu bōeki shi no kenkyū—Chūgokumuke yushutsu bōeki to kaisanbutsu*. As for the state of exports to China, Ogawa and Arai both refer to Matsuura, "Nisshin bōeki ni yoru tawaramono no Chūgoku ryūnyū ni tsuite": Ogawa for content concerning the Meiji period onward, and Arai for information regarding the Edo period.
70 *Kaban kōeki meisaiki*, 389.

Table 18 *Geographical origins of sea cucumber (Units:* kin*)*[71]

Region	Place	Quantity
Present-day Hokkaidō region	Matsumae 松前	62,100
Present-day Tōhoku region	Tsugaru 津軽	33,800
	Nanbu 南部	3,070
	Sendai 仙台	2,800
Present-day Kantō region	Awa 安房	3,100
	Kazusa 上総	1,060
	Musashi 武蔵	4,800
	Sōshū 相州	8,500
Present-day Chubu region	Owari 尾張	1,200
	Mikawa 三河	11,000
Present-day Hokuriku region	Noto 能登	18,800
	Echizen 越前	1,100
	Etchū 越中	450
Present-day Kinki region	Ise 伊勢	11,000
	Shima 志摩	7,100
	Harima 播磨	2,000
	Awaji 淡路	2,000
	Tango 丹後	1,330
	Kishū 紀州	850
Present-day Shikoku region	Awa 阿波	2,500
	Sanuki 讃岐	2,320
Present-day Chūgoku region	Aki 安芸	28,000
	Suō 周防	23,000
	Bizen 備前	15,000
	Nagato 長門	11,250
	Izumo 出雲	2,800
	Bitchū 備中	700
	Iwami 石見	500
Present-day Kyūshū region	Ōmura 大村	14,120
	Hirado 平戸	12,100
	Tsushima 対馬	8,580
	Karatsu 唐津	6,300
	Amakusa 天草	5,700
	Iki 壱岐	3,000
	Higo 肥後	2,400
	Satsuma 薩摩	1,200
	Chikuzen 筑前	320
	Bungo 豊後	270

71 Ibid., 388-89.

Part 2: Sino-Japanese Interaction based on Chinese Junks in the Edo period

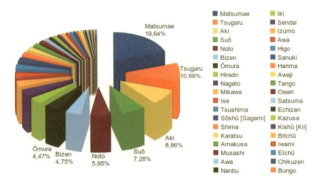

Figure 26 *Geographical origins of sea cucumber to Nagasaki in the early 19th century.*

Table 19 *Geographical origins of dried abalone (Units: kin)*[72]

Region	Place	Quantity
Present-day Hokkaidō region	Matsumae	210
Present-day Tōhoku & Hokuriku regions	Nanbu	9,100
	Sado 佐渡	2,230
Present-day Chūgoku region	Nagato	5,950
Present-day Kyūshū region	Chikuzen	3,050
	Bungo	860
	Amakusa	4,050
	Tsushima	20,770
	Iki	3,000
	Hirado	55,300
	Gotō 五島	28,450

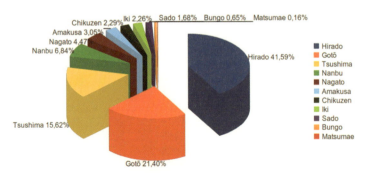

Figure 27 *Geographical origins of dried abalone.*

---

72 Ibid., 389.

152

8 Japanese Dried Marine Products and Chinese Markets

While we know that goods were exported from Nagasaki to Chinese markets by Chinese merchant ships, what might the demand have been for Japanese goods in China? Though I have mentioned this point before, I would like to discuss it briefly here.[73]

Dried sea cucumber, made by extracting, boiling and drying the intestinal tract of sea cucumbers, was called "ocean ginseng" in Chinese, suggesting that it was as highly valued as ginseng (*ninjin* 人参) for its beneficial efffects. Dried abalone had been regarded as an expensive gift since the Ming Dynasty. Dried shark fin was also widely regarded as a food item during the Ming Dynasty. Although poet and epicure Yuan Mei's 袁枚 *Suiyuanshidan* 随園食單 (printed in 1792) did not include seafood amongst its list of foods highly regarded since ancient times, it did contain a "sea food menu" that listed items that "now are popular," that is, highly regarded by Yuan's contemporaries. That list included items such as swallow's nest (*yanwo* 燕窩), sea cucumber, shark fin and dried abalone. These items were certainly dried marine products exported from Japan to China by Chinese merchant ships.[74]

While it is diffficult to concretely show the reception of these goods in Qing period Chinese markets, the situation at the end of the dynasty can easily be seen in Meiji period Japanese consular reports such as the "Status of Marine Goods in Tianjin Market, China" (Shinkoku Tenshin shijō kaisanbutsu keikyō 清國天津市場海産物景況), a report from the Japanese imperial consulate in Tianjin dated 1886/8/28.[75]

According to this report, "eight or nine out of ten marine goods [imported to Tianjin] are produced in Japan. Although Korean sea cucumber and Taiwanese shark fin try to compete with Japanese products, at this time they generally are shut out of the market by Japanese products." Thus we see how Japanese dried sea cucumber overwhelmed that produced in Korea, and likewise Japanese shark fin vastly outnumbered that produced in Taiwan. In fact, most dried marine products originated in Japan.[76]

---

73 See Matsuura, *Shindai kaigai bōekishi no kenkyū*, 388-97.
74 Ibid., 398.
75 "Shinkoku Tenshin shijō kaisanbutsu keikyō," 46-49.
76 海産物八十中八九ハ本邦産ニシテ、就中朝鮮産煎海鼠、臺灣産鱶鰭ノ如キ従前ハ本邦産ニ對シ競争セシモ、目下殆ント消滅ノ色ヲ現ハセリ」とあるように、日本産の干し海鼠が朝鮮産を圧倒し同様に日本産の鱶鰭も台湾産の鱶鰭を凌駕していた。さらに昆布に関しては「日本ヨリノ輸入ト掲ケタルハ昆布一項ノミニシテ、其他ノ海産物ニ

The same report describes the status of consumption of various marine products in Chinese markets (see table 20). Of the dried marine products exported from Japan in 1886, sea cucumber was highly regarded for its beautiful shape. Kelp became a daily comestible because of its supposed medicinal value, and it became popular even in Shanxi and Henan provinces. Shark fin with thick flesh was particularly well received. *Kanten* agar became popular in the Chinese interior, and *kanten* imported to Tianjin was often transported to Beijing, Shanxi, Shandong and Henan. Dried cuttlefish from Japan was popular, and that imported to Tianjin was transported to Bejing and Shanxi Province. A considerable amount of dried abalone came from Taiwan, but the thick flesh and high-quality drying of the Japanese product meant that Japanese abalone found its way to Beijing, Henan and Shandong provinces. Although domestic Chinese varieties of seaweed and *tosaka* 鶏冠 seaweed were also brought to market in Tianjin, Japanese versions were regarded more highly and, like the above dried marine products, were shipped to Henan and other provinces. In particular, *tosaka* seaweed was transported even to coastal Shandong.[77]

Although these accounts date from the Meiji period, we may imagine that similar tastes drove the consumption of goods exported during the Edo period.

至リテハ支那内地産及外國産ノ輸入若干トノミ記載アリテ、特ニ本邦ヨリノ輸入年額ヲ記載セサルヲ以テ、本邦ヨリハ絶テ輸入ナキニ似タレトモ實際市上ニ陳列賣買スル海産物ハ多ク本邦産ノモノニシテ支那商人モ亦日本産ト稱呼スルヲ見レハ、特ニ海関報告中ニ外國産ト記載スルモノハ【其中多少魯國産ト南洋産アルニモセヨ】概シテ本邦産ニ係ルモノトスルモ、蓋シ大過ナカルベシ。 on[Kelp is the only product listed as an import from Japan, and only a few other marine products are recorded as domestic or foreign import, with none listed as coming from Japan; it may seem that there were absolutely no imports from Japan. Yet, in actual fact the large proportion of marine products laid out and traded on the market are produced in Japan, and the Chinese merchants even called them products of Japan. Accordingly, we may particularly imagine that those goods recorded as 'foreign' in the marine goods reports (notwithstanding those few listed as Russian or from the southern Chinese coastal islands) are largely Japanese; this would certainly not be a misstatement.] ibid., 46-49.
77   Ibid., 47-49.

The Trade in Dried Marine Products from Nagasaki to China during the Edo Period

Table 20 *Status of consumption of various marine products in Chinese markets*[78]

Sea cucumber	Dried sea cucumber imported from Japan is predominantly of two varieties, number nine and number ten. Number ten is further divided into large and small. They are consumed in the greatest amount. Number nine is large, and perhaps because of its high price little is consumed. Those that have lots of spines and expand when boiled are highly regarded. At present, for every one hundred *kin* traded, number ten (large) fetches thirty-five *ryō*; number ten (small), twenty-six *ryō*; and number nine, forty-eight *ryō*. The so-called 'Koryŏ sea cucumber' (高麗參, Chinese *gongbieda* 工別大) is produced in Korea, and at present, one hundred *kin* of the large variety is worth twenty-three *ryō*, while the small is worth fifteen *ryō*. Sea cucumbers produced in Japan are highly regarded for their pleasing shape, while those from Korea are widely consumed for their low price and good flavour. The yearly value of these foreign imports is 55,430 *ryō* (The 1885 Maritime Customs Report, produced by Chinese offficials, records the same value).
Kelp (Chinese *haidai* 海岱)	A deep green colour and complete freshness are valued. If [the kelp] is even slightly aged, consumption falls drastically. Around August and September exports to the Shanxi and Henan regions are greatest. Moreover, the locals of those regions believe kelp to help reduce phlegm, and not a few incorporate [kelp] into their daily diet. Before kelp from Japan began to be imported, kelp produced in the Guangdong region was imported. Since Japanese kelp began to be imported, that from Guangdong has been almost completely shut out of the market, perhaps because of the low price and good taste [of the Japanese product]. At present, very little Guangdong kelp is imported. At present, the value of kelp imports for every 100 *kin* is 2 *ryō* 4 *sen* 錢. The yearly value of imports is 121,301 *ryō*. Red kelp comprises 1,993 *ryō*.
Shredded kelp (Chinese *daisi* 岱絲)	Although there are two types of shredded kelp, rough and fine, the fine is best suited to Chinese tastes. At present, 100 *kin* is worth 1 *ryō* 8 *sen*, for a yearly value of 3,049 *ryō*.
Dried scallops (伊多刺貝; Chinese *ganbei* 乾貝)	Of all the marine products produced in Japan, the most highly regarded are dried scallops, in particular for their round shape and large size. Demand for this product generally comes from the Shandong and Shanxi regions. There are truthfully very few dried scallops produced in China, and no [Chineseproduced scallops] are imported here. When dried scallops were first imported, they were highly regarded and valued, at five hundred *ryō* per one hundred *kin*; however, more recently the prices have fallen considerably, perhaps due to oversupply. Current prices are sixteen *ryō* per one hundred *kin*.
Shark fn	Consumption of both black and white varieties is greatest. Regardless of the variety, large fins with thick flesh are highly sought after. However, the Chinese are displeased when including useless flesh at the base of the fin needlessly increases the product's weight.

78 Ibid., 47-49.

155

Part 2: Sino-Japanese Interaction based on Chinese Junks in the Edo period

	Taiwanese shark fin has an excellent taste, and expands after boiling to become like snow. (It costs 110 *ryō* per 100 *kin*.) Despite high regard for it, its high cost keeps demand low. At present, 60 *ryō* of white shark fin to 40 *ryō* of black shark fin are sold (per 100 *kin* of shark fin, counted in *fuku* [副]; one *fuku* refers to the pair of fins behind the gills [頬]. The dorsal fin is not counted). There is a variety called *duichi* 堆翅, imported from the south, which is dried out after being cut. Consumption of this variety is very low, with no steady quantity being traded. The yearly value of foreign import runs to 26,341 *ryō* of white shark fin and 22,630 *ryō* of black shark fin; the value of imports from other Chinese ports runs to 6,464 *ryō* of white shark fin and, 2,946 *ryō* of black shark fin.
Kanten (寒天 agar) (Chinese *yangfen* 洋粉)	All the *kanten* imported from Japan is shredded *kanten* 絲寒天. Large, square items arrived as samples, but prove diffficult to sell. For the most part consumption is very low in Tianjin, and the bulk is exported to the Beijing, Shanxi, Shandong and Henan regions. There are three types of *kanten*: top grade 頭番, second grade 二番, and third grade 三番. White colour is also valued. Of the three, top quality agar is pure white, and thus consumed in greatest quantity. At present, top quality agar fetches 17 *ryō* 5 *sen* per 100 *kin*, and the yearly value of foreign imports is 19,515 *ryō*.
Dried cuttlefish (Chinese *youyu* 魷魚)	Large size and thick flesh are valued. In previous years, cuttlefish from Taiwan were in high demand compared to those from Japan, due to their large size (valued at 13 *ryō* per 100 *kin*). Yet they have been overwhelmed by Japanese imports, and recently only Japanese products are traded. A large proportion is exported to Beijing and Shanxi. At present, 100 *kin* fetches 8 *ryō*, and the yearly value of foreign imports is 2,173 *ryō*.
Abalone (Chinese *baoyu* 鮑魚)	Amongst the imports from Japan, there are three varieties: large, medium and small, of which the medium size sells in greatest quantity. A dried exterior, thick flesh and yellow-black colour are highly valued. A large quantity is exported to the Beijing, Shanxi and Henan regions. In previous years Taiwanese goods were imported, but were overwhelmed by Japanese products, and thus did not sell well. At present, one hundred *kin* fetches twentythree *ryō*.
Seaweed (Chinese *zicai* 紫菜)	A large size with red bands, and unadulterated by sand, is highly prized. Most is exported to Beijing and Henan, with little consumed here [in Tianjin]. Because [seaweed] is transported from Ningbo, some does arrive here by ship. Nevertheless, it is only a small amount, which does not play a significant role in the market. At present, 100 *kin* garners 20 *ryō*, with a yearly value of 20,434 *ryō*.
Tosaka 鶏冠 seaweed	[Seaweed] with a red band and unadulterated with sand is highly regarded. Much is exported to Henan and Shandong provinces. At present, every one hundred *kin* sold at market receives between three and five *ryō*. The so-called '*lincai* 鄰菜', with its round shape, reminds one of *hongcai*. Consumption is high of products from Guangdong and Xiamen. Yet it does not approach that of our *tosaka* seaweed. At present, one hundred *kin* barely fetches between three and six *ryō*.

9 Conclusion

Historical export records reveal the changes in export volumes of marine products, particularly sea cucumber, dried abalone and shark fin, from Nagasaki to China across the Edo period. The *Tōsen*, as Chinese merchant ships were called in Japan, often had two or three enormous masts to carry out their seafaring trade, and required stabilizing ballast for long-distance transport. For ships travelling to Nagasaki from Qing China, large quantities of sugar served as ballast.[79] In addition, the Chinese ships transported silk fabrics, books, and Chinese medicine. Chinese vessels returned home with cargoes of Japanese copper, eagerly sought after by the Qing government as the principal ingredient with which to mint coins. Known as "foreign copper" in China, Japanese copper constituted a significant and important proportion of China's copper supply sources during the early Edo period. Yet as time passed and Japanese copper production steadily declined, the amount of copper in the return cargoes of Chinese ships leaving Nagasaki for China decreased, until by the mid and late-Edo periods the Japanese authorities limited copper exports to one hundred thousand *kin* per ship.

In contrast, increasing demand in China for dried marine products made them a significant new export. Dried sea cucumber, dried abalone and shark fin bear particular attention as the three principle dried goods, representing a significant proportion of exports from the mid- to late Edo period. Above all the three dried goods of dried sea cucumber, dried abalone and shark fin were essential ingredients for the seafood cuisine that had grown popular from the mid-Qing period onwards. In addition, kelp and dried cuttlefish, as well as various sea plants such as *tengusa* seaweed, played an important role.[80] From the perspective of the Chinese junk trade, we may say that the decline in copper exports was balanced out by an increase in dried marine products.

---

79   Matsuura, "Edo jidai Tōsen ni yoru satō yu'nyū to kokunai shōhi no tenkai," 335-59.
80   Matsuura, "Nisshin bōeki ni yoru tawaramono no Chūgoku ryūnyū ni tsuite," 19-38, and Matsuura, *Shindai kaigai bōeki shi no kenkyū*, 382-402.

CHAPTER 9

The Import of Chinese Sugar in the Nagasaki Junk Trade and Its Impact

1 Introduction

An exemplary sweetener consumed around the globe, sugar seasons daily cooking and sweetens drinks in many regions. Yet it was not until production reached surplus levels around the world after the First World War that sugar entered the daily lives of people around the world.[1]

During the Edo period Chinese junks, called *Tōsen* 唐船, carried large amounts of Chinese sugar to Japan every year. A large part of this sugar was produced in the coastal regions of eastern Guangdong 廣東 and southern Fujian 福建 provinces, and in Taiwan. In the early Edo period ships transported sugar directly from these production areas to Japan; in the mid- and late Edo periods, coastal merchant ships transported sugar from these areas first to Zhapu 乍浦 in Zhejiang Province 浙江省, where it was transferred onto junks bound for Nagasaki. Much of the sugar shipped to Nagasaki was transported onwards to Osaka and then to the rest of Japan.

In the early 18th century, sugar cane harvesting began in Japan. The eighth Tokugawa shogun, Yoshimune (吉宗, r. 1716-1745), famously created the impetus to spread techniques for harvesting sugar cane, the basic ingredient of sugar. As a result, sugar consumption expanded during the Kyōhō years.[2] According to the record of Yoshimune's activities, the *Yūtokuin gojikki furoku* 有徳院御實記附錄 (volume 17), Yoshimune explored ways to reduce Japan's dependence on imports from China for the bulk of domestically consumed

---

* Paper translated by Michael Thornton.
1 Sekino, *Sekai tōgyō bunka shi*, 3.
2 Kobata, "Satō no shiteki kenkyū ni tsuite," 217. This paper is a revised version of an essay with the same title in *Taiwan jihō* 臺灣時報 186 and 187 (1935/5, 6). It is one of the most important fruits of historical research on the import and spread of sugar in Japan.

sugar.³ Yoshimune considered possibilities for domestic sugar production, particularly methods for harvesting sugar cane. In 1727 (Kyōhō 12), he approached the head of Shimazu domain 島津藩, Matsudaira Tsugutoyo 松平繼豊 (1701-1760) to study harvesting techniques in Satsuma. Furthermore, he transplanted sugar cane to Nagasaki and Suruga 駿河. He also studied Chinese texts on sugar cane harvesting technologies, ordering the magistrate in charge of imported books, Fukami Arichika 深見有鄰 (1691-1773), to conduct a survey of relevant Chinese literature. Yoshimune also sought to learn about sugar production from merchants who arrived in Nagasaki. In other words, records show that Yoshimune used three methods to study sugar cane harvesting: observations of the cane harvest in Ryūkyū and Satsuma; study of Chinese texts; and conversations with Chinese merchants in Nagasaki. In this way, not only did overall sugar production increase, but the quality of sugar also improved.

In this essay I shall discuss the import of sugar from China during the Edo period, and also the increase in sugar consumption in Japan. Furthermore, I will investigate the reception of Chinese culture through the lens of Chinese sugar imports during the Edo period, and in turn the Japanese transformation of that culture.

2 Chinese Sugar Imports in the Records of the Dutch Trading House at Nagasaki

Chinese records do not detail the quantity of sugar imported to Nagasaki, so I turn to the records kept by the Chinese merchants' Dutch competitors.⁴ Dutch traders were keenly aware of the Chinese ships entering Nagasaki, and kept meticulous daily records of the ships and their cargo capacity. Here I look at only those records that deal with sugar.

An entry dated 1641/7/5 in the *Nederlandsche Oost-Indische Compagnie, Comptoir Nangasackij* (長崎オランダ商館の日記 [Diary of the Dutch trading house at Nagasaki], henceforth *Diary*) states that merchant Zheng Zhilong 鄭芝龍 (1604-1661) sent twelve ships laden with sugar to Nagasaki in 1641.⁵

---

3 *Tokugawa jikki* 9, 316.
4 Details of sugar imported by Chinese and Dutch ships during the Edo period may be found in Iwao, "Edo jidai no satō bōeki ni tsuite," 1-33. Iwao exhaustively explores the Dutch records.
5 "According to one merchant, this year 'the offficial' is sending twelve ships of sugar here [Nagasaki]. The first entered the port around noon. Its cargo . . . included 19,800

On 1641/7/10, an entry records that "early this morning, one small junk arrived in port from Fuzhou 福州. Its cargo contained 16,000 *kin* of muscovado (*kurozatō* 黒砂糖, a type of unrefined brown sugar) . . . and 400 *kin* of white sugar (*shirozatō* 白砂糖)."[6] The same entry later mentions that "late at night a Chinese vessel arrived from Canton (Guangdong). Its cargo included 11,500 *kin* of white sugar, and 1,000 *kin* of muscovado."[7] On 7/12, "in the afternoon, the offfical's second ship arrived with 270,000 *kin* of white sugar."[8] On 7/13, "in the morning, a junk from Fuzhou arrived, laden with 70,000 *kin* of white sugar."[9] On 7/14, "two of the offfical's junks from the aforementioned location [Fuzhou] entered port, with a cargo of . . . 139,200 *kin* of white sugar, 10,300 *kin* of muscovado, [and] 30,000 *kin* of rock candy (*koorizatō* 氷砂糖)."[10] On 7/22, "in the evening, a Chinese junk from Fuzhou arrived. Its cargo included 4,200 *kin* of white sugar."[11] On 7/23, "shortly after noon, three junks entered port. The cargo of one ship from Guangnan 廣南 was 40,400 *kin* of muscovado."[12] As for the others, "the two ships from Fuzhou carried 77,050 *kin* of white sugar, [and] 8,300 *kin* of muscovado."[13] According to an entry from 7/24, "another of the offfical's junks from Zhangzhou 漳州 arrived. Its cargo included 1,660 *kin* of muscovado."[14] On 7/25, "at noon, four small junks arrived carrying the following goods: 275,700 *kin* of white sugar, 4,800 *kin* of muscovado, and 62,300 *kin* of rock candy."[15] On 7/26, "in the morning and afternoon five junks arrived in port. The three ships from Canton carried 55,000 *kin* of white sugar, and 1,200 *kin* of rock candy."[16] The remaining "two ships from Tonkin carried the following goods,"[17] though the records do not list sugar cargoes. According to an entry for 7/27, "today two junks arrived. One came from Canton, carrying 2,500 *kin* of white sugar,"[18] while "the ship from Quanzhou 泉州 carried 18,500

---

kin of sugar. . . ." Here 'the offfical' refers to Zheng Zhilong. 1 *kin* 斤 is approximately 600 grams". See *Nagasaki Oranda shōkan no nikki* 1, 56.
6   Ibid., 57.
7   Ibid., 58.
8   Ibid., 58.
9   Ibid., 58.
10 Ibid., 58.
11 Ibid., 62.
12 Ibid., 63.
13 Ibid., 64.
14 Ibid., 65.
15 Ibid., 66-67.
16 Ibid., 67.
17 Ibid., 67.
18 Ibid., 68-69.

kin of white sugar."[19] On 7/29, "a large junk arrived from Quanzhou. Its cargo included 10,000 *kin* of white sugar and 18,000 *kin* of muscovado."[20]

Chinese junks were not the only vessels shipping sugar to Nagasaki; the Dutch also carried sugar cargoes. On 7/30, "around nine in the morning, we started unloading the orange trees. By evening the textiles had mostly been finished, leaving only forty barrels of sugar [to be unloaded]."[21]

Records of the type and amount of goods brought to Nagasaki by Chinese vessels lie in the entry for 1641/10/11. On eighty-nine junks from China arrived "sugar: 5,427,500 *kin*; muscovado: 251,700 *kin*; rock candy: 47,300 *kin*."[22] Moreover, "three junks from Guangnan carried 4,000 *kin* of muscovado, [and] 20,000 *kin* of white."[23] Of the above totals, "the offficial wrote a memorandum of goods imported on six large junks," recording "4,000 *kin* of sugar and 35,000 *kin* of muscovado."[24]

The *Diary* entry for 1642/10/16 states that thirty-four merchant ships from China imported 32,800 *kin* of rock candy, 24,800 *kin* of [white] sugar, and 160,100 *kin* of muscovado.[25] According to the entry for 1644/11/15, 54 Chinese merchant vessels carried 489,800 *kin* of white sugar, 849,600 *kin* of muscovado, and 78,150 *kin* of rock candy to Nagasaki.[26] The following year, based on an entry dated 1645/11/25, seventy-six Chinese vessels brought 54,800 *kin* of rock candy, 1,770,000 *kin* of white sugar and 1,553,000 *kin* of muscovado to Nagasaki.[27] According to an entry for 1646/10/27, fifty-four ships transported 779,500 *kin* of white sugar, 145,500 *kin* of rock candy, and 258,100 *kin* of muscovado to Nagasaki over the course of the year.[28] "Between the end of the seventh month and 9/20," according to an entry for 1648/12/8, seventeen Chinese merchant ships transported 12,000 *kin* of white sugar, 91,000 *kin* of muscovado and 83 *kin* of rock candy to Nagasaki's market.[29] On 1649/11/5, the *Diary* records a total of fifty merchant ships carrying 685,800 *kin* of muscovado and 51,450 *kin* of powdered sugar (*konazatō* 粉砂糖);[30] according to an entry for

---

19　Ibid., 69.
20　Ibid., 71.
21　Ibid., 71.
22　Ibid., 108.
23　Ibid., 110.
24　Ibid., 111.
25　Ibid., 194, 197.
26　Ibid., 372, 374-75.
27　*Nagasaki Oranda shōkan no nikki* 2, 62-63.
28　Ibid., 103, 106.
29　Ibid., 224, 226-27.
30　Ibid., 265-66.

Table 21 *Volume of sugar cargo on Chinese Junks serving Nagasaki, 1642-1653 (in* kin*)*

Year	Total ships	Sugar 砂糖	White sugar 白砂糖	Muscovado 黒砂糖	Rock candy 氷砂糖	Total	Average load
1642	34	24,000		160,100	32,800	216,900	6,379.4
1644	54		489,800	849,600	78,150	1,417,550	26,250.9
1645	76		1,770,000	1,553,000	54,800	3,377,800	44,444.7
1646	54		779,500	258,100	145,500	1,183,100	21,909.3
1648	17		12,000	91,000	83	103,083	6,063.7
1649	50		51,450	685,800		737,250	14,745.0
1650	70	790,960			6,150	797,110	11,387.3
1653	54	152,100		584,870	37,250	774,220	14,337.4
Total	409	967,060	3,102,750	4,182,470	354,733	8,607,013	
Average	51.1	6,120.6	12,362.6	12,338.7	988.1		21,044.0

1650/10/25, some seventy ships imported 790,960 *kin* of white sugar and muscovado, as well as 6,150 *kin* of rock candy that year.[31] Between 1652/11/10 and 1653/11/10, fifty-four Chinese merchant ships carried 152,100 *kin* of Chinese sugar, 584,870 *kin* of muscovado, and 37,250 *kin* of rock candy to Nagasaki market, according to an entry from 1653/11/12.[32]

As seen above, Chinese merchants imported large amounts of sugar to Nagasaki every year. I would now like to consider how much each of these ships would have taken on as cargo.

As seen in table 21, between 1642 and 1653 yearly sugar imports on Chinese merchant vessels reached a maximum amount of 3,370,000 *kin* (ca. 2,022 tons), with cargoes in the leanest years still exceeding 700,000 *kin* (ca. 420 tons). The sugar represented by these values was all consumed domestically within Japan.

From the perspective of Chinese merchant ships travelling to Japan, even a lean year saw each ship carry roughly 6,000 *kin* of various types of sugar. Averaging these eight years, each ship carried roughly 12,000 *kin* of white sugar, 12,000 *kin* of muscovado and roughly 1,000 *kin* of rock candy, for a total of approximately 25,000 *kin* of sugar per cargo load. Given that one *kin* approximates 600 g today, each cargo works out to 15 tons. This was clearly the most appropriate ballast weight for Chinese sailing ships. Moreover, this demonstrates that demand for such a quantity of sugar existed in Edo-period Japanese society.

---

31 Ibid., 321-22.
32 *Nagasaki Oranda shōkan no nikki* 3, 248, 250.

3 Japanese Records of Nagasaki Sugar Imports

As described in the sixth volume of *Laoxuean biji* 老學庵筆記 by Sung-era poet Lu You 陸游 (1125-1209), sugar was imported to China by foreign envoys during the reign of the Taizong emperor (太宗, r. 626-649) of the Tang Dynasty. Thereafter sugar spread widely throughout China.[33] By the Edo period, Chinese sugar was regularly imported to Nagasaki on trading ships.

3.1 Japanese Records of the Import of Chinese Sugar

I would now like to investigate how the Japanese records portray the sugar cargoes of Chinese merchant vessels, in contrast to the records of the Dutch discussed above.

In the seventh month of 1686, a cargo ship from Xiamen 廈門 drifted ashore on Tsushima 対馬. Captain Chen Ang 陳昂 recorded a cargo of "4,000 *tan*[34] of white sugar and 2,000 *tan* of rock candy."[35]

We may summarize as follows the records of sugar extracted from the accounts of cargo imported to Nagasaki in 1729. These accounts are listed in the *Getsudō kenbunshū* 月堂見聞集, which recorded the comings-and-goings and hearsay of the Genroku 元禄 (1688-1704) through late Kyōhō periods, focusing on Edo, Kyoto and Osaka but covering the whole country.

Particularly noteworthy is the 67,000 *kin* of sugar transported on the No 17 ship from Tonkin (today Hanoi), which amounts to forty tons.

The cargo of a vessel shipwrecked upon Hachijō-jima 八丈島 on 1753/12/10, owned by Gao Shanhui 高山輝, included sugar. Despite losing a portion of the cargo to rough weather, "5,040 *kan*[36] of rock candy and 8,901 *kan* of white sugar" remained.[37] This ship's cargo was transferred to two Japanese ships, the *Wagōmaru* 和合丸 and *Ōsugimaru* 大杉丸, whose cargo records tell us that the vessel shipwrecked on Hachijōjima carried both white sugar and rock candy.[38]

---

33 *Laoxuean biji*, 80.
34 1 *tan* [擔, 担] = 100 *kin*.
35 *Ka-I hentai*, jō, 643; *Tsūkō ichiran* 5, 325.
36 1 *kan* [貫] is 3.75 kilograms.
37 "Gokaen zuihitsu", 56.
38 "Catalogue of Cargo for the Wagō-maru and Ōsugi–maru"
   – White sugar: 163 *ken* 件 (and 8 *tsutsumi* 包 for food supplies)
   – Rock candy: 132 *ken* (and 1 *tsutsumi* for supplies)

The Import of Chinese Sugar in the Nagasaki Junk Trade and Its Impact

Table 22   *Cargo carried on Junks entering Nagasaki harbor, tenth month*

Ship number	Origin	Date of entry	White sugar (in *kin*)	Muscovado (in *kin*)
8	Nanjing 南京		330	250[39]
9	Ningbo 寧波	10/22	15,000[40]	
10	Ningbo	10/23	18,000[41]	
11	Nanjing		18,000[42]	
15	Ningbo		22,500[43]	
16	Champa 占城		23,200[44]	
17	Tonkin 東京		67,000[45]	

On 1780/4/30, a trading ship owned by Shen Jingzhan 沈敬瞻 drifted ashore near Chikura 千倉, in Awa Province 房州. Combining the 262,500 *kin* of white sugar and 12,500 *kin* of rock candy, we reach a total of 275,000 *kin*—or 165 tons.[46] That a single ship imported this much sugar into Japan is noteworthy.

On 1807/1/7, a trading ship owned by Wang Zongding 王宗鼎 and bound for Nagasaki drifted into Chōshi Bay 銚子浦 in Shimōsa 下総. Its cargo was reported in "A general and detailed account of the cargo of the *Jinyuansheng* 金源盛." Adding together the highest-quality Chinese *sanbon* sugar 三盆 and *sentō*

   Catalogue of Remaining Goods
   – White sugar: 306 *ken*
   – Rock candy: 44 *ken*"
   Ken is an unknown measure, but probably refers to a quantity of goods placed into large sacks; the weight of those goods is also unclear. *Tsutsumi* were smaller bags, and likely contained some fraction of a *ken*. See "Junkairoku," 69-70.
39 *Kinsei fūzoku kenbunshū* 2, 174; *Tsūkō ichiran* 6, 36.
40 *Kinsei fūzoku kenbunshū* 2, 175; *Tsūkō ichiran* 6, 8.
41 *Kinsei fūzoku kenbunshū* 2, 175; *Tsūkō ichiran* 6, 9.
42 *Kinsei fūzoku kenbunshū* 2, 175; *Tsūkō ichiran* 6, 36.
43 *Kinsei fūzoku kenbunshū* 2, 175; *Tsūkō ichiran* 6, 9.
44 *Kinsei fūzoku kenbunshū* 2, 176.
45 Ibid., 176.
46 "A Nanjing trading vessel drifted into the waters of Awa Province. The magistrate at Uraga 浦賀 and shogunal offficials investigated the cargo of the ship, taking an aide from the *Rokujukken yakushu ton'ya* trading house in Edo, and submitted this report.
   Memorandum:
   – White sugar: 262,500 *kin*
   – Rock candy: 50 *oke* (桶, 12,500 *kin*)
   The latter was taken for fuel and burnt."
   See "Zokudankai," 94.

sugar 泉糖 from Quanzhou gives a total of 67,857 *kin*, or more than forty tons.[47]

In 1809 (Bunka 6, Jiaqing 14), the seventh ship of the year carried 18,300 *kin* (200 bags (*tsutsumi* 包)) of rock candy, 32,000 *kin* (265 bags) of *Sanbon*, and 45,550 *kin* (398 bags) of *sentō* sugar. This adds up to a total of 95,850 *kin*, or more than fifty-seven tons of sugar.[48]

In 1826/1, the ship *Detai* 得泰 drifted into Suruga, whence it was towed to Nagasaki and numbered the eighth ship of 1825. Owned by Ningbo merchants Liu Jingyun 劉景筠 and Yang Qitang 楊啓堂, the ship carried a cargo record (*tsūsen kasū* 通船貨数) that listed various types of sugar amongst its "670 items of cargo"[49]:

– white cake:	rock candy, 100 bundles [連 *ren*]
– *chōban* 頂番 sugar:	superior grade white sugar, 300 bags [包]
– *sanbon*:	high-grade sugar, processed as *sanbon*-grade, 650 bags
– *sentō* 泉糖 sugar:	middle grade; "Quan" refers to the place of production Quanzhou 泉州, 500 bags

The ship carried rock candy, *sanbon*, superior grade '*chōban* sugar,' and sugar from Quanzhou. There are no weights given for these amounts, but if we use the conversions from the seventh ship of 1809, we may calculate the values for the seventh ship of 1826: 200 bags of rock candy equaled 18,300 *kin*, meaning one bag equaled 91.5 *kin*; 260 bags of *sanbon* equaled 32,000 *kin*, meaning one bag equaled 123 *kin*; and 398 bags of *sentō* sugar came out to 45,550 *kin*, meaning one bag equaled 114 *kin*.

Thus for the *Detai*, 650 bags of *sanbon* works out to 79,950 *kin*; 500 bags of *sentō* sugar to 57,000 *kin*; if we presume *chōban* sugar weighed 100 *kin* per bag, then we reach a total of 30,000 *kin*; and similarly we may suppose that 100 bundles of rock candy, at roughly 100 *kin* a bag, totaled 10,000 *kin*. This adds up to 176,950 *kin*, or slightly more than 106 tons. This ship's cargo contained more than 100 tons of various types of sugar.

Turning to the Dutch records, an investigation into the quantity of sugar transported to Nagasaki by Chinese ships in the late Edo period (Tenpō 天保

---

47 "An investigation into various goods loaded onto the ship. The catalogue:
 – 250 units of Number One high-grade white sugar [*sanbon* 三盆], weighing 28,224 *kin* [16.9 tons].
 – 350 units of Number Two Quanzhou sugar, altogether weighing 39,633 *kin* [23.8 tons]." See "Bunka teibō Tōsen hyōchakuki", 6.
48 See *Matsuura, Shindai kaigai bōekishi no kenkyū*, 377.
49 Tanaka and Matsuura, *Bunsei kyūnen Enshū hyōchaku Detai sen shiryō*, 28-30.

2-3; 1831-1832) yields the following results:

Table 23 *Amount of sugar imported by Chinese Junks in 1831-1832 (Tenpō 2-3)*[50] *(in kin)*

1831 (Tenpō 2)					
[Ship number]	Rock candy	White sugar	Superior-grade sugar (最上砂糖)	Standardgrade sugar (並砂糖)	Totals
1	36,000	124,700			160,700
2	29,500	112,385			141,885
3	27,696				27,696
5	34,700	197,500			232,200
6	20,000	130,000			150,000
7	20,000	163,000			183,000
8	15,000	134,000			149,000
9	24,200	180,000			204,200
10	25,000	190,000			215,000
1832 (Tenpō 3)					
5	16,000	126,000			142,000
6	11,500		50,000	35,000	96,500
7	10,000		62,000	45,000	117,000
8	40,000		39,100	40,000	119,100
9	11,477		67,500	40,000	118,977
Totals	321,073	1,357,585	218,600	160,000	2,057,258
Average (per ship)	22,933.8	150,842.8	54,650	40,000	156,120.1

Note: The average per ship excludes the third ship of Tenpō 2.

The Chinese merchant ships travelling to Nagasaki in 1831 and 1832 carried 156,000 *kin* of sugar, white sugar and rock candy to Japan, nearly 100 tons.

3.2 The Collection of Chinese Sugar Products and the Structure of Exports to Japan

Now I turn to the question of how these varieties of sugar were collected and transported to Japan. For the Chinese merchant vessels that plied Nagasaki, the port of Zhapu in Zhejiang Province served as the centre of the Japan trade for roughly one hundred years between the mid-eighteenth century and the last

---

50 Nagazumi, *Tōsen yushutsunyūhin suryō ichiran 1637-1833 nen*, 249-52.

167

years of the Tokugawa Shogunate.⁵¹ This relationship between Zhapu and Japan in the Qing era was clearly recorded in the Daoguang-period *Zhapu beizhi* 乍浦備志, volume 14, "Qianming wobian 前明倭變," edited by Zou Jing 鄒璟. According to this record, Japanese copper was essential for China's domestic minting. In order to purchase this copper, state merchants (*guanshang* 官商) were established at Zhapu, from where they headed eastwards for Japan.⁵² Furthermore, the same document records details of the trade structure: a state and civil division of merchants was created, and each was allowed three ships a year. In midsummer, between *geshi* 夏至 and *shōsho* 小暑, a total of six vessels transported sugar and miscellaneous goods desired by the Japanese from Fujian and Guangdong east to Japan.⁵³ The period of trade with Japan, *geshi* to *shōsho*, corresponds roughly to 20 June through early July in today's calendar. During these twenty days, ships left Zhapu for Japan. The document further states that if westerly winds blew regularly, the voyage lasted four to five days.⁵⁴ If the winds were not favourable, the voyage required at least ten and up to thirty or forty days. In general, these ships returned in the middle of the ninth month carrying Japanese copper and dried marine products such as kelp and dried sea cucumber.⁵⁵

The ships then made a second voyage. Once they had unloaded the goods brought back from Japan, the vessels loaded up with sugar and other goods and once more set sail for Japan in the twenty days or so between *shōsetsu* 小雪 and *taisetsu* 大雪 —between the end of November and early December in today's terms. They then returned to Zhapu in the fourth or fifth month of the following year.⁵⁶ They carried Japanese copper and other miscellaneous goods on this return voyage as well. In this way they set a semi-annual pattern of trading voyages. Moreover, the documents state that every year 1,200,000 *kin* of Japanese copper was shipped to China, with each ship carrying 100,000 *kin* (ca. thirty tons).

Details about the sugar collected in Zhapu can be found in the sections "Guanliang 關梁" and "Haiguanshuikou 海關稅口" in the *Zhapu beizhi* (volume six). Sugar products brought to Zhapu were exported to the Hangzhou 杭州, Jiaxing 嘉興, Huzhou 湖州 and Jiangnan 江南 regions. Notably, during the Qianlong era (1736-1795) two-thirds of the sugar transported to Zhapu originated in Guangdong. Most of the sugar merchants in Zhapu were said to be people from

---

51 Matsuura, *Shindai kaigai bōekishi no kenkyū*, 98-117.
52 *Zhongguo difangzhi jicheng: xiangzhen zhi zhuanji*, 229.
53 Ibid., 229-30.
54 Ibid., 230.
55 Ibid., 230.
56 Ibid., 230.

Chaozhou 潮州, suggesting that the bulk of sugar traded in Zhapu was produced in the Chaozhou region of Guangdong. These merchants stayed in Zhapu the entire year. As ships laden with sugar arrived, transport workers known as *guotanghang* 過塘行 performed the customs procedures. In later years, it became common for most sugar to be transported to Shanghai rather than Zhapu.[57]

The records of a Ryūkyū offficial charged with investigating the wreck on Yaeyamajima 八重山島 of a merchant vessel from Chaozhou, dated 1814/12/25, appear in the *Rekidai hōan* (歷代寳案, 2: 118). This 149th Chenghai ship, a merchant vessel owned by Wu Yongwan 吳永萬 of Chenghai 澄海 County in Chaozhou Prefecture, left Donglong 東隴 port on 6/18 with fifty-eight people onboard (twenty-two passengers and thirty-six sailors, including the captain), carrying a cargo of muscovado and white sugar. On 8/7 it arrived in Tianjin Prefecture 天津府, where it sold its cargo.[58] From this example we may conclude that ships from Chaozhou regularly plied the seas offf northern China with sugar cargoes.

This pattern is also evident in the chapter "Customs and Occupations (Fengsu Shengye 風俗, 生業)" of the Jiaqing-era *Chenghai xianzhi*, which describes how sugar was gathered from every village in Chenghai County during the harvesting season, and loaded onto ships during the third and fourth months when southerly winds blew. The ships then travelled to Suzhou 蘇州 and Tianjin, where they reaped tremendous profits. Accordingly, we may imagine that much of the sugar from Chenghai County was exported to Zhapu.[59]

According to a palace memorial from Jiangnan provincial military commander Lin Junsheng (提督江南總兵官左都督 林君陞),[60] dated 1753/7/4, sugar ships from Fujian and Guangdong arrived at the ports of Liuhe 劉河, Chuansha 川沙, Wusong 吳淞, and Shanghai to trade during the season of southerly winds, in the fourth and fifth months. In the ninth and tenth months they purchased cotton and returned.[61] In this way, sugar produced in Chinese southeastern seaboard regions was transported to ports near Zhapu and Shanghai by ocean-going vessels from Guangdong and Fujian. Part of that sugar was transported from Zhapu to Japan by Nagasaki-bound trading ships.

---

57 Ibid., 149.
58 Matsuura, "18-19 seiki ni okeru Nansei shotō hyōchaku chūgoku hansen yori mita shindai kōungyō no issokumen", 17-75.
59 Chenghai-xianzhi vol. 6: 8.
60 Lin Junsheng was concurrently Left Commissioner-in-chief (*zuodudu* 左都督) in the Board of War, and also regional commander (*zongbingguan* 總兵官) of Zhenhai 鎮海 and Dinghai 定海.
61 A palace memorial submitted by Lin Junsheng, dated 1753/7/4, in [GDQZ], 5, 689.

4 The State of Sugar Consumption in Japan

Now we turn our focus to the consumption of sugar in Japan: how was the sugar brought to Japan by Chinese ships consumed?

4.1 Sugar Imported to Japan

Terashima Ryōan 寺島良安 wrote about sugar in a glossary appended to the passage on sugar cane (*kansho* 甘蔗) in the *Wakan sansai zue* 和漢三才 図会 (volume 9). According to Terashima, at the beginning of the 18th century 2,500,000 *kin*, or ca. 1500 tons, of white sugar was imported annually. This sugar was transported not only by Chinese vessels, but also by Dutch ships. Sugar was roughly divided into three types: rock sugar, white sugar and muscovado. These were all produced from sugarcane, which at the time did not grow widely in Japan. For that reason, sugar was imported through Nagasaki. White sugar imports totaled 2,500,000 *kin*, with Taiwanese sugar regarded most highly, followed by sugar from Jiaozhi [Cochin] in southern Vietnam, then sugar from Nanjing, Fujian and Ningbo. Indonesian sugar, imported from the Netherlands, was called "Dejima White" for its association with the Dutch settlement at Dejima in Nagasaki, and regarded as the lowest quality.[62]

Terashima described some foods that used sugar in "Candied sweets" (*satōzuke no kashi* 沙糖漬の菓子):

> In my view, items such as tangerines (*mikan* 蜜柑), citron (*busshukan* 佛手柑), dried asparagus root (*tenmondō* 天門冬), ginger (*shōga* 生薑) and winter melon (冬瓜 *tōgan*) are candied in sugar and made into sweets. Yet

---

62 "In my view, there are three types of sugar: rock sugar (*kōrizatō*), white sugar (*shirozatō*) and muscovado (*kurozatō*). Originally these are all the same thing, and differ only in the way that pig iron (*zuku*), iron (*kurogane*) and steel (*hagane*) differ. In our country, even sugarcane that is transplanted does not grow well. As a seasoning for rice cakes (*mochidango*), sugar is considered essential. The general outline of imports from other countries is as follows: Approximately 2,500,000 *kin* (1 *ton* is 175 *kin*. At Nagasaki it is divided into two crates (*hako*), each containing 86.5 *kin* [*sic*]) of white sugar arrive from various foreign countries. That which is pure and not damp is good. It contains large clumps of round, flat sugar in the shape of rice cakes. This sugar is called *sanbon*. When broken apart, it becomes very white. Everything from Taiwan is considered the highest grade, followed by sugar from Jiaozhi. The next grade comprises sugar from Nanjing, Fujian and Ningbo, while sugar from Calapa [咬留巴 present-day Jakarta] and Holland (阿蘭陀 [referring to Dejima]) is considered of the lowest quality."
See *Wakan sansai zue* 16, 81.

170

in order to preserve them for several months, they are soaked in limewater overnight and washed clean before being candied. . . .⁶³

Sugar thus served as an essential ingredient in important processed foods such as candied fruit.

As mentioned earlier, Tokugawa Yoshimune made great effforts to improve domestic sugar supply. In addition to ordering Fukami Arichika to comb imported texts for information on sugar, Yoshimune also had him gather information about sugar production from the captains of Chinese vessels arriving at Nagasaki. Li Daiheng 李大衡, of the sixth Xiamen ship, which arrived in the ninth month of 1726, recorded "Methods of Producing Muscovado 煮烏糖法" and "Methods of Producing White Sugar 煮白糖法." "Methods of Producing Muscovado" describes steps from the cutting of sugar cane and bamboo to the production of muscovado; "Methods of Producing White Sugar" describes several further steps including the addition of "ash made from barnacle shells" and further boiling to produce refined white sugar.⁶⁴

Li Daiheng had also travelled to Japan on the twenty-third Xiamen ship in 1723. While the ship originated in Xiamen, it took on thirty-nine people in Shanghai, left that port on the 1723/11/23, and arrived at Nagasaki on 11/28. A record from that visit indicates Li Daiheng had been a secretary in charge of financial afffairs on the twelfth ship of 1721. The trade permit (*shinpai* 信牌), which Li carried in 1723, had been issued to his fellow passenger, merchant Yan Qizong 顏啓惣, in 1721.⁶⁵ We can confirm Li Daiheng's arrival in Japan on the following ships shown in table 24:

Table 24 *Junks on which Li Daiheng arrived in Nagasaki*⁶⁶

Year, ship number, origin	Ship owner	Notes
1721, Number 12, Xiamen	Zhou Yuanji 周元吉	Permit holder: Wu Chuyu 吳楚譽 Secretary: Li Daiheng
1723, Number 23, Xiamen	Li Daiheng	Permit holder: Yan Qizong 顏啓總
1726, Number 6, Xiamen	Li Daiheng	
1727, Number 33, Xiamen	Li Daiheng	
1730, Number 12, Xiamen	Li Hongzhong 李弘中	In place of Li Daiheng
1731, Number 27, Nanjing	Li Daiheng Huang Ziyu 黃子欲	In place of Huang Xiangwan Penmit holden: Huang Hengwan 黃亨萬
1733, Number 11, Xiamen	Li Hongzhong	In place of Li Daiheng

63 *Wakan sansai zue* 18, 244.
64 *Tsūkō ichiran* 6, 24-27.
65 *Ka-I hentai* ge, 2984.
66 *Tōsen shinkō kaitōroku*, 74, 78, 82, 86, 90, 93, 96.

Based on these records, there is a very high probability that Li Daiheng came from Xiamen.

As a result of Yoshimune's effforts, by the late Edo period the state of domestic sugar supply had changed significantly. Kitagawa Morisada 喜多川守貞 recorded historical rumors and popular knowledge in *Morisada mankō* 守貞漫稿 and *Ruijū kinsei fūzoku shi* 類從近世風俗志, composed between 1837 and 1853. According to volume 28, "Foodstufffs 食類," sugar imported on Dutch vessels was called "Dejima White (*Dejimajiro* 出島白)" after the Dutch trading post at Dejima. Sugar imported from China fell into three categories: highest quality "*sanbon* 三盆", followed by "*jōhaku* 上白," and lowest-quality "*taihaku* 太白".[67] Sugar production in Japan had also spread, with Suruga and Enshū 遠州 growing sugarcane. By the Tenmei 天明 and Kansei 寬政 period (1781-1800), cultivation had spread to Shikoku. By the mid-nineteenth century, Sanshū 讚州 in Shikoku had become the largest producer, followed by Awa 阿波. Suruga, Tōtōmi 遠江, Mikawa 三河 and Senshū 泉州 also produced from Ryūkyū. Domestically, Kishū 紀州 and Doshū 土州 produced the greatest amount of muscovado, with Senshū, Suruga, Tōtōmi and Mikawa following. By the mid- and late Edo periods, sugar was used not only to make candied sweets, but also in a wide range of food products and cooking, including soba, tempura and fish sausage.

In 1823, Matsura Seizan 松浦静山 (1760-1841) was assigned to Suruga Castle, where he observed the state of sugarcane harvesting and sugar refinement. He recorded how the sugarcane harvest relied on oxen to liquefy the sugarcane, which was then used to make sugar.[68] Matsura also described how Tokugawa Yoshimune had championed the spread of sugar, and claimed that sugar's spread was a major contribution of Yoshimune's reign.[69] Seizan started chronicling events of his time in the *Kasshi yawa* 甲子夜話 in 1821, suggesting that by the middle of the century domestic sugar production had become a widely known fact. In other words, in the nearly one hundred years between the Kyōhō years (1716-1735) under Yoshimune (1684-1751) and the period when Matsura was writing *Kasshi yawa*, sugar production from sugarcane had become common across Japan.

A similar picture of the era emerges from two representative, well-known authors of agricultural texts. Miyazaki Yasusada 宮崎安貞 (1623-1697), an agronomist of the early to mid-Edo period, wrote *Nōgyō zensho* 農業全書 in 1697. In volume 5, "Plants of the countryside: sugarcane (山野菜之類：甘蔗),"

---

67   Kitagawa, *Ruijū kinsei fūzoku shi*, 441.
68   Matsura, *Kasshi yawa* 4, 78.
69   Matsura, *Kasshi yawa* 3, 295.

Miyazaki wrote that sugarcane would not grow except in hot regions. In the Genroku period (1688-1703) sugarcane seedlings were imported from Ryūkyū to Satsuma, and grown there. However the prohibitive cost required meant that cultivation by individuals was diffficult, especially if powerful men such as the local lord did not contribute.[70]

Yet by the time Ōkura Nagatsune 大蔵永常 (1768-1861), an agronomist of the late Edo era, wrote his *Kōeki kokusan kō* 広益国産考 in 1859, the situation had changed drastically. In the second volume, "Sugar 砂糖の事," Ōkura wrote:

> Until just over 200 years ago, only noble people knew about sugar, and those of humble birth never saw it. Yet from the Genroku period through the An'ei (1772-1780) and Kansei periods (1789-1800), a type of muscovado called "Chinese black 唐黒" was imported on Chinese ships. In the Bunka period (1804-1817) this ended and no more was imported. Compared to muscovado used today the grains were finer, and of higher quality.[71]

The role of sugar in Japan changed significantly over the two hundred years before Ōkura's 1859 *Kōeki kokusan kō*, dating back roughly to when Miyazaki Yasusada wrote *Nōgyō zensho*. As Ōkura noted, "until just over two hundred years ago, only noble people knew about sugar and those of humble birth never saw it," suggesting that the nobility, and particularly the residents of Edo Castle, were likely to be the greatest consumers of sugar. One study revealed the amount of sugar consumed at Edo Castle to be a surprising one thousand *kin* per day;[72] putting aside the question of whether this number was accurate, it is not diffficult to imagine that Edo Castle would have consumed more sugar than anywhere else. Although in the Genroku period only noble people encountered sugar, Ōkura Nagatsune's account shows that over the subsequent two hundred years domestically produced sugar became widespread. In particular, domestic producers began to make sugar equal in quality to that imported on Chinese merchant ships.

4.2 Expansion of Sugar Consumption in Japan

By the mid- to late-Edo period, the amount of sugar consumed and its uses had expanded considerably. One example of this spread lies in the use of sugar

---

70 Miyazaki, *Nōgyō zensho*, 391-92.
71 Ōkura, *Kōeki kokusan kō*, 98-101.
72 Kitamura, *Samidare zōshi*, 17; see also Asakura, "Kōki", in vol. 3, 355.

in iced drinks, sold by "iced water vendors" (*hiyamizuuri* 冷水売) in the Edo era, as described in *Morisada mankō* 守貞漫稿, volume 5, "Occupations 生業." In particular, in Kyoto and Osaka the job was known as "sugar water vendor" (*satōmizuuri* 砂糖水売).[73] Furthermore, candy known as "sugared beans" (*satōiri kintoki* 砂糖入金時)[74] and boiled dumplings made from rice called "rice flour dumplings" (*shiratamauri* 白玉)[75] were both sold with white sugar sprinkled on top. For the annual Boys' Festival, held on the fifth day of the fifth month, bean jam rice cakes (*kashiwamochi* 柏餅) were sold in Edo, Kyoto and Osaka, and contained red bean jam made with sugar. Some cakes in Edo used soybean paste (*miso* 味噌) made with sugar.[76] Children's sweets in the shape of bonito flakes (*katsuobushi* 鰹節) were made by knead-ing flour with sugar syrup, and hardening the mixture.[77] The well-known *Kinzanji miso* 金山寺味噌 was made with soybeans and malt barley, to which sugar was added.[78] *Kinton* 金團 was also made with sugar.[79] The bean paste used as a sauce for *konnyaku no dengaku* 蒟蒻の田楽 (*konnyaku* on skewers) was sweetened with sugar.[80]

The well-known "*konpeitō*" 金平糖, a small candy made by crystallizing sugar around a poppy seed core and first imported during the Azuchi Momoyama period (c.1573-1600), could not be made without sugar.[81] Sugar also became indispensable to jellied bean paste (*neriyōkan* 練り羊羹).[82] Moreover, steamed buns (*manjū* 饅頭) included sugar.[83] Naturally, expensive *manjū* used expensive sugar. By the Bunka period (1804-1818) *manjū* made with sugar had spread not only to the big cities such as Edo or Osaka, but also to provincial towns.[84] Although the bun of a *soba manjū* was made with buckwheat flour, the sweet jam filling incorporated high-grade imported sugar and *azuki* 小豆 beans.[85] This variety of *manjū* was quite popular in Edo.

In addition to these various sweets and food products, sugar was used in a variety of preserved foods. The Bunka-period *Bōkaen manroku* 卯花園漫録

---

73 Kitagawa, *Ruijū kinsei fūzoku shi*, 174.
74 Ibid., 177.
75 Ibid., 177.
76 Ibid., 270.
77 Ibid., 313.
78 Ibid., 418.
79 Ibid., 433.
80 Ibid., 435.
81 Ibid., 439-40.
82 Ibid., 443.
83 Ibid., 444.
84 Ibid., 445.
85 Ibid., 446.

(volume 2), contains records of plum wine and tangerines (*mikan* 蜜柑) preserved in sugar.[86] Goods such as plum wine and preserved tangerines, commonly used to this day, relatively regularly incorporated sugar. These records also appear in the late Tokugawa nativist scholar Oyamada Tomokiyo's 小山 田與清 (1783-1847) chronicle of events from the Bunsei years (1818-1830) onward, the *Matsuya hikki* (松屋筆記, volume 74), where the procedures for "Making plum wine" and "Making candied goods" are described in nearly identical language as the *Bōkaen manroku*.[87]

Takizawa Bakin 滝沢馬琴 (1767-1848) recorded the state of domestic sugar prices in the Tenpō years (1830-1843) in *Ibun zakkō* 異聞雑稿, volume 1.[88] He described a rapid inflation in the spring of 1833, which drove up prices of white sugar by a factor of 1.9, from 180 *mon* 文 to 350 *mon* per *kin*. Muscovado increased by a factor of 2.4, from 116 *mon* to 280 *mon* per *kin*. This drastic inflation curtailed sugar sales in the countryside, and by the tenth month of that year prices began to fall. Takizawa recorded that white sugar fell to 200 or 180 *mon*, and muscovado to 132 *mon*. In addition to sugar, *mochi* rice also sufffered high inflation, causing the size and sweetness of various sweets to diminish. Even after prices fell, sweets remained half the size as before the inflation, though their sweetness did increase somewhat. Similar episodes appear in the records of other periods.

5 Conclusion

From the early Edo period onward, Japan imported foreign-produced sugar on Chinese and Dutch vessels. Chinese coastal merchants transported sugar produced in Xiamen and Quanzhou in Fujian Province and Chaozhou in Guangdong Province to Zhapu in Zhejiang Province. There it was transferred to trading ships, known as *tōsen*, which plied Nagasaki. From Nagasaki it made its way to the merchant houses of Osaka, which distributed Chinese-produced sugar across Japan.

While the import of Chinese sugar continued throughout the Edo period, efffforts to increase the volume of domestic sugar production spread across Japan from the Kyōhō years onward. Under the eighth Tokugawa shogun, Yoshimune, Chinese methods of sugarcane cultivation and sugar production were studied

---

86 Isonokami, *Bōkaen manroku*, 154-55. See also Asakura, "Afterword" in vol. 5, 409.
87 Oyamada, *Matsuya hikki* 2, 124-25; also Ichijima, "Reigen", 1-5.
88 Takizawa, *Ibun zakkō* jō, 228. See also Asakura, "Afterword," in vol. 2, 434.

through books and also directly from the captains of Chinese ships calling at Nagasaki. Thereafter the *bakufu* urged sugarcane cultivation on shogunal lands and Tokugawa family lands in Suruga, Mikawa, Nagasaki and Kishū, contributing to the full-fledged development of sugarcane production. As a result, by the Bunsei period one hundred years later, Matsura Seizan, head of the Hirado domain, could describe the widespread cultivation of sugarcane and the production of sugar all over Japan in *Kasshi yawa*. Commoners in Edo turned that sugar into a variety of foodstufffs in their diet. Innumerable goods relied upon sugar, including sugar water drinks, rice flour dumplings, bean jam rice cakes, bonito flakes, *Kinzanji miso*, jellied bean paste, *manjū, soba manjū*, and more. By the end of the Edo period, Japanese people used large amounts of sugar on a daily basis, and many goods common then have persisted virtually unchanged to the present day.

CHAPTER 10

Imports and Exports of Books by Chinese Junks in the Edo Period

1 Introduction

The Edo Period was the period of Japan's so-called "seclusion policy" (*sakoku* 鎖国), during which foreign trade was limited to Chinese and Dutch merchant ships. Therefore most of the foreign books that arrived from abroad were Western books brought by the Dutch and Chinese books brought by the Chinese. Historian Ōba Osamu 大庭脩 made especially clear in *Edojidai ni okeru Tōsen mochiwatashisho no kenkyū* 江戸時代における唐船持渡書の研究 [Research on the cargo lists of Chinese trading vessels in the Edo period][1] that a large number of Chinese books were imported annually by Chinese junks.

It has long been known that the Japanese enjoyed Chinese books; their significance at the time is simply but vividly recorded in the *Wohao*[2] 倭好 (in Japanese *Wakō*). The *Wohao* reports that, of the Five Classics, the *Classic of History* (*Shujing* 書経 in Japanese *Shokyō*[3]) and *the Classic of Rites* (*Liji* 礼記 in Japanese *Raiki*) were well respected, whereas *the Classic of Changes* (*Yijing* 易経 in Japanese *Ekikyō*), the Classic of Poetry (*Shijing* 詩経 in Japanese *Shikyō*) and *the Spring and Autumn Annals* (*Chunqiu* 春秋 in Japanese *Shunjū*) were considered to be less important. As to the Four Books, we are told that *the Analects* (*Lunyu* 論語 in Japanese *Rongo*), *Great Learning* (*Dazue* 大学 in Japanese *Daigaku*) and *Doctrine of the Mean* (*Zhongyong* 中庸 in Japanese *Chūyō*) were well respected, whereas *the Mencius* (*Mengzi* 孟子 in Japanese *Mōshi*) was less well regarded. It is thought that *the Mencius* was particularly unpopular due

---

1 Ōba, *Edo jidai ni okeru Tōsen mochiwatashisho no kenkyū*; Ōba, *Edo jidai ni okeru chūgoku bunka juyō no kenkyū*.
2 *Riben-fengtu-ji*, page unknown.
3 Where Chinese book titles have a well-known English translation, the book is referred to using that translation. Otherwise book titles are in the original language. The English translation of these titles is in [ ].

to the spread of its reputation as a revolutionary text which went against the Shogunate's policy, an idea that is clearly represented in the *Wohao*. Buddhist and Taoist scriptures were also popular, and medical texts, too, were inevitably purchased. In his *Xiuhaibian* 袖海編, Wang Peng 汪鵬, who traded in Nagasaki at the beginning of the Meiwa period 明和年間 between 1772 and 1780, wrote that the *dongren* (東人 Easterners), as he called the Japanese, would purchase any Chinese book imported to Japan however high the price.[4]

Edo-period Sino-Japanese exchange was done by Chinese junks visiting Nagasaki, the only port at which international trade was permitted, from the middle of the 17th century until the 1860s.[5] Chinese goods such as silk, sugar and medicine were brought to Japan by these junks, which returned to China carrying Japanese goods such as copper, sea cucumber, and other dried goods and products of the sea.[6] As already indicated, a great many books were also among the goods brought to Japan from China. Because these were very expensive, they were primarily purchased for the collections of wealthy individuals such as the *shōgun* 将軍 (feudal military administrator) and various *daimyō* 大名 (feudal lords).[7] In return, as it were, older books that had originally been published in China and subsequently reproduced using Japanese wood-block printing were taken back to their original home by Qing Dynasty sailing vessels. This was made possible by a man named Wang Zhuli 汪竹里, the alternate name of the above-mentioned Wang Peng, who visited Nagasaki every year from 1772 to 1780, in the middle of the Qianlong Dynasty. He published *Xiuhaibian* on the occasion of the Chrysanthemum Festival in 1764. It can be called the Edo period's only account of Japan by a Chinese visitor to Nagasaki. Because Wang Peng used the name Wang Zhuli in his business dealings, few realized that they were one and the same person. The Japanese-reproduced books that Wang Peng brought back to China had more than a little influence on the academic community of the Qing Dynasty.[8] Some of these were included in the *Zhibuzuzhai-congshu* 知不足齋叢書 (in Japanese *Chifusokusai-sōsho*), which, together with *Yueyatang-congshu* 粵雅堂叢書 (in Japanese *Etsugadō sōsho*), is considered outstanding for the precision of its editing and the beauty of its printing in the Qing period.[9]

This paper has thus far described how Chinese books were brought to

---

4   Matsuura, *Edo jidai Tōsen ni yoru Nicchū bunka kōryū*; *Shōdai sōsho zokuhen*, issue 219, page unknown.
5   Matsuura, *Edo jidai Tōsen ni yoru Nicchū bunka kōryū*, 346-48.
6   Matsuura, *Shindai kaigai bōekishi no kenkyū*, 382-402.
7   Ōba, *Edo jidai ni okeru Chūgoku bunka juyō no kenkyū*, 128-29, 132-33, 212.
8   Matsuura, *Edo jidai Tōsen ni yoru Nicchū bunka kōryū*, 202-16.
9   Momose, "Chifusokusai sōsho", 157.

Nagasaki by Chinese junks during the Edo period, how books taken to China from Nagasaki were included in Bao Tinbo's 鮑廷博 *Zhibuzuzhai-congshu*, and the influence that books printed in Japan had on Qing Dynasty intellectuals. In the following sections, it will explore in more detail the impact that books traded across the sea had on Qing China and Tokugawa Japan.

2 Books Brought by Chinese Junks and Reproductions Printed by Edo Booksellers

Neo-Confucianism (*Zhuzixue* 朱子学, in Japanese *Shushigaku*) was the dominant school of thought among Edo-Period academics, and it can be said that the Confucian classics and Buddhist texts were the dominant printed works.[10] Of all Chinese book imports, the most popular were on scientific theories from the Ming Dynasty through to the beginning of the Qing Dynasty. Many Ming and Qing Dynasty works were imported, ranging from collections of poetry to *kogan* 古玩 (old books that were particularly rare or valuable), *sekifu* 石譜 (genealogies and suchlike, printed using a stone press), music and novels.[11]

Some Chinese junks carried a large quantity of books. For example, in 1753, the wreck of the *inuban gaisen* 戌番外船[12] drifted ashore at Hachijō-jima 八丈島, carrying 441 types of books, 490 copies in 1,476 sets, comprising 12,082 books in all.[13]

As an example of the books printed by booksellers in the Edo period, let us consider a catalogue of Chinese books published in 1798 as *Seireikaku zōhan shomokuroku* 青藜閣蔵板書目録 [Catalog of printing blocks owned by the Seireikaku bookshop]. This bookshop was owned by Suharaya Ihachi 須原屋伊八 and located at Asakusa Kayachō nichōme in Edo.

– *Sishu-jizhu* 四書集註 [a collection of Zhu Xi's commentated versions of *the Analects, the Mencius, Great Learning* and *Doctrine of the Mean*]. Phonetic readings (of the Chinese text) by Hayashi Dōshun 林道春.[14] Published by this

---

10 Yayoshi, *Mikan shiryō ni yoru Nihon shuppan bunka*, 119.
11 Ibid., 120-21.
12 The direct translation is "extra dog ship." The name refers to the fact that the ship arrived in the Year of the Dog, but it was not part of the port's regular trafffic.
13 Ōba, *Hōreki sannen hachijōjima hyōchaku Nankinsen shiryō*, 469.
14 Hayashi Dōshun is the Buddhist priest name Hayashi Razan 林羅山.

bookshop. Ten volumes.
- *Sishu-jizhu* (a diffferent printing of the same text), proofread by Zhu Xiqi 朱錫旂, additional annotations by Satō Issai 佐藤一齋. Ten volumes.
- *Zhouyiguzhu* 周易古註 [an annotated text on *the Classic of Changes*, one of the Five Classics]. Annotated by Wang Bi 王弼 of Wei 魏 and Han Kangbo 韓康伯 of Jin 晉. Five volumes.
- Original text of the Classic of the Changes. Proofread by Oda Kokuzan 小田穀山. Three volumes.
- *Wulixiaoshi* 物理小識 (in Japanese *Butsuri shōshiki*) [An encyclopedia of the science and art of the early Qing Dynasty compiled by Fang Yizhi 方以智]. By Fang Mizhi 方蜜之[15] of the Ming Dynasty. Twelve volumes.
- *Wenzi-quanshu* 文子全書 (in Japanese *Bunshi zensho*) [Works relating to Taoism]. Proofread by Irie Nanmei 入江南溟. Four volumes.
- *Qijin Mengzi-Kaowen-Buyi* 七經孟子考文補遺. [A text revised by editing the portions of *the Mencius* added to the seven texts that form the cornerstone of Confucianism: *The Classic of Changes, the Classic of History, the Classic of Poetry, the Classic of Rites, the Spring and Autumn Annals, the Analects*, and *the Classic of Filial Piety* (*Kōkyō* 孝經)]. Compiled by Yamai Tei 山井鼎. Supplement by Butsu Shukutatsu 物叔達.[16] 32 volumes.
- *Yantie-lun* 鹽鐵論 (in Japanese *Entetsuron*) [Text of pro and contra arguments regarding the monopolies on salt, iron and alcohol under Emperor Wu in the early Han Dynasty]. Compiled by Huan Kuan 桓寬 of the early Han Dynasty. Proofread by Cheng Rong 程榮 of the Ming Dynasty. Six volumes.
- *Zhuzi Xinxue lu* 朱子心學錄 (in Japanese *Shushi shingakuroku*) [A text on the Neo-Confucianism of Zhuzi 朱熹. Compiled by Jinxi Wangyi 金谿王萱 of the Ming Dynasty. Two volumes.
- *Daxue Zhangju Zuanshi* 大学章句纂釋 (in Japanese *Daigaku shōku senshaku*) [A commentary on *Great Learning*] and *Zhushuo Bianwu* 諸説辨誤 [A pro and contra investigation of various theories]. By Koga Seiri 古賀精里. Two volumes.
- *Sishu Bianjiang* 四書便講 (in Japanese *Shisho benkō*) [A text on *Great Learning, Doctrine of the Mean, the Analects* and *the Mencius*]. By Satō Naokata 佐藤直方. Six volumes.
- *Nujie* 女誡 (in Japanese *Jokai*) [A book on the behavior of women], by Cao Shishu 曹世叔 of the late Han Dynasty. Newly revised by Chū Chin 忠珍. One volume.

---

15   Fang Mizhi is the pen name (*azana* 字) of Fang Yizhi.
16   He is also known by the pen name Ogyū Hokkei 荻生北渓. Shukutatsu was a pen name, and Butsu was his Chinese surname. His given name (*na* 名) was Kan 観.

– *Tang-yin-bi-shi* 棠陰比事 (in Japanese *Tōin hiji*) [A text consisting of records of trials (interrogations and the passing of sentences) in ancient China, gathered to be used as a reference in trials]. By Gui Wangrong 桂萬荣[17] of the Ming Dynasty. Three volumes.
– *Xiaojing Huitong* 孝經會通 [An annotated text of the Classic of Filial Piety, considered a work of Confucius, in which he explains the way of filial piety, by which children pay respect to their ancestors and parents]. By Shen Huai 沈淮 of the Ming Dynasty. Proofread by Asakawa Zen'an 朝川善庵. One volume.
– *Xizhao-leshi* 熙朝樂事. By Tian Rucheng 田汝成 of the Ming Dynasty. Translated by Owari Nankō 尾張南康. One volume.
– *Song-shi-chao* 宋詩鈔 (in Japanese *Sōshishō*) [A representative collection of Song Dynasty poetry]. Compiled by Zhang Erming 張二銘 of the Qing Dynasty. Revised by Yamamoto Hokuzan 山本北山. Four volumes.
– *Jin-shi-chao* 金詩鈔 (in Japanese *Kinshishō*) [A representative collection of Jin Dynasty poetry]. Compiled by Gu Kuiguang 顧奎光 of the Qing Dynasty. Revised by Tate Ryūwan 館柳彎. Four volumes.
– *Yuan-shi-chao* 元詩鈔 (in Japanese *Genshishō*) [A representative collection of Yuan Dynasty poetry]. Compiled by Zhang Erming of the Qing Dynasty. Revised by Satō Issai. Four volumes.
– *Fang-qiu-ya-shi-chao* 方秋崖詩鈔 [A representative collection of the poetry of Fang Yue 方岳[18]]. Compiled by Wu Mengju 呉孟擧 of the Qing Dynasty. Proofread by Namikawa Tenmin 並河天民 and Sawa Tansai 佐羽淡齋. Two volumes.
– *Leng-zhai-shi-hua* 冷齋詩話 (in Japanese *Reisai shiwa*) [A collection of poetry]. By Seng Huihong 僧惠洪 (a Song Dynasty Buddhist priest). Two volumes.
– *Sui-yuan-shi-chao* 随園詩鈔 (in Japanese *Zuien shishō*) [A collection of poetry taken from a representative selection of the poetry of Yuan Mei 袁枚]. Compiled by Ichikawa Kansai 市河寛斎. Three volumes.
– *Quan-Tang-shi-yi* 全唐詩逸 (in Japanese *Zentō shiitsu*) (A collection of Tang Dynasty poetry that had made its way to Japan). Compiled and edited by Ichikawa Kansai. One volume.
– *Xi-yu-wen-jian-lu* 西域聞見録 (in Japanese *Saiiki bunkenroku*) (A Qing Dynasty text on the geography of the northwest). By Qishiyi 七十一[19] of the Qing Dynasty. Phonetic readings by Dōun 道雲. Three volumes.

---

17 Actually, Gui Wangrong lived during the Song Dynasty, and this book was revised by Wu Ne 呉訥 of the Ming Dynasty.
18 Fang Yue wrote under the pen name Qiuya 秋崖.
19 His pen name is Chunyuan 椿園.

– *Ji-xiao-xin-shu* 紀効新書 (in Japanese *Kikō shinsho*) [A text on military strategy]. By Qi Nantang 戚南塘 of the Ming Dynasty. Revisions by Hei Shiryū 平子龍.[20] Six volumes.
– *Xi-yang-huo-gong-shen-qi-shuo* 西洋火攻神器説 (in Japanese *Seiyō kakō shinkisetsu*) [A text on Western firearms and their military use]. By He Rubin 何汝賓 of the Ming Dynasty. Revised by Hirayama Heigen.
– *Xi-yang-huo-gong-shen-qi-shuo* (a diffferent printing of the same text), annotated with Japanese pronunciations and simple explanations.

From the above, one can see the sorts of Chinese books that were popular in Japan. Due to the low number of Chinese imports in circulation, many Japanese-made reproductions were published; a case in point is *Sui-yuanshi- chao* [Selected poems of Sui-yuan], one of the books contained in the above list.

It is well known that Sui-yuan 随園 was the name of a park in an outlying district of Nanjing 南京 in which the famous poet Yuan Mei (1716-1797) resided. But when did his poetry find its way to Japan? Let us consider some of the shipping records included in Ōba Osamu's *Edojidai ni okeru Tōsen mochiwatashisho no kenkyū*.

– 1791: One bound copy of *Sui-yuan-shi-hua* 隨園詩話 (in Japanese *Zuien shiwa*).[21] Listed in the *Shōhaku sairai shomoku* 商舶載來書目, a catalog of books imported by Chinese trading ships, vol. "su".
– 1793: One bound copy of *Xiaocang-shan-fang* 小倉山房 (in Japanese *shōsō sanbō*).[22] Listed in the *Shōhaku sairai shomoku*, vol. "se".[23]
– 1794: 15 bound copies of *Xiaocang-shan-fang*. Listed in *Kansei rokunen tora niban Nankinsen shoseki meimoku* 寛政六年寅貳番南京船書籍名 [a catalog of books shipped from Nanjing on the second ship that arrived in 1795].[24]
– 1798: One bound copy of *Xiaocang-shan-fang chidu* 小倉山房尺牘 (in Japanese *Shōsō sanbō sekitoku*) [a collection of Yuan Mei's correspondence]. Listed in *Shōhaku sairai shomoku*, vol. "se".[25]
– 1798: One bound copy of *Xiaocang-shan-fang wen-chao* 小倉山房文鈔 (in

---

20 This is the pen name of Hirayama Heigen 平山兵原, a vassal and military tactician.
21 Ōba, *Edojidai ni okeru Tōsen mochiwatashisho no kenkyū*, 739.
22 Xiaocang-shan is the name of a mountain in an outlying district north of Nanjing, on which Yuan Mei built a garden attached to a residence, which he named *Xiaocangshanfang*, literally "the room at Xiaocang-shan," a name which he also gave to many of the works he published.
23 Ōba, *Edojidai ni okeru Tōsen mochiwatashisho no kenkyū*, 733.
24 Ibid., 251.
25 Ibid., 738.

Japanese *Shōsō sanbō bunshō*) [Excerpts from Yuan Mei's works]. Listed in *Shōhaku sairai shomoku*, vol. "se".[26]

It is thought that the first of Yuan Mei's works to be shipped to Japan was *Suiyuan-Shi-hua*, probably the edition published in 1790. If this is the case, then it was shipped to Nagasaki the year after its publication.

According to *Sui-yuan-shi-chao fanli* 随園詩鈔凡例 (in Japanese *Zuien shishō hanrei*) [Explanatory notes to *Sui-yuan-shi-chao*], written in 1815/5 by Ichikawa Kansai (1749-1820), twenty years had already past since the arrival of *Sui-yuan-shi-hua*, and it had become much esteemed by the literati. However, because few copies had been imported, there were not so many people who recognized the significance of Yuan Mei's works.[27] Twenty years before 1815 is 1795. This is near enough to the year 1791 in which *Sui-yuan-shi-hua* arrived in Nagasaki according to Oba's research. Thus it is conceivable that *Sui-yuan-shihua* first arrived in Japan in 1791.

In Nagasaki, Kansai first acquired the 31-volume *Xiaocang-shan-fang shichao* 小倉山房詩鈔 (in Japanese *Shōsō sanbō shishō*) [Poetry taken from *Xiaocangshan-fang*], which contained over 1,500 poems. He subsequently purchased *Xiaocang-shan-fang quanji* 小倉山房全集 (in Japanese *Shōsō sanbō zenshū*) [The complete *Xiaocang-shan-fang*], and in later years recorded, in his own 1815 publication *Sui-yuan-shi-chao fanli* [Explanatory notes to *Sui-yuan-Shichao*], his amazement at the number of poems in that 37-volume collection.[28]

In *Zuien shishō jo* 随園詩鈔序 [Introduction to *Sui-yuan-shi-chao*], Ōkubo Kōna 大窪行, who learned Chinese poetry with Kansai and wrote under the pen name Ōkubo Shibutsu 大窪詩仏,[29] wrote the following:

In literature, all kinds of happy coincidences occur, but in one instance these coincidences conspired in a singular manner. Some twenty years ago, Ichikawa Kansai opened the private school *Kōkosha* 江湖社, where he taught the poetry of such authors as Bai Letian 白楽天, Li Bai 李白 and Wang Wei 王維. In addition, he recited the refreshing poetic works of Yuan Mei's *Xiaocang-shan-fang*. My only regret is that I was not able to see Yuan Mei's complete works. However, in 1813, Ichikawa Kansai travelled to Nagasaki, where he was able to acquire a copy of *Cang-shan ji* 倉山集 (in Japanese *Sōsan shū*), from which he shall publish a selection for a

---

26 Ibid., 738.
27 Nagasawa, *Wakokubon kanshi shūsei*, 192.
28 Ibid., 193.
29 Rai, "Ōkubo Shibutsu", 543.

number of intellectuals. He has asked me to write the introduction for that publication, which task I have hereby accomplished—Ōkubo Shibutsu.[30]

It thus appears clear, from both this text and Kansai's *Zuien shishō hanrei*, that Kansai travelled to Nagasaki in the course of his duties, and there acquired *Cang-shan ji*, i.e., the complete version of *Xiaocang-shan-fang shiji* 小倉山房詩集.

In *Ichikawa Shisei boketsumei* 市河子静墓碣銘 [epitaph for Ichikawa] in the third volume of *Jijitsu bunpen* 事実文編 [a biographical reference focused on famous intellectuals of the Edo period], Hayashi Taira 林衡 (the posthumous name of Hayashi Jussai 林述齋, 1768-1841) writes that Kansai travelled to Nagasaki.[31] The first volume of Kansai's *Keiho muyoroku* 瓊浦夢餘録 [Impressions of Nagasaki] is a record of one of his trips to Nagasaki. In it, he writes that he left in 1813/7 to accompany Makino Yamatonokami Shigetaka 牧野大和守成傑,[32] who had been appointed magistrate of Nagasaki, and that they arrived at the magistrate's offfice at Inasayama 稲佐山 in Nagasaki on 1813/9/7.[33]

In the winter section (Kiyū fuyu no jō 癸酉冬の条) of *Keiho Muyoroku*, Kansai wrote a poem in which he mourned the death of Yuan Mei while reading *Xiaocang-shan-fang*.[34] From it, one can surmise that Kansai experienced an extraordinary longing for Yuan Mei while reading the complete version of *Xiaocang-shan-fang* that had come into his possession in Nagasaki.

The poems of Yuan Mei's *Xiaocang-shan-fang* are arranged by time period. Based on that arrangement, let us specifically compare the diffferences between the selected works of *Xiaocang-shan-fang* that Kansai saw with the complete poetry collection. The following table compares the number of poems from each section of the complete collection and establishes how many of those poems are included in the selected works.

---

30 Nagasawa, *Wakokubon kanshi shūsei*, 191.
31 Gokyū, *Jijitsu bunpen*, 307.
32 Makino Yamatonokami Shigetaka 牧野大和守成傑 held the position of magistrate from 1813 to 1815. See *Zoku Nagasaki jitsuroku taisei*, 3.
33 Ichikawa, *Kansai yokō*, 265.
34 Ibid., 295.

Table 25 *Comparison of the complete* Xiaocang-shan-fang *(*Xiaocang-shan-fang shiji 小倉山房詩集*) and the collection of selected works (*Xiaocang-shan-fang shichao 小倉山房詩鈔*) bought by Ichikawa Kansai*[35]

Volume[36]	Published	Length[37]	Poems in complete collection	Poems in selected works
1	1736, 1737	14 (f.)	52	17
2	1739-1741	14 (f.3)	54	17
3	1742, 1743	19 (f.7)	98	55
4	1744, 1745	14 (r.8)	84	15
5	1746, 1748	25 (f.)	102	32
6	1749	17 (f.1)	72	20
7	1750, 1751	21 (f.1)	90	47
8	1752	28 (7)	149	95
9	1753		72	60
10	1754	26 (f.8)	125	78
11	1755	11 (r.8)	94	33
12	1756	11 (r.10)	31	21
13	1757	22 (r.)	102	75
14	1758	14 (r.8)	72	27
15	1759	30 (f.3)	152	98
16	1740, 1761	23 (r.1)	102	21
17	1762, 1763	23 (r.10)	133	30
18	1764	16 (r.4)	56	28
19	1765	19 (r,6)	92	28
20	1766, 1767	29 (r.10)	135	80
21	1768, 1769	22 (r.6)	70	70

---

35 The comparisons were made using books from the Shanghai Library 上海図書館. The complete collection values come from *Xiaocang-shan-fang shiji* 小倉山房詩集 [Collected *Xiaocang-shan-fang* poems], library identification number *zhang* 長 37124-33, dimensions 16.2 cm wide × 24.9 cm high, ten volumes. The selected works values come from *Xiaocang-shan-fang shiji buyi-* 小倉山房詩集補遺 [Collected *Xiaocang-shan-fang* poems, supplement], library identification number *zhang* 長 334533-36, dimensions 11.8 cm wide × 17.5 cm high, four volumes, small-sized version. The latter is clearly entitled *Xiaocang-shan-fang shiji* on its cover, but its title page reads *Xiao-cang-shan-fang shichao* [Selected *Xiaocang-shan-fang* poems].

36 Volume (*maki* 巻) here refers to the number of the volume in the complete collection in ten books.

37 The number listed here is the number of leaves the volume takes up (*chōsū* 丁数). An "f" in parentheses indicates the front side of the leaf, and an "r" indicates the reverse. The number following "f" or "r" refers to the number of lines.

Part 2: Sino-Japanese Interaction based on Chinese Junks in the Edo period

Volume	Published	Length	Poems in complete collection	Poems in selected works
22	1770, 1771	18 (r.9)	61	24
23	1772, 1773	16 (r.10)	79	29
24	1774, 1775	21 (f.6)	120	26
25	1776, 1777, 1778	37 (f.9)	190	103
26	1779, 1780	35 (r.3)	207	81
27	1781	17 (f.)	118	59
28	1782	41 (r.)	219	70
29	1783	20 (f.8)	101	10
30	1784	56 (r.7)	234	158
31	1785, 1786	11 (f.4)	137	55
32	1787-1789	38 (r.7)	32	
33	1791	16 (f.1)		
34	1793	12 (f.7)		
Total			3,435	1,562

From this it is clear that what Ichikawa Kansai found was a copy of the less comprehensive selected works, which explains the astonishment recorded in *Zuien shishō hanrei* that he could not help but experience when he later discovered an edition of the complete version.

It seems that Kansai, who was enthusiastic about Yuan Mei's *Sui-yuanshi-hua*, had a strong wish to popularize Yuan Mei's work in Japan. Thus he selected some poems from the selected work *Xiaocang-shan-fang shichao* and published the excerpt as *Zuien shishō* 隨園詩鈔. However, despite the similarity of this title to *Sui-yuan-shi-hua* 隨園詩話, it has nothing to do with *Sui-yuan-shi-hua* as regards contents. After this publication, Kansai learned of the existence of the complete version of *Xiaocang-shan-fang* and was amazed that many more works were contained in the complete version.

Seireikaku zōsho hansho mokuroku 青藜閣蔵板書目録 [Catalog of printing blocks owned by the Seireikaku bookshop], owned by Suharaya Isaburō 須原屋伊三郎 of Asakusa Sakayachō sanchōme in Edo and inserted in the back of volume three of Ichikawa Beian's 市河米菴 1812/10 publication *Beian bokudan* 米菴墨談, contains the following entry describing Ichikawa Kansai's *Zuien shishō*:

Zuien shishō—Edited by Ichikawa Kansai, three volumes
  400 of the 1,500 poems published in *Xiaocang-shan-fang*, selected for easy comprehension for the newcomer to poetry. The author, Zuien (Yuan Mei) is a master poet of the Qianlong period who revolutionized poetry in

the early Qing Dynasty. Any student of modern poetry must read this book.

In short, it was published as an essential reader for Edo-period students of Chinese poetry. Its table of contents indicates that it contained 441 poems in total:

- Volume 1: 58 five-line *koshi* 古詩 (ancient poems)
- Volume 2: 19 seven-line *koshi*
- Volume 3: 45 five-line *risshi* 律詩 (ancient Chinese verse form), 2 five-line *hairitsu* 排律 (long version of *risshi*)
- Volume 4: 96 seven-line *risshi*
- Volume 5: 9 five-line zekku 絶句 (a Chinese quatrain), 9 six-line *zekku*
- Volume 6: 203 seven-line *zekku*

As discussed previously, it is certain that Yuan Mei's *Sui-yuan-shi-hua* found its way to Japan some time immediately following publication. Its influence was huge and it was widely known by the Japanese literati. However one may surmise that only few copies of the text were available in Japan. It is reasonable to think that, because of this, these few available copies were lent out to be copied by hand and studied. It is also certain that Ichikawa Kansai, who regretted the rarity of printed books, visited Nagasaki on offficial business, where he acquired a collection of selected *Xiaocang-shan-fang* poems. He then arranged selected poems from that collection by form, and republished them as *Zuien shishō* 随園詩鈔. Despite their very similar names when written in Chinese characters (only the final character difffers), this text was, as previously indicated, difffferent from Yuan Mei's *Sui-yuan-shi-hua* 随園詩話. The complete *Xiaocang-shan-fang* fills 37 volumes, with an additional two supplementary volumes. The collection which Kansai initially acquired, and upon which *Zuien shishō* was based, was a simplified version and contained only 31 volumes. If one considers the state of Sino-Japanese relations at the time, this is an extraordinarily rapid reception of a written work.

3 Export of Chinese Books Published in Japan to China

To ascertain the kind of books published in Japan that were brought from Nagasaki to China on Chinese junks during the Edo period, let us begin with the records contained in *Nagasakishi zokuhen* 長崎志續編 [Sequel on the history of Nagasaki]. This was an Edo-period publication containing a chronological listing of events relating to Nagasaki, the main volume of which was entitled *Nagasakishi* 長崎志 [History of Nagasaki] or *Nagasaki jitsuroku taisei* 長崎實錄大成 [Nagasaki complete record of events]. The supplementary volume was called *Zoku Nagasaki jitsuroku taisei* 續長崎實錄大成 [Sequel on the Annals of Nagasaki].

The following descriptions are contained in *Tōsen shinkō narabi ni zatsuji no bu* 唐船進港并ニ雜事之部 [Various accounts of events related to the arrival of Chinese junks at port], found in volume eight of *Nagasakishi zokuhen*:

- 1794: The sixth ship of the year 1793 purchased one copy of *Shichikei Mōshi kōbun hoi* 七經孟子考文補遺 [Supplement to the seven Confucian classics and the Mencius] published in Japan, before setting sail.[38]
- 1801: Before leaving for China, the merchants of the first and second ships of the year 1801 took on board a total of eight volumes as samples, comprising the first and second volumes of *Yi-cun-cong-shu* 佚存叢書.[39]
- 1809: One each of a number of ancient books published in Japan was included among the volumes loaded on ships returning to China this autumn. These included: *Erya-zhushu* 爾雅註疏, *Yijing-benyi* 易經本義, *Nippon shoki* 日本書記, *Daxue-jie* 大學解, *Zhongyong-jie* 中庸解, *Shujing-guzhu-yinyi* 書經古註音義, *Liji-guzhu* 禮記古註, *Chunqiu-jizhu* 春秋集註, *Gongyangzhuan* 公羊傳, *Guliang-zhuan* 穀梁傳, *Zuo-zhuan-xida-yilu* 左傳觿大疑錄, *Hi-Sorai-gaku* 非徂徠學, *Lunyu-zheng-zhengwen* 論語徵正文, *Daxue-zhangju-xinshu* 大學章句新疏, *Guwen-Xiaojing-zhengwen* 古文孝經正文, *Xiaojing-dayi* 孝經大義, *Nippon shisen* 日本詩選, *Shishu-guzhuan* 詩書古傳, *Shijing-jizhu* 詩經集註, *Shujing-jizhu* 書經集註, *Yijing-jizhu* 易經集註, *Liji-jizhu* 禮記集註, *Zhao-zhu mengzi* 趙註孟子, *Lunyu* 論語, *Mengzi* 孟子, *Lunyu-zhushu* 論語註疏.[40]
- 1810: One copy of *Kobai enbokufu* 古梅園墨譜[41] exported on ships returning from Nagasaki to China this spring.[42]
- 1811: One copy of *Dongyi-baojian* 東醫寶鑑 published in Japan exported in autumn from Nagasaki on ships returning to China.[43]
- 1817: Thirteen copies of *Qunshu-zhiyao* 群書治要 published in Japan,

---

38 *Zoku Nagasaki jitsuroku taisei*, 196.
39 Ibid., 200.
40 Ibid., 211.
41 *Kobai enbokufu* is the name of an ink shop in Nara. This is a text on calligraphy published by Kobaien 古梅園, whose inks were also exported to China.
42 *Zoku Nagasaki jitsuroku taisei*, 213.
43 Ibid., 214.

exported from Nagasaki in spring and autumn on ships returning to China.⁴⁴
- 1818: Two copies of *Seizai sōroku* 聖済総録, published last year by the *Igakukan* 醫學館 (a medical school founded by the Tokugawa Shogunate). The *Igakukan* had them brought to the port by the magistrate of Nagasaki Tsutsui Izuminokami 筒井和泉守, whom they had asked to have the books given to Chinese merchants and shipped to China. Chinese merchants arriving in port this year brought ten bamboo artworks and suchlike in exchange for these books. Izumi no kami then returned to Edo and delivered the books to the Shogunate; the *Igakukan* was also informed.⁴⁵
- 1823: The following books, published in Japan, were exported to China this spring on the fourth ship of the year 1822 by merchant Liu Jingyun 劉景筠: *Yi-cun-cong-shu* 佚存叢書 vol. 1 (two copies), and vol. 2 and 3 (one copy each); two copies of *Qunshu-zhiyao* 群書治要; three copies of *Lunyu-jijie* 論語集解; one copy of *Shiji-pinglin* 史記評林; and one copy of *Kobaien bokufu kōhen* 古梅園墨譜後編.⁴⁶
- 1824: The following books, published in Japan, were exported to China this spring on the fourth ship of the year 1822 by merchants Liu Jingyun and Zhu Kaizhe 朱開折: One copy each of vols. 1, 2, 3 of *Yi-cun-cong-shu*; one copy each of *Qunshu-zhiyao* and *Lushi-chunqiu* 呂氏春秋. In addition, merchants Shen Qiquan 沈綺泉 and Jiang Yunge 江芸閣 took on the seventh ship of the year 1822: One copy each of *Sishu-jizhu* and *Shiji-pinglin*, as well as two copies of *Shanhanlun-jiyi* 傷寒論輯義.⁴⁷
- 1825: The following books, published in Japan, were exported to China by merchants Liu Jingyun and Yan Xuefan 顔雪帆 on the fourth ship of the year 1822: One copy each of *Qijin Mengzi-Kaowen-Buyi, Lunyu-zheng* 論語徵, and *Qunshu-zhiyao*, as well as ten copies each of vol. 1, 2, 3 of *Yi-cun-cong-shu*.⁴⁸
- 1837: This April, one copy of the 25-volume revised *Dongyi-baojian* 訂正東醫寶鑑, published in Japan, was exported from Nagasaki to China by merchant Shen Yungu 沈耘穀 on the third ship of the year 1836.⁴⁹

As recorded in the above entries, during the more than forty-year span from 1794 to 1837, Chinese merchants took books printed in Japan back to China on their own initiative, over and above the publications that the *Igakukan* wished to have brought to China. Table 26 contains the books of which more than one

---

44 Ibid., 218.
45 Ibid., 219.
46 Ibid., 225.
47 Ibid., 225.
48 Ibid., 225.
49 Ibid., 249.

Part 2: Sino-Japanese Interaction based on Chinese Junks in the Edo period

copy was shipped from Nagasaki to China by Chinese junks during this time.[50]

Table 26   *Multi-volume texts shipped to China by Chinese Junks from 1794 to 1837, grouped by similar or identical books*

Year of departure	Ship[51]	Text
1801	Numbers 1 and 2 of the year 1801	*Yi-cun-cong-shu-qian-bian hou-bian*, eight copies, hand-copied
1823	Number 4 of the year 1822	*Yi-cun-cong-shu*, two copies of vol. 1, one copy each of vols. 2, 3
1824	Number 3 of the year 1823	*Yi-cun-cong-shu*, one copy each of vols. 1, 2, 3
1825	Number 4 of the year 1825	*Yi-cun-cong-shu*, ten copies each of vols. 1, 2, 3
1809		*Yijing-jizhu*,[52] one copy
1809		*Yijing-benyi*, one copy
1817		*Qunshu-zhiyao*, 13 copies
1823	Number 4 of the year 1822	*Qunshu-zhiyao*, two copies
1824	Number 3 of the year 1823	*Qunshu-zhiyao*, one copy
1825	Number 4 of the year 1825	*Qunshu-zhiyao*, one copy
1810		*Kobaien bokufu*, one copy
1823	Number 4 of the year 1822	*Kobaien bokufu kōhen*, one copy
1811		*Dongyi-baojian*, one copy
1837	Number 3 of the year 1836	Revised *Dongyi-baojian*,[53] one copy consisting of 25 volumes
1823	Number 4 of the year 1822	*Shiji-pinglin*,[54] one copy
1824	Number 7 of the year 1823	*Shiji-pinglin*, one copy
1794	Number 6 of the year 1793	*Shichikei Mōshi kōbun hoi*,[55] one copy
1825	Number 4 of the year 1825	*Shichikei Mōshi kōbun hoi*, one copy

50   Similar books are counted as the same book, for example *Yijing-jzhu* and *Yijing-benyi*.

51   The year by which the ships are identified is the year of their arrival in Nagasaki and can thus differ from the year of their departure.

52   Possibly the *Yijing-jizhu* published in 1663. See Naikaku bunko, *Kaitei naikaku bunko kanseki bunrui mokuroku*, 2.

53   This is possibly the 1724 edition compiled by Heo Jun 許浚 of Korea. See Naikaku bunko, *Kaitei naikaku bunko kanseki bunrui mokuroku*, 232.

54   A Ming Dynasty text edited by Ling Zhilong 凌稚隆 with supplement by Li Guangjin 李光縉. The 130-volume Japanese edition with a two-volume main text was published in 1636, 1672, 1674 and 1786. See Naikaku bunko, *Kaitei naikaku bunko kanseki bunrui mokuroku*, 58.

55   This is known to be a 1731 publication of *Qijin Mengzi-Kaowen-Buyi* in 32 books with supplement by *Yamanoi Teisen* 山井鼎撰 and *Ogyū Kan* 荻生観 (also known as *Ogyū Hokkei* 荻生北渓, the younger brother of *Ogyū Sorai* 荻生徂徠). See Naikaku bunko, *Kaitei naikaku bunko kanseki bunrui mokuroku*, 604.

1809		*Chunqiu-jizhu,*[56] one copy
1809		*Chunqiu-jizhu,* one copy
1809		*Shujing-guzhu-yinyi,* one Copy
1809		*Shujing-jizhu,*[57] one copy
1809		*Daxue-jie,* one copy
1809		*Daxue-zhangju-xinshu,* one copy
1809		*Mengzi,* one copy
1809		*Zhaozhu Mengzi,* one copy
1809		*Liji-guzhu,* one copy
1809		*Liji-guzhu,* one copy
1809		*Lunyu,* one copy
1823	Number 4 of the year 1822	*Lunyu-jijie,* three copies
1809		*Lunyu-zhushu,* one copy
1825	Number 4 of the year 1825	*Rongochō* 論語徴, one copy (a commentary on the *Analects* written by Ogyu Sorai)
1809		*Rongochō seibun* 論語徴正文, one copy (a commentary on the *Analects* written by Ogyu Sorai)

As one can clearly see from this list, the great majority were woodcut reproductions of Chinese books, and Japanese books accounted for only a small share.

Between 1764 and 1837, the book most commonly exported from Nagasaki to China on Chinese trading junks was without question the Japanese printing of *Yi-cun-cong-shu*, a wood-block print edited by Hayashi Taira. 60 books were printed between 1799 and 1810, including the following works:

– Collection 1 (*daiicchitsu* 第一帙), Part 1 (*daiissaku* 第一冊): *Guwen Xiaojing* 古文孝經 [The text of the Classic of Filial Piety, said to have been discovered in a former residence of Confucius during the rule of the Han Dynasty emperor Wu-di 武帝], with commentary by Kong Anguo 孔安國 of the Han Dynasty. One volume.

– Collection 1, Part 2-6: *Wuxing-dayi* 五行大義 [Texts on the five elements:

---

56 A 37-volume publication of *Chunqiu-jizhu*, by Hu Anguo 胡安國 of the Song Dynasty, published in 1663 in Japan. See Naikaku bunko, *Kaitei naikaku bunko kanseki bunrui mokuroku*, 21.

57 A set of 58 books called *Gokyō jūchō* 五經集註 [Annotated collection of the Five Classics], a compilation of the 24-volume *Zhouyi-zhuanyi* 周易傳義, the 10-volume *Shujing-jizhu*, the 15-volume *Shijing-jizhu*, the 30-volume *Liji-jishou* 禮記集説 and the 37-volume *Chunqiu-jizhuan* 春秋集傳, was published in Japan in 1726. See Naikaku bunko, *Kaitei naikaku bunko kanseki bunrui mokuroku*, 26.

water, fire, wood, metal and earth]. By Xiao Ji 蕭吉 of the Sui Dynasty. Five volumes.
- Collection 1, Part 7-8: *Chengui* 臣軌 [A text on the correct behavior of the ruled]. By Wuhou 武后 of the Tang Dynasty. Two volumes.
- Collection 1, Part 9: *Leshu-yaolu* 樂書要錄 [A book about the music of Confucian texts], three hitherto existing volumes (Volume 5-7).
- Collection 1, Part 10: *Liangjing-xinji* 兩京新記 [A text about Changan 長安 and Luoyang 洛陽], one hitherto existing volume (Volume 3), by Weishu 韋述 of the Tang Dynasty. *Liqiao-zayong* 李嶠雜詠 [A poetry collection] by Li Qiao 李嶠 of the Tang Dynasty. Two volumes.
- Collection 2, Part 11-12: *Wenguan Cilin* 文館詞林 [A collection of Tang-Dynasty poetry], four hitherto existing volumes, by Xu Jingzong 許敬宗 of the Tang Dynasty.
- Collection 2, Part 13: *Wen-gong-zhu-xiansheng-ganxing-shi* 文公朱先生感興詩 [A collection of poetry by Zhu-xi] one volume, by Cai Mo 蔡模 of the Song Dynasty.
- Collection 2, Part 14-19: *Zhouyi-zhuan (Tai-xuan-yizhuan)* 周易傳 (泰軒易傳) [A commentated edition of *the Classic of Changes*], six volumes, by Li Zongzheng 李中正 of the Song Dynasty.
- Collection 2, Part 20: *Zuoshi Mengqiu* 左氏蒙求 [A collection of anecdotes of the ancients] taken from *Chunqiu-zuoshi-zhuan* 春秋左氏傳, with commentary by Zuo Qiuming 左丘明, one volume. By Wu Hualong 吳化龍 of the Yuan Dynasty.
- Collection 3, Part 21-25: *Tang-cai-zi-zhuan* 唐才子傳 [A collection of biographies of Tang Dynasty poets], ten volumes. By Xin Wenfang 辛文房 of the Yuan Dynasty.
- Collection 3, Part 26-30: *Wang-han-lin-ji-zhu Huangdi-bashiyi-nanjing* 王翰林集註黃帝八十一難經 [A medical text devoted to *kanpō* 漢方, a form of traditional Chinese medicine], five volumes, by Qin Yueren 秦越人 from Lu Guo (盧國 the name of a country in ancient times which was located in present-day Hubei province).
- Collection 4, Part 31-33: *Mengqiu* 蒙求 [A collection of anecdotes of the ancients], three volumes, commentated by Li Han 李瀚 of the Tang Dynasty.
- Collection 4, Part 34-40: *Cui-she-ren Yu-tang-leigao* 崔舍人玉堂類藁, 20 volumes, and *Cui-she-ren Xi-yuan-leigao* 崔舍人西垣類藁 [Poetry collection of Cui Dun 崔敦 of the Song Dynasty], 2 volumes and supplement 1.
- Collection 5, Part 41-50: *Zhouyi-xin-jiangyi* 周易新講義 [A commentated edition of *the Classic of Changes*], ten volumes, by Gong Yuan 龔原 of the Song Dynasty.
- Collection 6, Part 51-60: *Jingwensong-gong-ji* 景文宋公集 [A collection of

literature by Song Qi 宋祁 of the Song Dynasty].[58]

The entirety of *Yi-cun-cong-shu* had not yet been published in 1801, but one can assume that exports after 1825 included the entire collection.

The 50-volume *Qunshu-zhiyao*, compiled by Wei Zheng 魏徵 by order of the Tang emperor, was reprinted using copper type in 47 books. This edition, known as the Suruga edition (Surugaban 駿河版), was missing volumes 4, 13 and 20 of the original. In 1787, it was printed again in a 47-book edition under the title *Genna chūko katsuji insatu jūkan* 元和中古活字印本重刊 [Gennaperiod old-style movable type edition] by the *Meirindō* 明倫堂 (Meirin Temple) in the domain of Owari 尾張.[59] It is this edition that is thought to be the one exported from Nagasaki to China.

Zhibuzuzhai-congshu, an anthology of many works published by Bao Tinbo during the Qing Dynasty, includes the books that were reprinted in Japan. The contents shows that the anthology includes the following:

– Collection 1: *Guwen Xiaojing Kong-zhuan* 古文孝經孔傳, one volume. Japanese edition of *Guwen Xiaojing*, published in 1732, the original text of which was lost in China.
– Collection 7: *Lunyu-yishu* 論語義疏, ten volumes. A commentated edition of *the Analects* by Huang Kan 皇侃 of the Southern and Northern Dynasties, which had been lost in China and was published using texts that had made their way to Japan.
– Collection 21: *Xiaojing zhengzhu* 孝經鄭註, one volume. A commentated text on the Classic of Filial Piety, by Zheng Xuan 鄭玄, which had been lost in China and was published using texts that had made their way to Japan.
– Collection 26: *Wuxing-dayi* 五行大義, five volumes, Lost in China and published using texts that had made their way to Japan in ancient times.
– Collection 30: *Quan Tang-shiyi* 全唐詩逸 (in Japanese *Zentō shiitsu*), three volumes. A collection of Tang-Dynasty poetry that was lost in China and republished using texts that had made their way to Japan and collected by Ichikawa Kansai. Compiled by Nipponka Seinei 日本河世寗 (a penname of Ichikawa Kansai).

The inclusion of books reprinted in Japan in *Zhibuzuzhai-congshu* has to be credited to the trader Wang Zhuli, whose alternate name, as indicated earlier,

---

58 Naikaku bunko, *Kaitei naikaku bunko kanseki bunrui mokuroku*, 583.
59 Ibid., 277.

was Wang Peng.[60] Wang Peng had an extremely close relationship with Wang Danwang 王亶望, who had at one time served as governor of Zhejiang province 浙江巡撫.[61] According to the biography of Wang Danwang (*Wang Danwang zhuan* 王亶望傳) in *Qing-shi-gao* 清史稿 [a biographical history of the Qing Dynasty], vol. 339 *Liezhuan* 列傳 126, his reporting to the Qianlong emperor came under suspicion during a rebellion in Gansu province 甘肅, of which the former was then governor. It came to light that he had accumulated a fortune during his time as governor of Zhejiang province, which was found to amount to more than a million *liang* (両 silver currency) when his family properties were confiscated. Among the confiscated goods were a number of books.[62] The following are listed in *Chao yuanren Zhejiang Xungfu Wang Danwang liuzheshiwu-gubian-qingce* 抄原任浙江巡撫王亶望留浙什物估邊清冊 [Book on the market value of written materials in the possession of Wang Danwang in Zhejiang during his tenure as the governor of Zhejiang]:[63]

– 20 sets of *Ershiyi-shi* 二十一史 [History of the Dynasty], 164 books in total, valued at 16 *liang* and 4 *qian* (16 両 4 錢).
– 19 sets of *Ershiyi-shi*. 159 books in total, valued at 15 *liang* and 9 *qian*.
– 21 sets of *Ershiyi-shi*. 177 books in total, valued at 17 *liang* and 7 *qian*.
– 4 sets of *Zhibuzuzhai congshu* 知不足齋叢書.[64] 32 books in total, valued at 2 silver *liang*.
– 4 sets of *Lunyu-jijie-yishu* 論語集解義疏 (in Japanese *Rongo shikkai giso*).[65] Valued at 2 *liang* of silver and 2 *qian*.
– Two sets of *Zhibuzuzhai congshu* 知不足齋叢書.[66] 24 books in total, valued at 3 *liang* of silver.

This list demonstrates that Wang Danwang owned *Lunyu-jijie-yishu* and Bao Tinbo's *Zhibuzuzhai-congshu*, which Wang Peng had procured in Japan.

The *Zhibuzuzhai-congshu* included 765 volumes comprising 30 series and 198 diffferent kinds of texts. This is borne out by the following quotation, which is taken from *Zi-Zajia* 子雜家, in volume 270 *Jingji-kao* 經籍考 14 of *Xu wenxian tongkao* 續文獻通考, compiled by Liu Jinzao 劉錦藻.

---

60 Matsuura, *Edo jidai Tōsen ni yoru nicchū bunka kōryū*, 202-6.
61 Ibid., 206-9.
62 *Qing-shi-gao*, 11074-75.
63 *Qianlong chaocheng bantan wu dangan zhuan*, 1924-35.
64 *Qianlong chaocheng bantan wu dangan zhuanbian*, 1932-33.
65 Ibid., 1933.
66 Ibid., 1934.

Bao Tinbo's father moved from Huizhou 徽州, Anhui province 安徽 to a residence named *Zhibuzuzhai* 知不足齋 in Hangzhou 杭州, Zhejiang province. Bao Tinbo was fond of reading, and he would read his father's books and collect old texts. He borrowed books from famous Zhejiang libraries such as *Zhao-shi-xiaoshan-tang* 趙氏小山堂, *Lu-shi-baojingtang* 盧氏抱經堂, *Wang-shi-zhenqi-tang* 汪氏振綺堂, *Wu-shi-baijinglou* 吳氏拜經樓 and made revised versions of them, and collected various books.[67]

As described above, many of the books brought to China on Qing-Dynasty junks in the Edo period were Chinese books that had been reproduced in Japan. Because many of these books had been lost in China, the deep interest shown by Qing Dynasty intellectuals is easy to understand. Let us consider this phenomenon taking the example of one of these intellectuals, named Xu Zongyan 許宗彥. Xu Zongyan had already mastered the Classics at the age of nine, and he lived in the Deqing district of Huzhou prefecture in Zhejiang province 浙江省湖州府德清縣, quite close to Zhapu in the Pinghu district of Jiaxing prefecture, also in Zhejiang province 浙江省嘉興府平湖縣乍浦, which was the center of Chinese trade with Japan. Because price was no object for him when acquiring rare books, one may suppose that he was most keen to purchase *Yi-cun-cong-shu* when that book was brought from Nagasaki. Then, he learned of the existence of *Wuxing-dayi*, which was included in *Yi-cun-congshu*, and of which he made a revised version in 1804/03. Thus, it is reasonable to assume that Xu Zongyan had a strong interest in a copy of *Yi-cun-cong-shu* which was brought by the first and second ships of the year 1801 from Nagasaki in 1801. Considering the time required for transportation and the revision, this book made its mark in China surprisingly quickly.

4 Conclusion

As a case study of cultural exchange across national borders and across the sea, this essay has shed light on the flow of books carried by Chinese junks between Qing Dynasty China and Tokugawa Japan. Although the people of Japan had a great interest in many of the academic texts brought to Japan by Qing Dynasty trading vessels and appreciated their value, their high prices and low supply meant that the circulation of such books was not very extensive. However, Edo period book sellers were able to overcome this problem by

---

67 *Qingchao xu wenxian tongkao*, Kao 考, 10148.

printing reproductions. This also had a negative side effect, as seen in the example of Ichikawa Kansai's partial publication of *Sui-yuan-shi-chao* rather than the complete works of Yuan Mei. This was unavoidable given the lateness of the import of Yuan Mei's complete works.

In the other direction, the *Zhibuzuzhai-congshu*, which contained Japanese publications that had been brought to China by Chinese junks, had a huge influence on Qing Dynasty academics.[68] It is certain that this kind of publication, known as *sōsho* 叢書 (collection of written works), which afforded many more people the opportunity to read a work, resulted in the collection being well known among intellectuals. The sudden and unexpected arrival of a Chinese work from Japan, which had long been lost in its homeland, gave the Chinese academic community an opportunity to re-recognize the erudition of their predecessors. One could even speak of an academic Renaissance brought about by the return of this book from Japan to its native home.

As this paper illustrates, trade between Japan and China in the Edo period was by no means limited to economic exchange and material goods. It also included the exchange of cultural and scientific knowledge that cannot be overlooked.

---

68 Matsuura, *Kinsei Higashi Ajia kaiiki no bunka kōshō*, 334-47.

Epilogue

Conflicts among the Shipping Companies over the Ocean Traffic in the Asian Seas

CHAPTER 11

Conflicts among the Shipping Companies over the Ocean Traffic in the Asian Seas

1 Introduction

During the first half of 19th century, the demand for steamers arose in East Asian countries after the English steamers came into China. The first steamer company set up by the Chinese government was China Merchants' Steam Navigation Company in Shanghai in 1872. However, the European steamers had already been sailing in the waters along China's coast and they even sailed to the Hankou port at Yangtze River. These steamers played an important role not only in the international trade but also in the inner transportation of China.[1]

During the same period, Japan also noticed the importance of steam ships. At the beginning of Meiji period, the Sino-Japan route was mainly controlled by those steamer companies of America, Britain and France. In 1875, the Japanese government authorized Mitsubishi Yūsen Kaisha to set up the first foreign route, which connected Yokohama, Kobe, Shimonoseki, Nagasaki and Shanghai. Later on, Mitsubishi Yūsen Kaisha became Nippon Yūsen Kaisha, running main marine routes between Japan and China.[2] Likewise, China Merchants' Steam Navigation Company would also like to set up the route toward Japan, but failed because of the resistance on the Japan side.[3]

After Sino-Japan war, Nippon Yūsen Kaisha took use of three lent ships (*Can-long* (蒼龍), *Xian-yi* (顕益) and *Hai-long* (海龍)) which were owned by the government and started to operate the business with the Kyōdo Kisen Kaisha (Cang-long 共同汽船會社) on the Korean Peninsula. The latter inherited the

---

1 NIE, Bazhang ed., *Zhongguo jindai hangyun si ziliao*, vol. 1, Shanghai: Shanghai Renmin Chubanshe, 1983, pp. 34-41, 245-263.
2 MATSUURA Akira, *Kindai nihon chugoku taiwan kōro no kenkyū*, Osaka: Seibundō, 2005.
3 MATSUURA Akira, "Shinkoku rinsen shōshōkyoku no nihon kōkō", *Bulletin of the Institute of Oriental and Occidental Studies*, No.39, 2006.4, pp. 1-48.

Conclusion

legacy of Korea's first steamers achievements which was founded in Busan.

Through analyzing the conflicts among China Merchants' Steam Navigation Company, Nippon Yūsen Kaisha and Kyōdo Kisen Kaisha, this paper is attempted to discuss the beginning and the development of steamer business in East Asia.

2 The founding and development of China Merchants' Steam Navigation Company

The founding of China Merchants' Steam Navigation Company related to the supply transportation to Beijing. Before its founding, the ship transportation from Jiangsu and Zhejiang were the main method to transport the supply from Yangtze River to Tianjin. Therefore, the smaller quantity of these ships caused great problems in supply. According to LI Hongzhang's *Shiban zhaoshang lunchuan zhe* (試辦招商輪船摺)[4], China were trying to build steamers but they were not as suitable as merchant ships. So it seemed to be quite feasible to hire Chinese merchants to ease the burden of supply transportation from Jiangnan area to Beijing. In 1872, China Merchants' Steam Navigation Company was founded. After the severe competition with an American company, Russell & Co, it became the biggest transporting company in China.

Figure 28   Map of CMSNCD's Asian branch 1920s

Soon after the founding of the company, it set up several costal routes including the routes from Shanghai to Shantou (汕頭), Hongkong and Tianjin. As for the inner ones, the routes from Shanghai to Zhenjiang, Jiujiang, Hankou were set up to compete against the English companies, such as the famous Jardine Matheson and Swire Pacific Limited.[5]

---

4   LI Hongzhang, "Shiban zhaoshang lunchuan zhe", *Liwenzhonggong Zougao*, vol. 20
5   LIU Kwangching ,*Anglo-America Steamship Rivalry in China, 1862-1874*, Havard University Press, 1962.

Figure 29　Map of CMSNCD's Line 1920s

Figure 30　The model of *Aden*, collection of China Maritime Museum

The ships bought from foreign countries were named in Chinese: Liyun (利运), sailing between Shanghai and Tianjin; *Fuxing* (福星) to Amoy; *Yuqing* (永清), from Zhenjiang to Guangdong; *Aden* (伊敦) to Japan[6]. These steamers were also planned to be used in the eastern costal routes and the routes of Yangtze River, from Zhenjiang, Jiujiang to Hankou. Therefore the question of setting up the branches was being considered. In 1874, the company renamed as China Merchants' Steam Navigation Company. Then in 1880 it becomes a private company.

China Merchants' Steam Navigation Company was also attempted of building the Sino-Japan route. In 1873, steamer *Aden* (伊敦) was sent to Japan, and then followed by *Tahyew* (大有) in 1877, *Hwai-yuen*(怀远) in 1882, *Haeting* (海定) and *Chiyen* (致远) in 1886. However all of these were not regular sailings. Hae-ting and Chi-yen even encountered the resistance from Japan in 1886, which caused the failure of the plan.[7]

　　MATSUURA Akira, *Kindai nihon chugoku taiwan kōrō no kenkyū*, pp. 11-15.
6　"Shurun zhi shengxuanhuai han", *Lunchuan zhaoshang ju shengxuanhuai dangan ziliao xuanji*, vol. 8, Shanghai: Shanghai renmin chubanshe , 2002, p. 8.
7　MATSUURA Akira, "Shinkoku rinsen shōshōkyoku no nihon kōkō", *Bulletein of the*

Conclusion

The report in *Kobe Yūshin Nippo* (神戸又新日報) No.524 with the title *Chi-yen without passengers* (致遠号に船客無し) was one of the most representative article at that time. This article was reprinted by *Tokyo Yokohama Mainichi Shinbun* (東京横濱毎日新聞), No. 4,560. Although Chi-yen planned to expand its business and attract the Japanese passengers, there was still no passenger onboard while it sailed from Yokohama to Kobe or then leaving for Shanghai. Because of the failure, the plan of setting up the regular route between China and Japan was terminated.

3 The rise of Osaka Shōsen Kaisha (大阪商船会社) and Nippon Yūsen Kaisha

The first regular route between China and Japan was built by Peninsular and Oriental Steam Navigation Company in 1864[8]. The route connecting Shanghai with Yokohama served twice a month. In 1865, French steamers also started a regular sailing between Shanghai and Yokohama, and it has one service a month.[9] In 1867, America's Pacific Mail Steam Ship Company built the route from San Francisco, Yokohama to Hong Kong. Besides "Colorado", the other newly built steam ships, such as "Great Republic", "China", "Japan", "America" also joined for service. Later, P & O built a branch route, which started from Yokohama, via Kobe, Nagasaki and Shanghai.[10] The P & O steam ships were called "Beihikyakusen" (米飛脚船) in Japan. In 1870, the first issue of *Yokohama Daily News* printed the ads of P & O, informed readers about the newly built route from San Fraccisco via Yokohama to Hong Kong. When it came to the next year, the form of the ads greatly changed. In *Yokohama Daily News*,

---

Institute of Oriental and Occidental Studies, No.39, 2006.4, pp. 1-48.
8   Boyd Cable, *A Hundred Year History of the P. & O. Peninsular and Oriental Steam Navigation Company 1837-1937*, London: Ivor Nicholson and Watson, 1937.
    NAKAGAWA Keiichiro, "P. & O. kisen kaisha no seiritsu- igirisu tōyō kaiun si no hitokoma", *Shihonshugi no seiritsu to hatten-Tsuchiya takao kyoju kanreki kinen ronbunshu*, Tokyo: Yūhikaku, 1959.3, pp. 276-301.
9   KOKAZE Hidemasa, Eikoku P&Okisen no nihon shinshutsu to mitsubishi to no kyosō ni tsuite, *Nihon Rekishi*, 1990.4, pp. 94-100.
    KOKAZE Hidemasa, *Teikokushugi ka no nihon kaiun- Kokusai kyosō to taigai jiritu*, Tokyo: Yamakawa, 1995.2, p27.
10 John Haskell Kemble, *A Hundred Years of the Pacific Mail*, The American Neptune, Mariners' Museum, 1950, p.131.

No. 29, Jan. 20, an whole page ads were printed to show that five steam ships ("Golden Age", "New York", "Costa Rica", "Oregon" and "Ariel") started their regular service from Kobe via Nagasaki to Shanghai.[11]

According to the ads printed in *Japan Daily Herald*, No. 3201, Apr. 4, 1874, Pacific Mail Steam Ship Company started its service from China and Japan to America, and it was also available of sailing across America, from San Francisco to New York. From New York and Aspinwall, passengers were accessible to the steamships bound for other European countries, including England, France, and Germany. This route was used by the heroes in Jules Verne's *Le Tour du Monde en Quatre-Vingts Jours* published in 1873.

The international steamer service in Japan was an oligopoly controlled by American companies before 1875. After that, Japan started its serious competition in this business and the first attempt was the regular route connecting Japanese ports and Shanghai.

Mitsubishi was the first company to set up the regular route between Japan and China. In 1875, Mitsubishi started the regular route between Yokohama and Shanghai under the guidance of the Japanese government. According to *Yokohama Daily News* No. 1241[12], Tokyo Maru and the other three steamers owned by Mitsubishi Company set out from Yokohama, via Kobe, Shimonoseki, Nagasaki to Shanghai, every Wednesday from Jan. 3rd, Meiji 8. According to the ads printed in *Tokyo Nichi Nichi Shinbun* No. 928, the name of the other three steamers were *Nigata Maru* 新潟丸, *Kanagawa Maru* 金澤丸, *Takasago Maru* 高砂丸. The same ads also went on *Japan Daily Herald*.

As for Tokyo Maru, *Shenbao*, No.854, mentioned that Tokyo Maru was originally bought by Wolf & Co. and was named as "New York", then renamed as "Tuo ju mai lu" (託局麥魯). From the pronunciation, "Tuo ju mai lu" must be the same ship as *Tokyo Maru* 東京丸. The same report also mentioned the opening of Mitsubishi's Shanghai office and the popularity of the new route by Chinese, which came into being because of the foreseeing vision of the Sino-Japan trade. Furthermore, in the "Gaobai" (告白) section, an ad titled "the Founding of the Steamer Company" (創設火輪船公司) was printed for several issues. In this ad, the founding of a regular route from Shanghai to Yokohama was announced. The steamer would stop at Kobe, Shimonoseki and Nagasaki. The steamer, Tokyo Maru, formerly named as "New York", sailed from Yokohama on Feb. 2nd and from Shanghai on Feb. 17th. The steamer was with the western style and the crews were all westerners.

The cover page of *Shenbao*, No. 856, Feb. 13, 1875 mentioned the price

---

11 *Yokohama Mainichi Shinbun*, vol.1, Tokyo: Fujishuppan, 1989, p5.
12 *Yokohama Mainichi Shinbun*, vol.10, p67.

Conclusion

competition between Mitsubishi and Wolf & Co. and it suggested its Chinese readers to make the tour to Japan while the tickets were cheap. However, it also reminded Chinese readers that they should be prudent because of the perils encountered by those travelers who were attracted by cheap tickets of American steamers. The other example can be found in the report of *"Encouraging Chinese to Join the International Expo in Japan"* (奉勸華人往東洋赴博覽會説), printed on the cover page of *Shenbao*, No.860, Feb. 18, 1875. One of the reasons of recommending the visit to Japan Expo was the cheap travelling fees. In the same issue, there was also the ad, about "the Great Eastern Expo" (東洋大博覽會) held in Kyoto.

In 1875, Mitsubishi Kaisha received thirteen steamers and the sponsorship of 250,000 Yen per year from the Japanese government. The company name was also changed to "Yūbin Kisen Mitsubishi Kaisha" (郵便汽船三菱会社). Then in 1885, because of the affiliation with "Kyōdo Unyu Kaisha" (共同運輸会社), "Nippon Yūsen Kaisha" was formally founded in Tokyo.

In 1884, OKA Senjin (岡千仞) traveled from Yokohama to Shanghai by Tokyo Maru, and wrote his travelling experience in Chinese. In the first volume of *Guan guang ji you* (観光紀游), OKA described the experience during the journey. The middle level of Tokyo Maru was dinning space, and the two sides were rooms for passengers. The room was clean and the toilet sets were well-supplied. There were around 200 passengers staying in the rooms of lower level.[13] This steamer arrived Kobe on May. 31st,[14] passing Awajishima (淡路島) and Harimanada (播磨灘) on Jun. 1st, and finally anchored in Nagasaki port at Jun. 2nd.[15] Around half of these 200 passengers got off at Kobe, and another 40-50 people got off at Shimonoseki. Only 20-30 people left while it sails from Nagasaki to Shanghai. At last, it passed the mouth of Yangtze River on Jun. 5th, ascended the Huangpu River, and finally arrived in Shanghai at the noon of Jun. 6th.

Besides OKA, CHEN Yidong (陳翼棟), who was from Hunan province, also travelled on Kōsai Maru (弘濟丸) through the same route to Japan. According to the record of his *"Ji zi zhai yi you dong you ri ji"* (寄自齋己酉東遊調查日記), dated on May, 1st, 1909, Kōsai Maru sailed from Shanghai at 8 a.m.. At noon they heard the sound of beating a gong, and the crews started to prepare the lunch. When the lunch was prepared, the gong was beaten again; then the passengers of first class cabin came, sat at table and dined in decent manner. CHEN's servant was in third class cabin and the food was simple. Kōsai Maru arrived in Nagasaki at May 13th. At 6 a.m. of the next day, the immigration

---

13 OKA Senjin, *Guan guang ji you*, vol. 1, p1.
14 OKA Senjin, *Guan guang ji you*, vol. 1, p2.
15 OKA Senjin, *Guan guang ji you*, vol. 1, p2.

Conflicts among the Shipping Companies over the Ocean Traffic in the Asian Seas

inspection was imposed on the passengers. The inspection in the first and second class cabins was quite loose while passengers in the third class cabins were gathered at the west side of the ship and were inspected one by one. Kōsai Maru arrived in Kobe at 16th. After an interview with a Chinese consul, CHEN took a train to Tokyo at 6 p.m. While the night train passed the city, the illumination lighting streets amazed him greatly.

4   Chosen Yūsen Kaisha and the coastal route of Korean Peninsula

The most details of steamer sailing around Korea Peninsula were still unknown. However, some clues could be found from the newspaper ads which were published in Korea after 1905. By arranging the sailing ads in the first issue of *Chosen Nippo* (朝鮮日報) which was published in Busan, dated 1905.1.15, Table 27 was concluded.

Table 27   Sailing Steamers from Busan port in Jan. 1905[16]

Date of sailing	Name	Port of embarkation	Port of Destination	Store Dealing In	Date of embarkation	Name	Port of embarkation	Port of Destination	Store Dealing In
Jan. 17	Nito-maru 日東丸	Busan	Incheon, Chefoo	Nippon Y.	Jan. 18	Ohayo-go ヲハヨー號	Busan	Incheon	Nippon Y.
Jan. 22	Fushiki-maru 伏木丸	Busan	Monji, Kobe	Nippon Y.	Jan. 17	Gunzan-maru 群山丸	Busan	Mokpo, Incheon	Osaka
Jan. 15	Amoy	Busan	Mokpo Incheon	Osaka	Jan. 22	Amigo	Busan	Incheon	Osaka
Jan. 18	Daisan-Kotohira-maru 第三琴平丸	Busan	Incheon	Osaka	Jan. 21	Mokpo Maru	Busan	Masanpo, Mokpo, Gunsan	Osaka
Jan. 15	Kanjo-maru 漢城丸	Busan	Gunsan, Incheon	Osaka	Jan. 16	Gishu-maru 義州丸	Busan	Shimonoseki, Kobe, Osaka	Osaka

16   The table is based on *Chosen Nippo*, no.1, 1905.1.15 ~ no.16, 1905.2.7.

Conclusion

Jan. 18	Anto-maru 安東丸	Busan	Shimonoseki, Kobe, Osaka	Osaka	Jan. 19	Kanjo-maru 漢城丸	Busan	Shimonoseki, Kobe, Osaka	Osaka
Jan. 19	Daigo-Hijikawa-maru 第五肱川丸	Busan	Shimonoseki, Kobe, Osaka	Osaka	Jan. 19	Amoy	Busan	Shimonoseki, Kobe, Osaka	Osaka
Jan. 18	Tedorigawa-maru 手取川丸	Busan	Izuhara, Nagasaki, Hakata, Shimonoseki	Osaka	Jan. 28	Shiro-maru 城丸	Busan	Wonsan	Osaka
Every Wednesday	Zuiyo-maru 瑞鷹丸	Busan	Gunsan <=> Incheon	Osaka	Jan. 22	Sukei-maru 崇敬丸	Busan	Shimonoseki, Osaka	Amazaki
Jan. 18	Kamishiro-maru 神代丸	Busan	Incheon	Amazaki	Jan. 25	Daiyu-maru 大有丸	Busan	Incheon	Amazaki
Jan. 15	Daihachi-Nagata-maru 第八永田丸	Busan	Wonsan	Okinaga	Jan. 16	Daruma-go ダルマ號	Busan	Monji, Kobe	Okinaga
Jan. 16	Daini-Uramon-maru 第二浦門丸	Busan	Incheon	Mitsugi	Jan. 16	Bocho-maru 防長丸	Busan	Incheon	Mitsugi
Jan. 17	Kamishiro-maru 神代丸	Busan	Incheon	Mitsugi	Jan. 18	Tensho-maru 天照丸	Busan	Incheon	Mitsugi
Jan. 17	Daini-Heian-maru 第二平安丸	Busan	Shimonoseki, Osaka	Mitsugi	Jan. 18	Daiyu-maru 大有丸	Busan	Busan	Mitsugi
Jan. 16	Taieki-go 泰盛号	Busan	Wonsan	Yamakawa	Jan. 17	Keisho-maru 慶尚丸	Busan	Wonsan	Yamakawa

*Nippon Y. = Nippon Yūsen Kaisha, Osaka = Osaka Shōsen Kaisha, Amazaki = Osaka Amazaki Kisen, Okinaga = Edward Meyer & Co. ; Okinaga Kaisōten, Mitsugi = Mitsugi Kaisōten

According to Table 27, it is clear that Busan was the starting point of all routes, and most of the steamer companies were Japanese companies. Apart from the major ones like Nippon Yūsen Kaisha and Osaka Shōsen Kaisha, there were also minor ones like Osaka Amazaki Kisen. Such situation continued until the founding of Chosen Yūsen Kaisha.

Before the founding of Chosen Yūsen Kaisha, Japan and Korea were connected by the steamers, such as Umega Maru (梅ヶ丸), Ikki Maru (壹岐丸), Tsushima Maru (對馬丸), Sakura Maru (櫻丸), and Satsuma Maru (薩摩丸), which were sailed every two days between Busan and Shimonoseki.[17]

Keijō Shinppo (京城新報), dated on Jan. 9, 1912, published the interview of the president of Nakahashi Osaka Shōsen Kaisha. He talked about the future of the Chosen Yūsen Kaisha in positive tone. In *Keijō Shinppo*, dated on Jan. 16, 1912, the sponsorship for Chosen Yūsen Kaisha was published, which showed the great expectation for this newly founded company.[18] The main reason of the expectation came from the shortage of steamers in Korean costal transportation. In *Keijō Shinppo*, dated on Jan. 20, 1912, the amount of the steamers in Korea was counted.[19] According to this record, there were only 3 steamers over 1,000 tons, 7 steamers over 500 tons. Considering that these steamers had to fulfill the transportation need of the whole Korea, it was obvious that the quantity of the steamers was far from enough.

When the 1911 revolution broke out, lots of Chinese escaped from Shandong Peninsula to Korean Peninsula. In *Keijō Shinppo*, No. 877, dated on Feb. 3, 1912, more than 30 Chinese took Chinese steamer "Jiang-cheng" (姜成号) and sailed from Chefoo to Incheon. They were the rich families from Huang Prefecture (黃縣). Even though they lived near Chefoo, they still had to take Chinese steamer to Incheon. Therefore, new Korean steamer companies were in urgent need at that time.

Keijō Shinppo, No. 878, dated on Feb. 4th, 1912, referred to the problems of founding Chosen Yūsen Kaisha and the most serious one was that the ships were old and that none of them were over 800 tons.

In 1912, Chosen Yūsen Kaisha's main office started its service in Keikido keijo (京畿道京城), and the branch in Busan and Wonsan. Its two main routes connected Busan and Unggi, and connected Wonsan and Unggi. Busan-Unggi route started from Busan, sailing more than 3 times a month, while Wonsan-Unggi route started from Wonsan, sailing more than 6 times a month.[20] The were also some other routes, such as Mokpo route which started from Busan; Mokpo-Gunsan route; Incheon-Gunsan route; Incheon- Chinnampo route and Incheon-Haeju (海州) route.[21]

---

17   *Keijō Shinppo*, p30.
18   *Keijō Shinppo*, p34.
19   *Keijo Shinppo*, p50.
20   *Keijo Shinppo*, p41-42.
21   *Keijo Shinppo*, p42-44.

Conclusion

Table 28　Sailing Steamers of *Chosen Yūsen Kaisha* in Aug. 1920[22]

Date of sailing	Name	Port of embarkation	Port of Destination	Store Dealing In	Date of sailing	Name	Port of embarkation	Port of Destination	Store Dealing In
Aug.3	Heian-maru 平安丸	Wonsan	Osaka	Yoshida	Aug.6	Keki-maru 京畿丸	Wonsan	Osaka	Yoshida
Aug.2	Kanjo-maru 漢城丸	Wonsan	Gangwonko	Yoshida	Aug.8	Echigo-maru 越後丸	Wonsan	Tsuruga	Yoshida
Aug.4	Echigo-maru 越後丸	Wonsan	Chongjin	Yoshida	Jul.31	Keiga-maru 慶賀丸	Wonsan	Unggi	Yoshida
Aug.5	Seishin-maru 清津丸	Wonsan	浦鹽	Yoshida	Jul.31	Shingi-maru 新義丸	Busan	Osaka	Ōike
Aug.5	Heian-maru 平安丸	Busan	Osaka	Ōike	Jul.30	Heikei-maru 平慶丸	Busan	Shimonoseki	Ōike
Jul.30	Yuki-maru 雄基丸	Busan	Sinuiju	Ōike	Aug.15	Keiki-maru 京畿丸	Busan	北鮮 (Hokusen?)	Ōike
Aug.3	Seishin-maru 清津丸	Busan	浦鹽	Ōike	Aug.3	Kinkai-maru 金海丸	Busan	Ulleungdo	Ōike
Aug.2	Rajo-maru 羅城丸	Busan	Gangwonko	Ōike	Aug.1	Shohei-maru 昌平丸	Busan	Jeju Island	Ōike
Jul.30	Soshin-maru 宗信丸	Busan	Mokpo	Ōike	Aug.2	Kankyo-maru 咸鏡丸	Mokpo	Osaka	Yamano
Jul.30	Shogen-maru 昌原丸	Mokpo	Busan	Yamano	Aug.3	慶興丸	Mokpo	Jeju Island	Yamano
Aug.1	Koshu-maru 公州丸	Mokpo	Dadohae	Yamano	Aug.6	全州丸	Mokpo	Incheon	Yamano
Jul.31	Yuki-maru 雄基丸	Mokpo	Sinuiju	Yamano	Jul.31	Kankyo-maru 咸鏡丸	Incheon	Osaka	Hori
Aug.3	Yuki-maru 雄基丸	Incheon	Sinuiju	Hori	Aug.1	Zenshu-maru 全州丸	Incheon	Mokpo	Hori
Jul.30	Kaishu-maru 海州丸	Incheon	Keumgang	Hori	Aug.1	Yuki-maru 雄基丸	Incheon	Chinnampo	Hori
Aug.5	Kogen-maru 江原丸	Incheon	Qingdao	Hori					

*Wonsan store = Yoshida Unyu Kaisha, Busan store = Ōike Kaisōbu, Mokpo store = Yamano Kaisōbu, Incheon store = Hori Kaisōbu

22　The table is based on *Keijo Nichinichi Shinbun*, No. 29, 1920.8.1~No. 33, 1920.8.5.

According to the business record[23], during 1925 to 1926, Chosen Yūsen Kaisha owned 34 steamers and had 21 routes. The total tonnage registered 31,484.43 tons, which equaled 927 tons for one. There were also 8 chartered ships and the average tonnage registered 1,362 tons. Generally in one day Chosen Yūsen Kaisha's steamers sailed 4 times, transported 622 tons of cargos and 155 passengers.

In 1915, Chosen Yūsen Kaisha opened the route among Incheon, Dalian and Chefoo. In 1931, the route starting from Incheon, via Chinnampo, Sinuiju, Chefoo, Dalian, Qingdao, and then back to Incheon was called Kōline (甲線). Otsu line (乙線) were operated in the opposite direction. In 1936, Yingkou (営口) was also added into the route.[24]

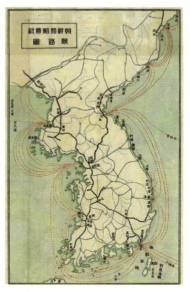

Figure 31　Map of CYK's Line

The route to Shanghai opened in 1925. It started from Incheon, via Chinnampo, Gunsan, Mokpo, Busan, Shanghai, Qingdao and then back to Incheon. In 1931, 慶安丸, which weighted 2,091 tons started its service.

5　Conclusion

In the 19th century, the steamers were gradually in place of the sailboats and played the most important role in costal transportation of East Asia. In order to compete with European steamers, China and Japan founded their own steamer companies at the end of 19th century. China Merchants' Steam Navigation Company and Nippon Yūsen Kaisha, Osaka Shōsen Kaisha were the pioneers.[25]

23　*Chosen yūsen kaisha eigyō hōkokusho nado*, p2.
24　Kobuke Yoshibē ed., *Chosen yūsen kaisha nijugonen si*, Chosen Yūsen Kabushiki Kaisha, 1937.6, pp.149-150.
25　*Osaka shōsen kabushiki kaisha gojunen si*, Osaka: Osaka shōsen kabushiki kaisha, 1934.6, pp. 189-280.
　　Nippon yūsen kabushiki kaisha gojyunen si, Nippon Yūsen Kabushiki Kaisha, 1935.12, pp.174-176.

Conclusion

Later on in 1907, Nissin Kisen Kaisha, sponsored by the Japanese government, was founded, which absorbed the Yangtze routes of Nippon Yūsen Kaisha, Osaka Shōsen Kaisha, Hunan Kisen Kaisha and Daitō Kisen Kaisha.

In the Korean Peninsula, under the guidance of Chosen Sōtokufu, Chosen Yūsen Kabushiki Kaisha started its service of costal transportation.[26] The North China Steamer Company which was founded in Dalian and later it was reconstructed and renamed as Dalian Steamer Company.

In 1938, after Tōa Kaiun Kabushiki Kaisha was founded, almost all of the Asian routes belonged to the Japanese steamer company and they were all under its operation until 1945.

MATSUURA Akira, *Kindai nihon chugoku taiwan kōrō no kenkyū*, Osaka: Seibundō, 2005.

YANG Lei, "19 seiki matsu kara 20 seiki shoki ni okeru nihon- tenshin kisen teiki kōrō", *Higashiajia bunkakanryu*, 3rd issue, No.1, Tokyo: Tōhōshoten, 2010. 1, p101-127.

LIU Jing, "20 seiki shoki no nihon to dairen kan no kōrō no kaisetsu", *Higashiajia bunkakanryu*, 3rd issue, No.1, Tokyo: Tōhōshoten, 2010. 1, p128-143.

26　Kobuke Yoshibē ed., *Chosen yūsen kaisha nijugonen si*, Chosen Yūsen Kabushiki Kaisha, 1937.6, p6132.

Appendix I: The Situation of Chinese Migrants Abroad in the Newspaper of Singapore

Migrants abroad Fujian southern coast especially southern coast of China, from Hiroshi east northeastern coastal area is famous, but not been studied in detail immigrants or were conducted in any area specifically from these areas. But it is the time of, 1907 -1909 years you look at the newspaper articles that were published in Singapore, one end of passengers number of arrival of ships to Singapore from Shantou(Swatow) and Xiamen(Amoy) can be seen.

So I made it clear specifically referring to the newspaper article about the number of Chinese who arrived from Singapore to Shantou and Xiamen 1907-1909 year in this paper.

Articles of 1827-1828 on *"Singapore Chronicle"*

1 *"Singapore Chronicle"*,[1] No.74, 18 January, 1827
Within these few days two Junks have arrived from Canton, being the tust of the □□□. We are □□□□ aware that these is anything new or peculiar in the mature of their cargoes, but those who feel any curiosity on that head will find detailed list of them in the Commercial Register. One of these Junks has brought 450 Passengers, the other has not been reported as bringing any.

2 *"Singapore Chronicle"*, No.75, 1 February 1827
Since our last three Junks have arrived, two from Canton and one from Emmoi; one of the former has brought an addition to our population of 700 men, the other 300, and the one from Emmoi 200.

---

1 *"Singapore Chronicle"* on microfilm of Indian Office Library, London.

3   *"Singapore Chronicle"*, No.76, 15 February 1827
    Since our last several junks have arrived from Siam and one from Emmoi, the latter bringing 440 passengers.

4   *"Singapore Chronicle"*, No.77, 1 March 1827
    Two Junks have arrived since our last from Emmoi, one bringing 240 and the other 276 Passengers.

5   *"Singapore Chronicle"*, No.77, 28 February 1828
    The number of Junks which have already arrived this year is three, all of the from Canton. One of them has brought 500 passengers, another also 500, and third 200, altogether 1,200.
    The people of one of these vessels were reduced to the last extremity by famine, having been out much longer than they had calculated on, owing to the junk having sustained some damage by striking on a rock which obliged them to use only one sail; besides which they state that they had more of calms and light winds on the passage than is usually experienced.
    Since writing the foregoing another Junk of estimated burthen of 600 Tons has arrived from Amoy bring 423 passengers. The cargoes of all these vessels will be found detailed in the Commercial Register.

Articles of 1907 on *"The Straits Times"*

6   *"The Straits Times"*, 29 May 1907, Page 6.
    There were 1,154 passengers from Swatow and Amoy on the Dutch steamer Merapi, which arrived from those ports, this morning, en route to Sauiarang.

7   *"The Straits Times"*, 26 June 1907, Page 6.
    There were 1,272 passengers on the British steamer Hong Bee, which arrived from Amoy and Swatow, this morning.

8   *"The Straits Times"*, 16 July 1907, Page 6.
    Over 1,600 passengers came, yesterday, from Swatow and Amoy, by the Hong Moh. This is an exceptionally large passenger list for a local steamer.

9   *"The Straits Times"*, 14 August 1907, Page 4.
    About 400 passengers arrived, this morning, from Calcutta and Penang by the Nam Sang, and 427 from Swatow and Amoy by the Simongan. The steward of the latter ship is very ill and has been sent to hospital.

Appendix

10 *"The Straits Times", 5 September 1907, Page 6.*
    Almost a thousand passengers from Swatow and Amoy arrived by the Hong Bee, yesterday afternoon.

11 *"The Straits Times", 14 September 1907, Page 6.*
    Nearly 800 passengers came down from Amoy and Swatow by Wee Bin and Company's steamer Glennfalloch, this morning.

12 *"The Straits Times", 21 September 1907, Page 6.*
    A total of 1,469 passengers arrived from Amoy and Swatow, this morning, by the steamer Glenogle.

13 *"The Straits Times", 8 October 1907, Page 6.*
    Twelve hundred and sixty-two passengers arrived from Amoy and Swatow, this morning, by the Wee Bin and Company's steamer Hong Bee.

14 *"The Straits Times", 14 November 1907, Page 6.*
    Over 500 passengers arrived from Swatow this morning, by the North German Lioyd steamer Tsintau. Over 900 more, from Amoy and Swatow, arrived by the local steamer Hong Bee.

15 *"The Straits Times", 30 November 1907, Page 8.*
    Over 800 passengers arrived from Amoy and Swatow, yesterday, by the local steamer Chong Chew. An infant died on board on Tuesday, and was buried at sea.

Articles of 1908 on *"The Straits Times"* and *"The Singapore Free Press and Mercantile Advertiser"*

16 *"The Straits Times", 17 January 1908, Page 8.*
    Over fifteen hundred passengers arrived from Amoy and Swatow by the British steamer Glenogle, yesterday afternoon.

17 *"The Straits Times", 4 March 1908, Page 6.*
    From Amoy and Swatow, this morning, 1,842 passengers arrived by the British steamer Glenogle.

18 *"The Straits Times", 2 March 1908, Page 6.*
    Messrs. Wee Bin and Company's steamer Hong VWan I. arrived from Amoy and Swatow, yesterday, with 1,140 passengers.

19 *"The Straits Times"*, *31 March 1908, Page 6.*
   The Russian steamer Meteor arrived, this morning from Shanghai in ballast. By Messrs. Wee Bin and Company's steamer Hong Wan I, there arrived from Amoy and Swatow, 1,465 deck passengers, and by the German steamer Devawongsee, from Swatow. 917 deck passengers.

20 *"The Straits Times"*, *28 April 1908, Page 6.*
   Three infants died on the Dutch steamer Merapi, which arrived from Amoy and Swatow, on Saturday, on the way down from China. There were 771 passengers on board.

21 *"The Straits Times"*, *17 June 1908, Page 6.*
   From Amoy and Swatow 674 passengers arrived, yesterday, by Messrs. Wee Bee and Company's steamer Hon Wan I. The German steamer Deva-wongsee arrived from Swatow, this morning, with 272 passengers.

22 *"The Singapore Free Press and Mercantile Advertiser"*[2], *7 July 1908, Page 8, SHIPPING NOTES.*
   It is notified that Quarantine Restrictions against the ports of Swatow and Amoy on account of small-pox are withdrawn. The homeward German mail steamer Kleist came m last night about 7 p.m. She leaves for Europe to-day. On the arrival of the "Kistna" from Malacca yesterday, Chinese youth, a cripple, was found concealed in a box on board. He is to be sent back Malacca. Quarantine restrictions with regard to smallpox have been with draw on vessels arriving from Amoy and Swatow.

23 *"The Straits Times"*, *24 August 1908, page 6.*
   At noon on Saturday, the British steamer Glenfalloch arrived from Amoy and Swatow with 731 passengers. There were four deaths eh route, two from cholera. The passengers were landed at St. John's Island and the ship was fumigated and released.

24 *"The Straits Times"*, *10 September 1908, page 6.*
   From Amoy and Swatow, yesterday, 1,269 passengers arrived by Messrs. Wee Bin and Company's steamer Hong Moh. Captain Bainbridge reports that a Chinese woman died of heart failure and was buried at sea, on Tuesday.

---

2 *"The Singapore Free Press and Mercantile Advertiser"* had been published from 1884 to 1942.

Appendix

25 *"The Straits Times"*, 23 September 1908, page 6.
Over a thousand passengers arrived from Amoy and Swatow by Messrs. Wee Bim and Company's steamer Glenfalloch.

26 *"The Singapore Free Press and Mercantile Advertiser"*[3], 13 October 1908, page 8, SHIPPING NOTES.
The Imp. German mail steamer Kleist having left Colombo on the 11th instant at 10 am may be expected to arrive here on Friday afternoon. The N.D.L. steamer Luetzow arrived at 11am yesterday, from Yokohama and she will leave at 1 pm to-day for Bremen with the German mail for Europe via Naples.
The Hong Moh from Amoy and Swatow brought down 1768 deck passengers, all well.

27 *"The Straits Times"*, 20 October 1908, page 6.
From Amoy and Swatow, 725 passengers arrived by the local steamer Cheang Chew, this morning.

28 *"The Straits Times"*, 27 October 1908, page 6.
From Amoy and Swatow, 1,166 passengers arrived, on Sunday, by the British steamer Glenfallock, belonging to Messrs. Wee Bin and Company. The Captain reports that, at 4.30 p.m. on October 21, he passed an upright spar, standing 10 feet above water, apparently attacked to a submerged junk, in latitude 14.35 and longitude 112.2 East.

29 *"The Straits Times"*, 3 November 1908, page 6.
Messrs. Wee Bin and Company s steamer Hong Bee arrived from Amoy and Swatow, yesterday, with 1,484 passengers.

30 *"The Straits Times"*, 15 December 1908, page 6.
The Chinese coolie trade seems to have begun again in earnest. Messrs. Wee Bin and Company's steamer Hong Wan I. arrived from Amoy and Swatow, this morning, with 1,330 passengers.

---

3 *"The Singapore Free Press and Mercantile Advertiser"* had been published from 1884 to 1942.

Articles of 1909 on *"The Singapore Free Press and Mercantile Advertiser"* and *"The Straits Times"*

30   *"The Singapore Free Press and Mercantile Advertiser"*[4], 12 January 1909, page 8, SHIPPING NOTES.
The Hong Bee arrived from Amoy and Swatow on Sunday with 1,439 Chinese passengers.

31   *"The Straits Times"*, 23 February 1909, page 7, Local Shipping News.
The Dutch steamer Merapi arrived from Amoy and Swatow, this morning, with a case of small-pox on board. Capt. Uldall of the Dutch Steamer Amerapi, which arrived this morning from Amoy, reports a case of small-pox on board. She brought 630 passengers for Singapore, Penang and Samarang. The Italian steamer Iscbia also came in, this morning, from Hongkong, with 220 passengers.

32   *"The Straits Times"*, 4 May 1909, page 8, Local Shipping News.
The British steamer Den of Kelly arrived from Saigon, this morning, en route to Bordeaux, with a cargo of rice. Over 1,400 passengers arrived from Amoy and Swatow, last night, by Messrs. Wee Bin and Co.'s steamer Hong Bee. The Indo China Steam Navigation Co.'s steamer Fook Sang brought from Hongkong, yesterday, twelve Chinese Chow pups tp be trans-shipped to the steamer Indrasamba, which is bound for New York. There were nearly a thousand passengers on board.

33   *"The Straits Times"*, 11 May 1909, page 8, Local Shipping News.
From Amoy and Swatow, 2,081 Chinese passengers arrived, this morning, by Messrs. Wee Bin and Co.'s steamer Hong Moh.

34   *"The Straits Times"*, 1 June 1909, page 5, Local Shipping News.
From Amoy and Swatow, 835 passengers arrived, this morning, by the German steamer Sexta.

35   *"The Straits Times"*, 3 September 1909, page 5, News Items.
From Amoy and Swatow, 846 passengers have arrived by Messrs. Wee Bin and Co.'s steamer Glenfalloch: 225 more have come Swatow by the N D. L. steamer Samsen.

---

4   *"The Singapore Free Press and Mercantile Advertiser"* had been published in Singapore from 1884 to 1942.

Appendix II: The Situation of Chinese Migrants Abroad in the Records of Chinese *Maritime Customs*

In the record of Chinese Maritime Customs, the records of Chinese visitors is known from Shantou and Xiamen to Singapore in the early of 1881 (Guangxu 8 years).

China. Imperial Maritime Customs, Returns of Trade at the Treaty Ports, for the year 1882-1892.

1 *'Swatow Trade Report, for the year 1882'*
   Passenger Traffic Never has the Swatow passenger traffic been so brisk as in the year under review. 71,301 Chinese left the port in Foreign vessels, against 49,356 in 1881, the last total being higher than that of any previous year. Most of the passengers embarked for Singapore, Bankonk, or Hongkong. Constant emigration hence to Bankonk is a novelty, being inaugurated last year by the establishment of regular steamer communication. The passenger traffic generally was greatly stimulated by the low rates of passage offered by the competing steamer companies. Fares (including board) have been as low during as low during the years as $2,50 to Singapore, $2 to Bankok, and 10 cents to Hongkong.[5]

2 *'Amoy Trade Report, for the year 1889'*
   The passenger traffic, though not attaining to the unprecedentedly high figures of 1888, surpassed that of all years previous, the total number of Chinese who left and returned having been 123,038, or nearly 5,000 more than in 1887, when the highest known record had been achieved. The largest traffic, as usual, took place with the Straits, to which place same quarter being given as 23,997 only. Manila took away 12,029, and sent back 8,873. The average rate of passage for coolies to Singapore during 1889 was $4.93, including food, per head; to Penang the cost was $1.50 more. These rates are about half what used to prevail eight or nine years

---

5 *"Zhonguo Haiguan shilio* (中國舊海關史料)" Vol.9（All. vol. 170）、Jinghua Chubanshe (京華出版社), 2001, p. 806.

ago.[6]

3 *'Swatow Trade Report, for the year 1889'*
Passenger Traffic As compared with 1888, outward traffic steadily increased----to the Straits, from 38,401 to 42,258; and to Siam, from 8,555 to 9,171. The Deli traffic worked smoothly, and 3,825 emigrates left, against 1,341 in 1888. Including passengers to and from Hongkong and coast ports, 77,317 Chinese left, and 57,462
Chinese returned to, Swatow during 1889.
The system of controlling emigration here works very well, and no serious complaints of kidnapping have reached me. But here, as everywhere else, some Chinese "jump the bounty," as it is termed, i.e., jump overboard from the outgoing steamers between Swatow and Bill Island, in order to earn cheaply the advance which their friends obtain as an earnest of future remittances. Such emigrants are not victims of fraudulent inducements to go abroad.[7]

4 *'Swatow Trade Report, for the year 1892'*
Passenger Traffic. The total number of departure of Chinese passengers amounted to 62,465, and the arrivals to 50,261. Since the middle September last competition has been very keen between the various lines of steamer engaged in the passenger traffic between Swatow and the Straits, and a cutting down of rate has resulted. The average charge for a passage to Singapore has been as low as $2.50, and is now $3.50. A considerable number of emigrants from parts of the country along the confine of the Fukkien province, whose outlet according to geographical position should have been Amoy, took ship at this port. Amoy rates of passage money were maintained at figures about $1.50 higher than those ruling here, a sufficient difference to make it worth the while of intending emigrants from the borders to commence their sea voyage from Swatow. The benefit of the reduction in rates did not, how, ever, fall to the share of the passenger alone, but also the coolie hongs.[8]

---

6 *"Zhonguo Haiguan shilio"* Vol.15, Jinghua Chubanshe, 2001, p.390.
7 *"Zhonguo Haiguan shilio"* Vol.15, Jinghua Chubanshe, 2001,p. 420.
8 *"Zhonguo Haiguan shilio"* Vol.18, Jinghua Chubanshe, 2001,p. 454.

References

Primary Sources

Japanese Primary Sources

Annan-koku hyoryu monogatari 安南国漂流物語, Ishii Kendou korekushon 石井研堂コレクション *Edo hyoryu-ki soushu* 江戸漂流記総集, vol. II, Nipponn hyouron-sha 日本評論社, 1992.

*Annan-sen yori gaikoku hyouchaku no mono shichinin okuri-kirarishi koto*安南船ヨリ外國漂着之者七人送來事>、Nagasaki jituroku taisei 長崎実録大成, vol. XII, Nagasaki Bunken Sousho 長崎文献叢書, collection I, vol. 2, Nagasaki jituroku taisei seihen 長崎實録大成正編, Nagasaki bunkensha長崎文献社, 1973.

Bunka gannen nedoshichū shuppan hikiawasechō, 17-113. [Falsche Seitenzahl?] Momose, "Chifusokusai sōsho", 157.

Gaikoku Shinbun ni Miru Nihon, (Japan As Seen in Foreign Newspapers),Volume 1, 1851-1873, *Mainichi Komyunikeshonzu* (Mainichi Communications), September 1989.

Horeki roku ushi nenn nanabann nankinnsenn kihann nimotu kaiwatashi chou (寶永六丑年 七番南京船帰帆荷物買渡帳) 船頭 沈秋堂 七月十日 [Sixth year of Hōei [1709], Year of the Ox: Record of the Purchase of Return Cargoes for the Seventh Nanjing Ship; Captain Shen Qiutang 沈秋堂. Tenth day of the seventh month]" in *Tōban kamotsu chō*, 1:2-7.

Kai hentai (Chinese Metamorphosis), Vol. 1, Tōyō Bunkō, Nonprofit Corporation, March, 1958; Reprinted by Tōhō Shoten, Nov. 1981.

Kampō 官報, 4148, 4 May 1897, 45.

Midoshi nanabann ninposenn kaiwatashi nimotuchou (巳年七番 寧波船買渡荷物帳 宝暦十二年 午四月廿二日帰帆) [Seventh Ningbo Ship: Record of Return Cargo, Returning on the twenty-second day of the fourth month, 1762, Captain: Cao Tisan 曹體三 Crew: 83 Chinese]." See *Nagasaki hiroku*, 2:10-12.

Nagasaki jitsuroku taisei (*A compilation of veritable records on Nagasaki*) (Nagasaki: Nagasaki Bunkensha, 1973), pp. 289-290.

Murakami Naojiro tr., Nagasaki oranda shōkan no nikki, vol I, Tokyo: Iwanami shoten, 1956 first printing, 1980 second printing.

Murakami Naojiro tr., Nagasaki oranda shōkan no nikki, vol II, Tokyo: Iwanami shoten, 1957 first printing, 1980 second printing.

Murakami Naojiro tr., *Nagasaki oranda shōkan no nikki*, vol III, Tokyo: Iwanami shoten, 1958 first printing, 1980 second printing.

Tōban kamotsu chō [Lists of cargoes from China and Europe], parts 1 and 2, Tokyo: Naikaku bunko, 1970.

Ōba Osamu ed., *Hōreki sannen hachijōjima hyōchaku nankinsen shiryō,* 469.

Yayoshi, *Mikan shiryō ni yoru nihon shuppan bunka,* 119.

Nisshin ryōkokukan sōnanmin kyūjo hiyō shōkan yakuyō ikken (2-6-1-9) (*An agreement on payment for the fees incurred in rescuing the castaways from Japan and China*) (preserved at the diplomatic archives, Ministry of Foreign Affairs).

Nagasaki bunken sōsho daiisshū 1, daiinimaki, Nagasaki jitsuroku taisei seihen (Nagasaki Documents Series, Series 1, vol. 2, Principal Compilation of the Authentic Account of Nagasaki), Nagasaki Bunkensha, December 12, 1973.

'Shinshiki hansen bōeki gaikyō', in *Tsūshō hōkoku* (Dai ni kai, 1886).

Ofuregaki Kampo shūsei (Tokyo: Iwanami Shoten, 1934; reprint 1989).

Ryūkyū shiryō sōsho (4) (*Historical materials on Ryūkyū Series*) (First published in 1940. Reprint, Hōbūn shokan, 1990).

Tanaka and Matsuura, *Bunsei kyūnen Enshū hyōchaku Detai sen shiryō,* 28-30.

Tōsen shinkō kaitōroku, 74, 78, 82, 86, 90, 93, 96.

Kitagawa, *Ruijū kinsei fūzoku shi,* 441.

Matsura, *Kasshi yawa* 4.

Matsura, *Kasshi yawa* 3.

Miyazaki, *Nōgyō zensho,* 391-92.

Ōkura, *Kōeki kokusan kō,* 98-101.

Kitagawa, *Ruijū kinsei fūzoku shi,* 174.

Kitamura, *Samidare zōshi,*17; see also Asakura, "Kōki", in vol. 3, 355.

Isonokami, *Bōkaen manroku,* 154-55. See also Asakura, "Afterword"in vol. 5, 409.

Nagasaki-shi shi tsūkō bōeki-hen tōyō shokokubu (The History of Marine Trade in Nagasaki City with Far Eastern Nations), Nagasaki City Office, April, 1938, p. 462.

Oka Senjin, *Guan guang ji you* 観光紀游, 1886.

Oyamada, *Matsuya hikki* 2, 124-25; also Ichijima, "Reigen", 1-5.

Takizawa, *Ibun zakkō* jō, 228. See also Asakura, "Afterword,"in vol. 2, 434.

Wakan sansai zue 18, 244.

Tsūkō ichiran 6, 24-27.

Zoku Nagasaki jitsuroku taisei, 196.

Tokugawa Jikki 9, 316.

Kobuke Yoshibē ed., *Chosen yūsen kaisha nijugonen si,* Chosen Yūsen Kabu-

shiki Kaisha, 1937.
Osaka shōsen kabushiki kaisha gojunen si, Osaka: Osaka shōsen kabushiki kaisha, 1934.
Nippon yūsen kabushiki kaisha gojyunen si, Nippon Yūsen Kabushiki Kaisha, 1935.
Yokohama Mainichi Shinbun, vol.1, Tokyo: Fujishuppan, 1989.
"Shinkoku Tenshin shijō kaisanbutsu keikyō", 46-49.

Chinese Primary Sources

He Ruzhang, *Shidong zaji* (Miscellany of an Envoy in Japan), *Xiaofanghu zhai yudi congshao, dishizhi suoshou* (Geographical Essays from the Xiaofanghu Studio, Collection Bound in the Tenth Volume).

Gongzhongdang Daoguang chao zouzhe (*Memorials of the Daoguang reign period preserved at the Imperial Archives),* no.2 (3) (Taibei: Palace Museum, unpublished documents), pp.749-750.

Gongzhongdang Qianlongchao zouzhe, 16:655-57.

Gongzhongdang Qianlongchao zouzhe, 48:837 (858).

Gongzhongdang Yongzhengchao zuozhe, diyiwu ji (Report to the Yongzheng Court, Inner Palace Files, Compilation No. 15), *Gongli gugong bowuyuan* (National Palace Museum), January 1979, p. 424.

Riben-fengtu-ji, page unknown.

Shangyu Tiaoli, hubu, "bantong tiaoli" (上諭條例 戶部、辦銅條例 *Edicts and Regulations,* Finances Section, "Regulations for the procurement of copper," 1736; Matsuura, *Edo jidai Tōsen ni yoru nitchū bunka kōryū,* 111.

HOU Jigao, *Quan Zhe Bing Zhi Kao* (全浙兵制考), National Archives of Japan, volume 2, *Fu Lu Jin Bao Wo Jing* (附錄近報倭警).*Qinding Da Qing huidian (Jiaqing chao)* (*Statutory precedents of the Qing dynasty approved by His Majesty (The Jiaqing reign period*) (*Jindai Zhongguo ziliao congkan sanbian* edition. Taibei: Wenhai Chubanshe, 1992), vol. 64, .

Qingdai zhupi zouzhe caizhenglei guanshui, document no. 0371-012 (Jiaqing period).

Qingji Zhong Ri Han guanxi shiliao (*Historical materials concerning China, Jana, and Korea during the late Qing dynasty*) (Taipe: Zhongyang Yanjiuyuan Jindaishi Yanjiusuo, 1972), vol. 3, pp. 1350-1353.

Xiaocang-shan-fang shiji 小倉山房詩集 [Collected *Xiaocang-shan-fang* poems].

*Xiaocang-shan-fang shiji buyi-*小倉山房詩集補遺 [Collected *Xiaocang-shan-fang* poems, supplement].

"Shurun zhi shengxuanhuai han", *Lunchuan zhaoshang ju shengxuanhuai dangan ziliao xuanji,* vol. 8, Shanghai: Shanghai renmin chubanshe , 2002, p. 8.

Korean Primary Sources
Dongmun hwigo (Seoul: Daikan Minkoku Bunkyōbu Kokushi Hensan Iinkai, 1978).
Zōsei kōrin shi (*Enlarged and revised records on foreign relations*) (Soul: Ajia Bunka Sha, 1974).
Keijo Nichinichi Shinbun, No. 29, 1920.8.1~No. 33, 1920.8.5
Chosen Nippo, no.1, 1905.1.15 ~ no.16, 1905.2.7.

Vietnam Primary Sources
Le Quy Don tuyen tap tap 3, PHU BIEN TAP LUC (Phan2), 2008.
PHU BIEN TAP LUC (Phan2)

English Primary Sources
Arthur W. Hummel, ed., Eminent Chinese of the Ch'ing Period (1644-1912) (Washington, D.C.: U.S. Government Printing Office, 1943).
China. Imperial Maritime Customs, Decennial Reports, 1881-91, Kiungchow,
Narrative of The Expedition of American Squadron to the China Seas and Japan, Performed in the Years 1852, 1853, and 1854, Under the Command of Commodore M. C. Perry (United States Navy, Washington, 1856).
John Crawfurd, *Journal of an Embassy to the Courts of Siam and Cochin China*, 1828.
Report from the Select Committee on the affairs of the East India Company and the trade between Great Britain, the East Indies and China, 1830, Irish University Press Area Studies Series British Parliamentary Papers, China 37, Irish University Press, 1971.

Secondary Sources

Arai Eiji 荒居英次, *Kinsei kaisanbutsu bōeki shi no kenkyū—chūgokumuke yushutsu bōeki to kaisanbutsu* , Tokyo: Yoshikawa koubunnkann,1975.
Boyd Cable, *A Hundred Year History of the P. & O. Peninsular and Oriental Steam Navigation Company 1837-1937*, London: Ivor Nicholson and Watson, 1937.
Chen Jinghe. Qing-chu Hua-bo zhi Changqi maoyi ji rinan yunhang, Nanyang xuebao,vol. 13, no.1, 1957, pp. 1-52.
Feng Chengjun(annotation), *Zhu Fan Zhi Jiao Zhu annotation*, Peking, The Commercial Press,1940Kawashima, "Saisho ni kokoromita Shanhai bōeki," 115-66.
Iwao Seiichi, "Edo jidai no satō bōeki ni tsuite," 1-33.
Ogawa Kuniharu 小川国治, *Edo bakufu yushutsu kaisanbutsu no kenkyū—*

tawaramono no seisan to shūka kikō , Tokyo: Yoshikawa koubunnkann, 1973.
I.A. Donnely, *Chinese junks and other native craft* (Shanghai, 1924), 1-142.
KOKAZE Hidemasa 小風秀雅, Eikoku P&O kisen no nihon shinshutsu to mitsubishi to no kyosō ni tsuite, *Nihon Rekishi*, 1990.4, pp. 94-100
KOKAZE Hidemasa, *Teikokushugi ka no nihon kaiun- Kokusai kyosō to taigai jiritu*, Tokyo: Yamakawa, 1995.2, p27
John Haskell Kemble, *A Hundred Years of the Pacific Mail, The American Neptune*, Mariners' Museum, 1950, p.131.
Kanazashi Shōzō, *Kinsei kainan kyūjo no kenkyū* , Tokyo: Yoshikawa kōbunkan, 1968.
Kobata, "Satō no shiteki kenkyū ni tsuite," 217, *Taiwan jihō* 臺灣時報 186 and 187 (1935/5, 6).
LI Hongzhang, "Shiban zhaoshang lunchuan zhe", *Liwenzhonggong Zougao*, vol. 20.
LIU Kwangching, *Anglo-America Steamship Rivalry in China, 1862-1874*, Havard University Press, 1962.
MATSUURA Akira, *Kindai nihon chugoku taiwan kōrō no kenkyū*, pp. 11-15
Matsuura, "Nisshin bōeki ni yoru tawaramono no chūgoku ryūnyū ni tsuite".
Matsuura, *Kinsei higashiajia kaiiki no bunka kōshō*, 334-47.
Matsuura Akira, *Edo jidai tōsen ni yoru nitchū bunka kōryū* (Sino-Japanese Cultural Interaction via Chinese Junk in the Edo Period), Shibunkaku Press, July 2007, p.248.
   Matsuura Akira, *Shindai Shanghai shasen kōungyō shi no kenkyū* (Osaka, 2004).
Matsuura Akira, *Shindai kaigai bōeki shi no kenkyū* (Kyoto, 2002).
NAKAGAWA Keiichiro, "P. & O. kisen kaisha no seiritsu- igirisu tōyō kaiun si no hitokoma", *Shihonshugi no seiritsu to hatten-Tsuchiya takao kyoju kanreki kinen ronbunshu*, Tokyo: Yūhikaku, 1959.
NIE, Bazhang ed., *Zhongguo jindai hangyun si ziliao*, vol. 1, Shanghai: Shanghai Renmin Chubanshe, 1983.
Matsuura Akira, *Shindai kaigai bōekishi no kenkyū* (Research on the History of Foreign Trade in the Qing Period).
Matsuura Akira, *Shindai kaigai bōekishi no kenkyū* (Research on the History of Foreign Trade in the Qing Period), Hōyū Shoten, January 2002, pp 382-402.
Matsuura Akira, *Qingdai Taiwan haiyun fazhanshi* (Taipei, 2002), 1-152; 'Rizhi shidai Taiwan yu Fuzhou zhijian rongke maoyi shiliao Tongshang huizuan jieshao'. *Taibei wenxian (zhizi)*, 152 (2005), 269-324, 153 (Taipei, 2006), 206-66.

Matsuura Akira, 'Rizhi shiqi Taiwan he Zhongguo dalu zhijian de fanchuan hangyun', *Taibei wenxian (zhizi)*, 150 (Taipei, 2004), 51-82.

Matsuura, "Nisshin bōeki ni yoru tawaramono no Chūgoku ryūnyū ni tsuite", 19-38; Matsuura, *Shindai kaigai bōekishi no kenkyū*, 382-402.

Matsuura Akira, "Mindai ni okeru Chōsensen no Chūgoku hyōchaku ni tuite (*The encounters of Korean ships in Ming China*)," *Kansai Daigaku Bungaku Ronshū*, 51:3 (2002), pp.25-45.

Matsuura Akira, "Shindai makki no shasengyo ni tsuite," Kansai daigaku bungaku ronshu 39:3 (1990), pp. 1-71.

Matsuura Akira, "18~19 seki ni okeru nansei shotō hyōchaku Chūgoku hansen yorimita Shindai kōungyo no ichisokumen," *Kansai Daigaku Tōzai Gakujyutsu kenkyūsho Kiyō*, no. 16 (1983), pp. 17-75.

Matsuura Akira, "Richō hyōchaku Chūgoku hansen no 'monjō bettan' nituite," *Kansai Daigaku Tōzai Gakujyutsu kenkyūsho Kiyō*, no.17 (1984), pp. 25-83; no. 18 (1985), pp. 33-96.

Matsuura Akira, *Shindai Shanghai sasen kōunshi no kenkyū*, Suida: Kansai Daigaku Shuppankai, 2004.

Matsuura Akira, *Edo jidai tōsen ni yoru nitchū bunka kōryū*, Kyoto: Shibunkaku, 2007.

Matsuura Akira, *Kindai nihon chugoku taiwan kōrō no kenkyū*, Osaka: Seibundō, 2005.

MATSUURA Akira, *Studies in the History of Qing Period Maritime Trade*, Kyoto, 2002.

MATSUURA Akira, *The sailing ship of Qing Dynasty in East Asia and maritime commerce and pirate* (清代帆船東亞航運與海商海盜), Shanghai Lexicographical Publishing House, 2009.

Matsuura Akira, "Shinkoku rinsen shōshokyoku no nihon kōkō", *Bulletein of the Institute of Oriental and Occidental Studies*, No.39, 2006.4, pp. 1-48.

Matsuura Akira, Shindai Senshu Shinko Hansen niyoru kaiyou bunnka koushou 清代泉州晋江帆船による海洋文化交渉, Higashi Ajia Bunka kousho kennkyu 東アジア文化交渉研究, Kansai University, No. 2, 2009 March, pp.145-164.

Nagazumi Yoko, *Tōsen yushutsunyūhin sūryō ichiran* 1637-1833, Soubunsha, 1987.

Nagasaki kenshi hensan iinkai ed., Nagasaki kenshi shiryouhenn, Nagasaki: Nagasaki ken, 1965.

Ng Chin-Keong, *Trade and Society The Amoy Network on the China Coast 1683-1735 (Second Edition)*, Singapore, 2015.

Ōba Osamu, 'Hirado Matsuura shiryō hakubutsukan zō 'Tōsen no zu' ni tsuite– Edo jidai ni raikō shita Chūgoku shōsen no shiryō', *Kansia Daigaku Tōzai*

Gakujutsu Kenkyūjo Kiyō, 5 (Osaka, 1972), 13-49;

Ōba Osamu, 'Scroll paintings of Chinese junks which sailed to Nagasaki in the 18th century and their equipment', *Mariner's Mirror*, 60:4 (1974), 351-62.

Ōba Osamu, *Edo jidai ni okeru Chūgoku bunka juyō no kenkyū* , Kyoto: Douhousha, 1984.

Ōba Osamu, *Edo jidai ni okeru tōsen mochiwatashisho no kenkyū*; Ōba, *Edo jidai ni okeru chūgoku bunka juyō no kenkyū*.

Sakuma Shigao, A Study of Relations between Japan and the Ming Dynasty, Tokyo, 1992.

Sekino Tadakazu, *Sekai tōgyō bunka shi*, 3.

Yan, *Qingdai Yunnan tongzheng kao*, 3. The treasury of the Board of Finances and the mint of the Board of Works in Beijing required over 4,400,000 *jin* of copper every year to mint coins (Ibid., 4).

Soda Hiroshi, "Kinsei hyōryūmin to Chūgoku (The castaways and China in recent times)," *Fukuoka Kyōiku Daigaku shakaika kiyō*, 31:2 (1982), pp. 1-20.

Sasaki Masaya 佐々木正哉, 19seiki-shoki chuugoku jyanku no kaigaiboueki ni kansuru shiryou 十九世紀初期中国戎克の海外貿易に関する資料、 Kindai Chugoku 近代中国, Vol. 3, 1978 May, pp. 56-74.

Thomas Allom & G, N. Wright, *China, in a Series of Views, Displaying the Scenery, Architecture, and Social Habits, of that Ancient Empire,* 1843, Vol. III, p. 49.

Tang Xiyong, "Shindai zenki chūgoku ni okeru Chōsenkoku no kainansen to hyōryūmin kyūjo ni tuite (*The salvage of shipwrecks and the rescue of castaways from Korea during early Qing China*)," *Nantou Shigaku*, no.59 (2002), pp. 18-43. See also his "Shindai Chūgoku ni okeru Betonamu kainansen no kyūjo hōhō ni tuite (*The practices of salvaging Vietnamese shipwrecks during Qing China*)," *Nantou Shigaku*, no.60 (2002), pp. 38-56.

Saeki Tomi 佐伯富, *Gazoku kango yakkai* 雅俗漢語訳解 (*Understanding Classical and Colloquial Chinese*), Kyoto: Douhousha shuppannbu, 1976.

Tian Rukang, *Zhonguo fanchuan maoyi yu duiwai guanxi shi lunji* (*Collected essays on the history of China's junk trade and foreign relations.* Hangzhou: Zhejiang Renmin Chubanshe, 1987), pp. 1-99.

Xiamen zhi (*Zhongguo fangzhi congshu* edition. (Taipei, 1967), 108.

Ymawaki Teijirou , Kinsei Nichuu bouekishi no kennkyuu , Tokyo: Yoshikawa kobunnkan, 1959.

Yamawaki Teijirou 山脇悌二郎, "*Tōban kamotsu chō* kaidai" 唐蠻貨物帳解題 ["Explanatory Notes on *Tōban kamotsu chō*"], pp. 1-12, "*Tōban kamotsu chō*", Tokyo: Naikaku bunko, 1970.

Ymawaki Teijirou, Nagasaki no Tojin bouki, Tokyo: Yoshikawa kobunnkan,

1964.

Zhou Shide, 'Zhongguo shachuan kaolue', *Kexue shi jikan*, 5 (Beijing, 1963),34-54.

Zheng Zuan, *Shanghai diming xiaozhi*, (Shanghai, 1988), 18.

Ōba, *Edojidai ni okeru tōsen mochiwatashisho no kenkyū*, 733.

Nagasawa, *Wakokubon kanshi shūsei*, 192.

Naikaku bunko, *Kaitei naikaku bunko kanseki bunrui mokuroku*, 58.

Kobuke Yoshibē ed., *Chosen yūsen kaisha nijugonen si*, Chosen Yūsen Kabushiki Kaisha, 1937.6, p6132.

Lin Jing, "20 seiki shoki no nihon to dairen kan no kōrō no kaisetsu", *Higashiajia bunkakanryu*, 3rd issue, No.1, Tokyo: Tōhōshoten, 2010. 1, p128-143

Yang Lei, "19 seiki matsu kara 20 seiki shoki ni okeru nihon- tenshin kisen teiki kōrō", *Higashiajia bunkakanryu*, 3rd issue, No.1, Tokyo: Tōhōshoten, 2010. 1, p101-127.

Afterword

This book is summarizes mainly English paper presented at study life so far.

The first Part of three papers, chapter, third, 4th and 6th are have been translated by Wang Zhenping of Professor of National Institute of Education, Nanyang Technological University (NIE/NTU), Singapore.

The first chapter of the second part are those that have been published in the Society for Cultural Interaction in East Asian's magazine *"Journal of Cultural Interaction in East Asia"* vol.1, 2010. Other three papers (Chapter 8-10) is intended to Dr. Keiko Nagase-Reimer, Technical University Berlin, Germany gave me the translation, were recorded rely to those that have been published from the famous publisher Brill of the Netherlands.[1]

The English translation of the other papers, Nian Xu and Zhao Siqian of Kansai University Graduate School of East Asian Cultures and Pekin University MA Ms. Chen Lu, were the cooperation of each paper.

Also during the publication, your efforts our was Kansai University authorities as well as Nobuo Nakatani Director, Institute of Oriental and Occidental Studies, the Secretariat Tomoko Nasu and the Yasuko Akai.

Although there is at the end, I would like to thank for everyone.

---

1 Keiko Nagase-Reimer ed., *Copper in Early Modern Sino-Japanese Trade,* Brill, Netherlands, 2016, pp.118-195 (pp.1-224).

Index & Glossary

A

Aden 伊敦　53, 121, 139, 160, 161, 169, 201
Aki 安芸　15-18, 20, 22, 23, 30-32, 34, 51, 52, 58, 60, 67, 83, 86, 92, 94-96, 98, 104-106, 109-116, 118-123, 125-129, 131, 132, 134-137, 139, 143, 144, 146-150, 153, 157, 159, 160, 162-167, 169-173, 175, 176, 178, 179, 183, 184, 187-191, 193, 195, 199, 202-204, 206
Amakusa 天草　128
An'ei 安永　113, 173
Anhui 安徽　164, 195
Asakawa Zen'an 朝川善庵　181
Ashikaga Yoshiteru 足利義輝　48
Awajishima 淡路島　204
Awa 阿波　19, 27, 31, 48, 53, 68, 70, 86, 89, 94-98, 105, 106, 109, 110, 112, 113, 115, 116, 118, 120-123, 147, 148, 150, 159, 160, 165, 168, 171, 172, 175, 176, 179, 181, 183, 184, 186, 187, 189, 193, 195, 196, 203

B

bageniao 八哥鳥　132
Bai Letian 白楽天　183
Bantam　50
Bao Tinbo 鮑廷博　179, 193-195
baoyu 鮑魚　115
Beian bokudan 米菴墨談　186
Beihikyakusen 米飛脚船　202
birds boats 鳥船　13, 14
Bōkaen manroku 卯花園漫録　174, 175
Bohai Sea 渤海　48, 57-59
brown sugar 黒砂糖 kurozatō　161

Bunka 文化　105, 110, 112, 122, 123, 146, 166, 173, 174
Bunsei 文政　105, 175, 176
bupi　30
Busan 釜山　200, 205-207, 209
Butsu Shukutatsu 物叔達　180

C

Cambojia　79
Cang-shan ji 倉山集　183, 184
Canton カントン 廣東　80, 83, 84, 86-88, 111, 161
Champa 占城　39, 46, 47, 79, 80
Chang Lai 常賚　82
Chaozhou 潮州　50, 52, 53, 85, 169, 175
Chen Facai 陳發材　93
Chenghai 潮澄　169
Chen Yidong 陳翼棟　204
Chikura 千倉　105, 165
China Merchants' Steam Navigation 招商局輪船公司　199-201, 209
Chinese herbal medicine 漢方薬剤　23
Chinese Junks　13-16, 20, 22, 23, 34, 35, 58, 59, 80, 85, 87, 88, 111, 113, 114, 117, 118, 121, 122, 125, 131, 132, 134, 148, 159, 162, 177-179, 187, 188, 190, 195, 196
Chi-yen 致遠　201, 202
Chongming-dao 崇明島　71
Chosen Nippo 朝鮮日報　205
Chuansha 川沙　169
Chunqiu-zuoshi-zhuan 春秋左氏傳　192
citron 佛手柑 busshukan　170
cloves 丁子 丁香　33, 48
Cochin-china　79
Copper 銅　16, 22, 23, 114, 115,

228

125-129, 132-139, 143, 144, 146-148, 157, 168, 178, 193
Cui-she-ren Yu-tang-leigao 崔舍人玉堂類藁 192

D

dadu dufu 大都督府 46
Dai Biao-yuan 戴表元 72
Daigaku 大學 123, 177, 180
daimei 30
Da Ming huidian 大明會典 91
Daoguang 道光 18, 20-22, 32, 66, 68, 71, 72, 74, 168
Da Qing huidian shili 大清會典事例 91, 92
Daxue Zhangju Zuanshi 大學章句纂釋 180
Dazue 大學 177
Dejima White 出島白 Dejima-jiro 170, 172
Detai 得泰 29, 44, 63, 66, 69, 90-92, 97, 112, 143, 150, 160, 165, 166, 168, 179, 205
Ding Ri-chang 丁日昌 76
Donghai 東海 90
Dongmun hwigo 同文彙考 92, 99
dongren 東人 178
Dongyi-baojian 東醫寶鑑 188, 189
Dongyi-baojian 訂正東醫寶鑑 188, 189
Doshū 土州 172
dried abalone 干し鮑、鮑魚 115, 126-131, 144, 147, 150, 151, 153, 154, 157
dried abalone 干鮑 hoshi-awabi 115, 126-131, 144, 147, 150, 151, 153, 154, 157
dried abalone 鰒魚 fuyu 115, 126-131, 144, 147, 150, 151, 153, 154, 157
dugang 都綱 40
Dutch merchant ships 177

E

East China Sea 52, 53, 58, 59, 70
en kung-sheng 恩貢生 74
Ennin 円仁 38
Enshū 遠州 104, 105, 172
Ershiyi-shi 二十一史 194

F

Fai-fo 海防 84, 85
Fang-qiu-ya-shi-chao 方秋崖詩鈔 181
Fang Yizhi 方以智 180
Fang Yue 方岳 181
Fu bian za lu 撫邊雜録 82
fu-chuan 福船 13, 14
Fujian boats 福船 13, 14
Fujian 福建 14, 15, 18-23, 30, 31, 33, 34, 40-44, 46-56, 58-61, 63, 66-68, 70, 77, 79-82, 87, 88, 92, 93, 109, 114, 116, 118, 126, 134, 159, 168-170, 175
Fujian 福建 14, 15, 18-23, 30, 31, 33, 34, 40-44, 46-56, 58-61, 63, 66-68, 70, 77, 79-82, 87, 88, 92, 93, 109, 114, 116, 118, 126, 134, 159, 168-170, 175
Fujita Toyohachi 藤田豊八 28
Fukami Arichika 深見有隣 160, 171
Fukuda Dennoshin 福田傳之進 129
Fuqing 福清 30, 68, 134
fuyu 鰒魚、鮑魚 80, 115, 126, 184
Fuzhou 福州 27, 40, 47, 57, 67-69, 88, 93, 94, 98, 106, 116, 134, 161

G

Gangnam 江南 71
Gansu 甘肅 194
Gaobai 告白 203
Genna 元和 193
Genroku 元禄 15, 114, 119, 126-128, 164, 173

229

geshi 夏至　168
Gia Long 嘉隆帝　88
ginger 生薑 shōga　31, 170
ginseng 人参 ninjin　21, 153
guan-chuan 廣船　13, 14
Guangnan 廣南　37, 87, 161, 162
Guan guang ji you 観光紀游 Kanko
　-kiyu　204
guanshang 官商 kansho　168
Gu Kuiguang 顧奎光　181
guotanghang 過塘行　169
Guo-zi jian 國子監　74
Guwen Xiaojing Kong-zhuan 古文孝經
　孔傳　193
Guwen Xiaojing 古文孝經　119, 191,
　193

H

Hae-ting 海定　201
Haiguanshuikou 海關稅口　168
haihan chiken 廃藩置県　95
Haijin 海禁　46, 80, 81
Hainan Island 海南島　79, 85, 87, 88
Hai Phong 海防　87
haishen 海參　115, 126
Hangzhou 杭州　20, 30, 39, 42-44,
　53, 80, 113, 114, 117, 161, 168, 195
Hankou 漢口　199-201
Hao Yulin 郝玉麟　17, 20
Harimanada 播磨灘　204
Hayashi Akira 林燧、復斎　89
Hayashi Jussai 林述斎　184
Hei Shiryū 平子龍　182
Hōei 宝永　13, 15, 16, 18, 20-23,
　27-30, 32-35, 37-52, 54-56, 58-61,
　63, 64, 66-72, 74, 76, 77, 79-81,
　83-87, 90-98, 105, 106, 110-123,
　126-132, 134, 137, 143, 146, 150,
　153, 154, 157, 159, 160, 162-164,
　166-169, 171-184, 186-189, 192,
　193, 195, 196, 199-204, 207, 209
He Ruzhang 何如璋　115, 122, 126
Himemiya-maru 姫宮丸　83

Hirado 平戸　131, 150, 176
Hoi An 會安　88
Hou-Han shu 後漢書　73
Hōreki 宝暦　135
huameiniao 畫眉鳥　132
Huang Prefecture 黃縣　207
Huan Kuan 桓寬　180
huaqiao 華僑　51
Hue 会安　80, 84, 85, 87, 88
Huizhou 徽州　53, 195
Hu Yuji 胡球基　22
Huzhou silk 湖絲　31
Huzhou 湖州　168, 195
Hué 順化　71-74, 79-90, 94, 96, 98,
　104, 106, 109-115, 117, 119-123,
　125-128, 130-132, 135, 137, 146,
　147, 149, 150, 154, 156, 159, 160,
　164, 168, 172, 173, 175-184,
　186-188, 191-195, 199-205, 207,
　210
Hwai-yuen 懷遠　201

I

iced water vendors 冷水売
　hiyamizuuri　174
Ichikawa Beian 市河米菴　186
Ichikawa Kansai 市河寬斎　181, 183,
　186, 187, 193, 196
Ichikawa Shisei boketsumei 市河子静墓
　碣銘　184
Igakukan 醫學館　189
Ikki Maru 壹岐丸　207
Inasayama 稲佐山　184
Incheon 仁川　207, 209
Indonesia インドネシア　27, 43, 50,
　170
Irie Nanmei 入江南溟　180
Ise 伊勢　28, 36, 42, 43, 46, 48, 49,
　69, 73, 96, 109, 112, 114, 116, 123,
　126, 127, 133, 136, 143, 144, 153,
　168, 179-182, 184, 187-189, 195,
　199, 200, 202, 204, 206, 210
Ishida Mikinosuke 石田幹之助　28

Izumi no kami 筒井和泉守　189

J

Jiang-cheng 姜成号　207
Jiangnan 江南　31-33, 42, 44, 53, 113, 116, 117, 121, 134, 168, 169, 200
Jiangsu 江蘇　31, 33, 48, 53, 56, 65, 76, 87, 117, 200
Jiangxi 江西　73, 80
Jiang Yunge 江芸閣　189
jian-sheng 監生　74
Jianzhen 鑑真　38, 39
Jiaqing 嘉慶　52, 61, 63, 66, 91, 92, 166, 169
Jiaxing 嘉興　66, 117, 126, 168, 195
Jijitsu bunpen 事実文編　184
Jing He Tang Ji 敬和堂集　80
Jingwensong-gong-ji 景文宋公集　192
Jin-shi-chao 金詩鈔　181
Jinyuansheng 金源盛 Junk's registered name　165
Jinzhou 錦州　54, 57-59, 61, 63, 93
Jiu-shao 秦九韶　72, 73
Ji-xiao-xin-shu 紀効新書　182
Ji zi zhai yi you dong you ri ji 寄自齋己西東遊調査日記　204
Junk ジャンク　13, 14, 17, 19-23, 32, 34, 35, 51, 52, 55, 57-61, 63-66, 68-70, 79, 80, 84-86, 109-111, 113-118, 121, 122, 125, 127, 128, 131, 134, 148, 157, 159, 161, 162, 177-179, 187, 188, 190, 191, 195, 196

K

kago 籠　95
Kanagawa Maru 金澤丸　203
Kan'ei 寛永　113
Kangxi 康熙　13, 15, 16, 81, 82, 90, 97, 113, 114, 126

Kansei 寛政　16, 116, 172, 173, 182
kansho 官商 guanshang　170
Kasshi yawa 甲子夜話　172, 176
Keiho muyoroku 瓊浦夢餘錄　184
Keikido 京畿道　207
kelp 昆布 海帶　126, 130-132, 134, 144, 147, 150, 154, 157, 168
Kinzanji miso 金山寺味噌　174, 176
Kitagawa Morisada 喜多川守貞　172
Kiungchow 瓊州　87
Kobai enbokufu 古梅園墨譜　188
Kobe 神戸　199, 202-205
kogan 古玩　179
Koga Seiri 古賀精里　180
Kong Anguo 孔安國　191
Koxinga 国姓爺、鄭成功　53, 113

L

Laoxuean biji 老學庵筆記　164
Leng-zhai-shi-hua 冷齋詩話　181
Leshu-yaolu 樂書要錄　192
Liangjing-xinji 兩京新記　192
Liaodong 遼寧　69, 71, 93
Li Bai 李白　183
Li Daiheng 李大衡　171, 172
Liji 礼記　31, 177, 188
Lin Junsheng 林君陞　169
Liuhe 劉河　169
Liu Huaqian 劉華謙　130
Liu Jingyun 劉景謙　166, 189
Luerhmen 鹿耳門　17
Lunyu-jijie-yishu 論語集解義疏　194
Lunyu-jijie 論語集解　189
Lunyu-yishu 論語義疏　193
Lunyu-zheng 論語徵　188, 189
Lunyu 論語　177, 188
Lushi-chunqiu 呂氏春秋　189
Lu Xin-yuan 陸心源　77
Lu You 陸游　164

M

Makino Yamatonokami 牧野大和守成傑 184
Mao Wenquan 毛文銓 81
Marco Polo 44
Maritime ban 海禁政策 46, 48, 50
Maritime History 27, 29, 35
Matsudaira Tsugutoyo 松平繼豊 160
Matsura Seizan 松浦靜山 172, 176
Matsuya hikki 松屋筆記 175
Meiwa 明和 16, 116, 178
Mengqiu 蒙求 192
Mikawa 三河 172, 176, 181
Miyazaki Yasusada 宮崎安貞 172, 173
Mokpo 木浦 33, 207, 209
Muromachi Bakufu 室町幕府 49, 116

N

Nagakubo Sekisui 長久保赤水 119
Nagasaki jitsuroku taisei 長崎實錄大成 116, 123, 188
Nagasakishi zokuhen 長崎志續編 188
Nagasakishi 長崎志 188
Nagasaki 長崎 15-17, 20, 22, 23, 30, 34, 51, 52, 58, 67, 83, 92, 94-96, 98, 109-116, 118-123, 125-129, 131, 132, 134-137, 139, 143, 144, 146-150, 157, 159, 160, 162-167, 169-171, 175, 176, 178, 179, 183, 184, 187-191, 193, 195, 199, 202-204
Namikawa Tenmin 並河天民 181
Nanjing 南京 88, 129, 131-133, 146, 170, 182, 192
Nan Juyi 南居益 109, 110
Nanshi 南市・上海 63-66
Nha Le 黎朝 88
Nha Nguen 阮朝 88
niao-chuan 鳥船 13, 14

Nigata Maru 新潟丸 203
Ningbo 寧波 27, 31, 32, 39-41, 44, 47, 51, 52, 58-60, 67, 68, 70, 92, 113, 114, 116, 128, 130-132, 166, 170
Niuzhuang 牛莊 31, 32, 57, 59, 61, 63-66, 68

O

ocean ginseng 海參 haishen 115, 153
ochinchina 交阯 80
Ohshu 奧州 83
OKA Senjin 岡千仞（鹿門） 204
oke 桶 30, 46, 53, 86, 92, 112, 113, 119, 133, 177, 182, 184, 196, 207
Owari 尾張 181, 193
Oyamada Tomokiyo 小山田與清 175

P

Philippine 19, 20, 27, 31, 50, 86, 87, 92
Pinghu 平湖 117, 126, 195
powdered sugar 粉砂糖 konazatō 162
Pu Shougeng 蒲壽康 28, 43

Q

Qianlong 乾隆 16, 18, 21, 31, 53, 54, 90, 92, 97, 106, 126, 134, 168, 178, 186, 194
Qijin Mengzi-Kaowen-Buyi 七經孟子考文補遺 180, 189
Qingdao 青島 209
Qing-shi-gao 清史稿 194
Qingzhu 范清注 137
Quan Tang-shiyi 全唐詩逸 193
Quan-Tang-shi-yi 全唐詩逸 181
Quanzhou 泉州 20, 33, 34, 40-44, 47, 53, 67, 79, 161, 162, 166, 175
Qunshu-zhiyao 群書治要 188, 189, 193

R

Raiki 礼記　177
rock candy 氷砂糖
　koorizatō　161-167
Rongo 論語　177, 194
Ryukyu 琉球　20-23, 27, 31, 32, 47, 110

S

sakoku 鎖国　112, 113, 177
Sakura Maru 櫻丸　207
sanbon sugar 三盆　165
sanbon 三盆　166, 172
sand boats 沙船　13, 14
Satsuma Maru 薩摩丸　207
Sawa Tansai 佐羽淡齋　181
sea cucumber 海參 haishen
　115, 126-132, 134, 144, 147, 150, 153, 154, 157, 168, 178
sea cucumber 海鼠、海參　115, 126-132, 134, 144, 147, 150, 153, 154, 157, 168, 178
sea cucumber 煎海鼠 iriko　115, 126-132, 134, 144, 147, 150, 153, 154, 157, 168, 178
seaweed 海草 海藻　60, 130, 144, 154, 157
Seikado bunko靜嘉堂文庫　77
Senzai-maru 千歳丸　120, 121, 147
sha-chuan 沙船　13, 14, 71
shaluo　30
Shanghai　22, 27, 32, 33, 44, 51, 52, 56, 57, 60, 63-68, 71, 74, 76, 82, 116, 117, 120, 121, 147, 148, 150, 169, 171, 199-204, 209
Shanhanlun-jiyi 傷寒論輯義　189
shark fin 魚翅 yuchi　126-132, 144, 153, 154, 157
shark fin 鱶鰭 fuka-hire　126-132, 144, 153, 154, 157
Shen Huai 沈淮　181
Shen Jingzhan 沈敬瞻　165
Shen Qiquan 沈綺泉　189

shibosi 市舶使　39, 40, 44, 48
Shi bo ti ju si 市舶提擧司　82
Shidong zaji 使東雑記　115, 122
Shiji-pinglin 史記評林　189
Shimazu domain島津藩　160
Shimonoseki 下関　150, 199, 203, 204, 207
shinpai 信牌　115, 116, 171
shoshiki 諸色　150
Shu-Han 蜀漢　72, 73
shuinsen 朱印船　30
Shujing 書経　177, 188
Shu-shu jiu-zhang 數書九章　72
silk 絹　20, 30, 33, 34, 39, 40, 48, 50, 51, 56, 84, 86, 87, 94, 112, 117, 126, 157, 178
Sishu Bianjiang 四書便講　180
Sishu-jizhu 四書集註　179, 180, 189
Song-shi-chao 宋詩鈔　181
Soo-loo Islands 蘇禄　86
South China Sea 南シナ海 南海　27, 49-52, 58, 70, 79
steamed buns 饅頭 manjū　174
sugar cane 甘蔗 kansho　159, 160, 170, 171
Suharaya Ihachi 須原屋伊八　179
Sui-yuan-shi-chao 随園詩鈔　181, 183, 196
Sui-yuan-shi-hua 随園詩話　182, 183, 186, 187
Sui-yuan-shi-hua 随園詩話　182, 183, 186, 187
Sui-yuan 随園　182, 183, 186
Sumiyoshi-maru 住吉丸　83
sumu　30
Suo 周防　44, 122, 174
surugaban 駿河版　193
Suruga 駿河　160, 166, 172, 176, 193
Suzhou 蘇州　31, 68, 109, 117, 118, 122, 134, 169

T

taihaku 太白　172

Taiping Rebellion 太平天国の乱 63, 120, 121
Taiping yulan 太平御覧 42
taisetsu 大雪 168
Taiwan 台湾 13, 14, 17-19, 27, 33, 50, 52, 53, 55, 58, 60, 67-69, 81, 90, 91, 93, 106, 113, 127, 129, 130, 153, 154, 159, 170
Takasago Maru 高砂丸 203
Takizawa Bakin 滝沢馬琴 175
Tang-cai-zi-zhuan 唐才子傳 192
tangerines 蜜柑 mikan 59, 60, 170, 175
Tangguan 唐館 118
tawaramono 俵物 115, 150
Tenmei 天明 172
Tianjin 天津 27, 31, 32, 51, 52, 56, 58-61, 67, 69, 94, 153, 154, 169, 200, 201
Tianqi 天啓 61, 109
Tian Rucheng 田汝成 181
Tokugawa Bakufu 徳川幕府 109, 110, 113, 118, 120-122, 147, 148
Tokugawa Yoshimune 徳川吉宗 171, 172
Tokyo Maru 東京丸 203, 204
Tokyo Nichi Nichi Shinbun 東京日日新聞 203
Tokyo Yokohama Mainichi Shinbun 東京横濱毎日新聞 202
Tongshang Riben shuo 通商日本説 125
Tonquin 東京・越南 84-86
Torai 東莱 93
Trade License 信牌 shinpai 126
Tsushima Maru 對馬丸 207
Tungking 東京、越南 79
Twelve Families 十二家 136, 146

U

Umega Maru 梅ヶ丸 207

W

Wakan sansai zue 和漢三才図会 170
Wang Danwang 王亶望 194
Wang-han-lin-ji-zhu Huangdi-bashiyi-nanjing 王翰林集註黄帝八十一難經 192
Wang Peng 汪鵬 119, 178, 194
Wang Shengwu 汪繩武 119
Wang Tao 王韜 125
Wang Wei 王維 183
Wang Xianzhi 王仙之 37
Wang Zaijin 王在晋 29
Wang Zhuli 汪竹里 119, 178, 193
Wang Zongding 王宗鼎 165
Wang 王 30, 45, 48, 53, 80, 81, 98, 126, 136, 146, 180, 181, 183, 192, 195
Wei Yuanlang 魏元烺 93, 94
Wendeng 文登 65, 93
Wen-gong-zhu-xiansheng-ganxing-shi 文公朱先生感興詩 192
Wenguan Cilin 文館詞林 192
white sugar 白砂糖 shirozatō 30, 115, 126, 161-167, 169-171, 174, 175
winter melon 冬瓜 tōgan 170
Wuhumen 五虎門 79
Wulixiaoshi 物理小識 180
Wusong 吳淞 169
Wuxing-dayi 五行大義 191, 193, 195
Wu Yongwan 吳永萬 169

X

Xiamen 厦門 17-19, 21, 27, 34, 51, 59, 67-69, 130, 164, 171, 172, 175
Xiaocang-shan-fang chidu 小倉山房尺牘 182
Xiaocang-shan-fang quanji 小倉山房全集 183
Xiaocang-shan-fang shichao 小倉山房詩鈔 183, 186

Xiaocang-shan-fang wen-chao 小倉山房文鈔　182
Xiaocang-shan-fang 小倉山房　182-184, 186, 187
Xiaochangdao 小長島　93
Xiaojing Huitong 孝經會通　181
Xiaojing zhengzhu 孝經鄭註　193
Xinbao 申報　120
Xiong Xuepeng 熊学鵬　137
Xiuhaibian 袖海編　178
Xiuhaibian 袖海編　178
Xi-yang-huo-gong-shen-qi-shuo 西洋火攻神器説　182
Xiyu dufu 西域都護　36
Xi-yu-wen-jian-lu 西域聞見録　181
Xizhao-leshi 熙朝樂事　181
Xizong Shilu 熹宗実録　109
Xu Fuyuan 許孚遠　80
Xu-Han shu 續漢書　72
"Xu Weihuai 徐惟懷,"　134
Xu wenxian tongkao 續文獻通考　194

Y

Yaeyamajima 八重山島　169
Yamai Tei 山井鼎　180
Yamamoto Hokuzan 山本北山　181
Yangchou 揚州　74
Yang Hui suan-fa 楊輝算法　72
Yang Hui 楊輝　72, 73
Yang Qitang 楊啓堂　166
Yangtze River 長江　14, 27, 57-61, 63, 70, 71, 87, 113, 116, 199-201, 204
Yang Wenqian 楊文乾　81
Yano Jinichi 矢野仁一　111
Yantie-lun 鹽鐵論　180
Yan Xuefan 顏雪帆　189
Yao Fuqing 姚福慶　93
Yellow Sea 黄海　52, 58, 59, 90
Yi-cun-cong-shu 佚存叢書　188, 189, 191, 193, 195
Yi Fan 程益凡　130

Yijianzhi 夷堅志　42
Yi-jia tang cong-shu 宜稼堂叢書　71
Yijing 易経　177, 188
Yingkou 営口　60, 69, 70, 209
Ying Ya Sheng Lan 瀛涯胜覽　79
Yokohama 横浜　96, 199, 202-204
Yongle dadian 永楽大典　45
Yongzheng 雍正　16, 18-20, 53, 90, 97, 117, 122
Yuan Jue 袁桷　72
Yuan Mei 袁枚　153, 181-184, 186, 187, 196
Yuansheng 源盛 Junk's registered name　165
Yuan-shi-chao 元詩鈔　181, 183, 196
yuchi 魚翅　115
Yue Jian 越鐫　29
Yueyatang-congshu 粤雅堂叢書　178
Yunnan 雲南　114, 127
Yu Run-nian 郁潤年　74
Yu Sen-sheng 郁森盛　74
Yu Sung-nien 郁松年　71
Yu Xing 于興　93

Z

Zhang Erming 張二銘　181
Zhangzhou 漳州　20, 30, 53, 80, 113, 114, 161
zhanhailing 展海令　113
Zhao Rugua 趙汝适　79
Zhapu beizhi 乍浦備志　68, 168
Zhapu 乍浦　20, 34, 52, 66, 68, 116-118, 122, 126, 137, 139, 159, 167-169, 175, 195
Zheng Chenggong 鄭成功　13, 58, 81, 113
Zheng He 鄭和　47, 50, 79
Zheng Keshuang 鄭克塽　113
Zheng Zhilong 鄭芝龍　160
Zheng 鄭　16-20, 30, 40, 53, 61, 79, 90, 97, 117, 122, 127, 188, 189, 192, 193
Zhenla feng tu ji 真臘風土記　45

Zhibuzuzhai congshu 知不足齋叢書 194

Zhibuzuzhai-congshu 知不足齋叢書 178, 179, 193, 194, 196

Zhibuzuzhai 知不足齋 195

Zhong Yin 鐘音 134

Zhongyong 中庸 177, 188

Zhouyiguzhu 周易古註 180

Zhouyi-xin-jiangyi 周易新講義 192

Zhu Junwang 朱均旺 80, 81

Zhu Xiqi 朱錫旂 180

Zhu Yuanzhang 朱元璋 46

Zhuzi Xinxue lu 朱子心學錄 180

Zhuzixue 朱子学 179

Zhuzi 朱熹 180

Zoku Nagasaki jitsuroku taisei 續長崎實錄大成 188

Zou Jing 鄒璟 168

Zuoshi Mengqiu 左氏蒙求 192